THE CARTOON HISTORY OF THE UNIVERSE III

ALSO BY LARRY GONICK

THE CARTOON HISTORY OF THE UNIVERSE, VOLUMES 1–7

THE CARTOON HISTORY OF THE UNIVERSE II, VOLUMES 8–13

THE CARTOON HISTORY OF THE UNITED STATES

THE CARTOON GUIDE TO THE COMPUTER

THE CARTOON GUIDE TO THE ENVIRONMENT (WITH ALICE OUTWATER)

THE CARTOON GUIDE TO GENETICS (WITH MARK WHEELIS)

THE CARTOON GUIDE TO (NON)COMMUNICATION

THE CARTOON GUIDE TO PHYSICS (WITH ART HUFFMAN)

THE CARTOON GUIDE TO SEX (WITH CHRISTINE DEVAULT)

THE CARTOON GUIDE TO STATISTICS (WITH WOOLLCOTT SMITH)

THE CARTOON HISTORY
OF THE
UNIVERSE III

From the Rise of Arabia
to the Renaissance

Larry Gonick

W. W. NORTON & COMPANY

NEW YORK   LONDON

FOR INFORMATION ABOUT PERMISSION TO REPRODUCE SELECTIONS FROM THIS BOOK,
WRITE TO PERMISSIONS, W. W. NORTON & COMPANY, INC.,
500 FIFTH AVENUE, NEW YORK, NY 10110

THE TEXT OF THIS BOOK IS COMPOSED IN AVAR MEDIUM WITH THE DISPLAY SET IN BOUNCY ROMAN
MANUFACTURING BY R. R. DONNELLEY, WILLARD DIVISION
PRODUCTION MANAGER: JULIA DRUSKIN

ISBN 0-393-05184-6
ISBN 0-393-32403-6 (PBK.)

W. W. NORTON & COMPANY, INC., 500 FIFTH AVENUE, NEW YORK, N.Y. 10110
WWW.WWNORTON.COM

W. W. NORTON & COMPANY LTD., CASTLE HOUSE, 75/76 WELLS STREET, LONDON W1T 3QT

1 2 3 4 5 6 7 8 9 0

Table of Contents

THIS BOOK IS DEDICATED TO
ALL THE SKEPTICS WHO HAVE EVER LIVED.

CHRISTIANITY, AS THE OFFICIAL RELIGION OF THE ROMAN EMPIRE, HAD SPREAD ACROSS EUROPE AND AROUND THE MEDITERRANEAN SEA, UNTIL AT LAST ALL PAGAN TEMPLES WERE ORDERED CLOSED IN THE YEAR 395.

THE ROMANS MAY HAVE OUTLAWED PAGANISM, BUT WHAT ABOUT **JUDAISM?** JEWS, EXILED FROM JUDAEA IN THE 2ND CENTURY, HAD SETTLED ALL OVER THE EMPIRE AND BEYOND. HOW DID THE ROMAN CHURCH VIEW THE JEWS?

(EVEN THE GERMAN TRIBES WHO PILLAGED ROME WERE CHRISTIANS OF A KIND!)

WE **ARE** IN THE SAME BOAT, AREN'T WE?

NO CHRISTIAN WOULD ACCUSE THE JEWS OF WORSHIPPING FALSE GODS—CHRISTIANS AND JEWS WORSHIPPED THE **SAME** GOD, AND JEWISH SCRIPTURES WERE SACRED TO CHRISTIANS—BUT CHRISTIANS DID NOT OBSERVE JEWISH LAW, AND JEWS DID NOT ACCEPT JESUS AS DIVINE. JEWS WERE NOT CHRISTIAN!

THE CHURCH TOOK THE POSITION THAT THE JEWS SHOULD BE **CONVERTED,** NOT BANNED... AND TO "ENCOURAGE" THEM TO CHANGE THEIR FAITH, ROMAN LAW DISCRIMINATED AGAINST JEWS IN MANY WAYS, RESTRICTING THEIR WORSHIP, PROPERTY, MOVEMENTS, AND SPEECH.

THE GREATEST CHRISTIAN POWER SAT ON THE EDGE BETWEEN EAST AND WEST: **CONSTAN-TINOPLE**, CAPITAL OF THE **"ROMAN"** EMPIRE,* EVEN AFTER THE FALL OF ROME ITSELF. IN THE EAST, **ARMENIA** HAD ADOPTED CHRISTIANITY, AND IN THE SOUTH SO HAD **ETHIOPIA**. CHRISTIAN CHURCHES HAD ALSO SPRUNG UP IN ARABIA, PERSIA, INDIA, AND BEYOND.

IN **PERSIA**, THE OTHER GREAT POWER IN THE REGION, THE RULERS WORSHIPPED **MAZDA**, GOD OF THE MAGI, WHOSE FAITH WAS FOUNDED LONG AGO BY ZOROASTER OF BALKH. THE PERSIANS MISTRUSTED CHRISTIANS AS POSSIBLE ROMAN AGENTS BUT HAD NO PROBLEM WITH JEWS.

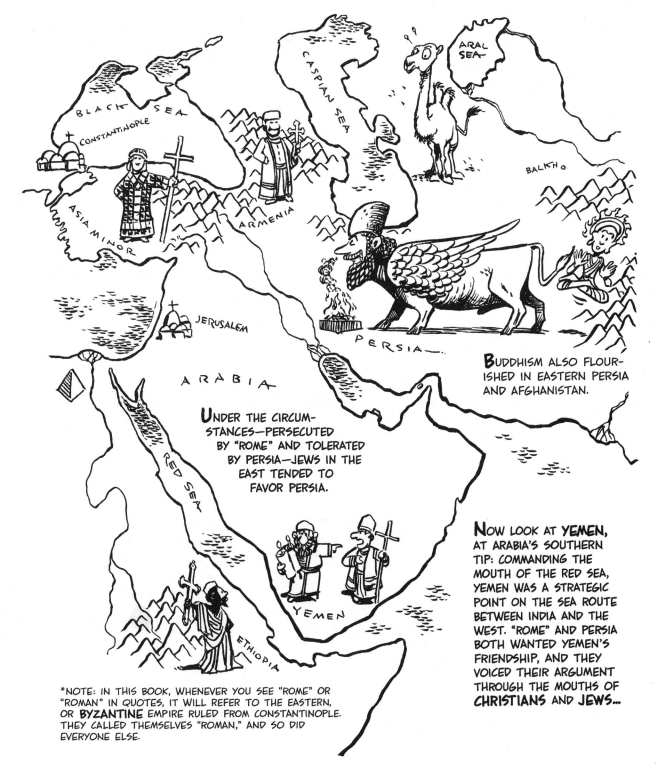

BUDDHISM ALSO FLOUR-ISHED IN EASTERN PERSIA AND AFGHANISTAN.

UNDER THE CIRCUM-STANCES—PERSECUTED BY "ROME" AND TOLERATED BY PERSIA—JEWS IN THE EAST TENDED TO FAVOR PERSIA.

NOW LOOK AT **YEMEN**, AT ARABIA'S SOUTHERN TIP: COMMANDING THE MOUTH OF THE RED SEA, YEMEN WAS A STRATEGIC POINT ON THE SEA ROUTE BETWEEN INDIA AND THE WEST. "ROME" AND PERSIA BOTH WANTED YEMEN'S FRIENDSHIP, AND THEY VOICED THEIR ARGUMENT THROUGH THE MOUTHS OF **CHRISTIANS** AND **JEWS**...

*NOTE: IN THIS BOOK, WHENEVER YOU SEE "ROME" OR "ROMAN" IN QUOTES, IT WILL REFER TO THE EASTERN, OR **BYZANTINE** EMPIRE RULED FROM CONSTANTINOPLE. THEY CALLED THEMSELVES "ROMAN," AND SO DID EVERYONE ELSE.

IN THE LATE 300s, CHRISTIANS AND JEWS PREACHED TO THE RULERS OF YEMEN.

AROUND 395, THE YEMENITE KING CONVERTED TO **JUDAISM** (OR ELSE A JEW BECAME KING—IT'S HARD TO SAY!)

GET THOSE **CROSSES** OUT OF THE PALACE!

FOR OVER A CENTURY JEWISH KINGS RULED YEMEN, UNTIL, IN THE EARLY 520s, KING **JOSEPH DHU-NUWAS** HEARD RUMORS OF AN IMPENDING CHRISTIAN REVOLT.

MUTTER

MUTTER

MUTTER

DHU-NUWAS STRUCK FIRST AND SLAUGHTERED THOUSANDS.

A SURVIVOR MADE HIS WAY TO **CONSTANTINOPLE** SEEKING AID... THE EMPEROR SAID YEMEN WAS TOO FAR AWAY, BUT SUGGESTED ASKING **ETHIOPIA** FOR HELP... SO, ON TO ETHIOPIA...

THE KING OF ETHIOPIA, A FERVENT CHRISTIAN, VOWED TO AVENGE THE DEATHS.

AND ADD YEMEN TO MY KINGDOM WHILE I'M AT IT!

HE RAISED AN ARMY AND INVADED YEMEN IN 525.

THE AFRICANS DEFEATED DHU-NUWAS'S YEMENITES, AND THE JEWISH KING GALLOPED INTO THE OCEAN AND DISAPPEARED.

NO FAIR! IT PARTED FOR **MOSES!**

4

AND SO THE YEAR 570 WAS REMEMBERED IN MECCA AS THE **YEAR OF THE ELEPHANT!**

CLINK CLINK CLINK CLINK CLINK CLINK CLINK CLINK CLINK CLINK

THE ETHIOPIAN GENERAL, **ABRAHAM THE SPLIT-FACED,** WON HIS COMMAND BY CHALLENGING A RIVAL GENERAL TO A **DUEL.** DURING THE FIGHT, ABRAHAM TOOK A CHOP TO THE FACE, BUT HIS **SERVANT** STEPPED IN, KILLED THE OPPONENT, AND SAVED ABRAHAM'S LIFE.

THANK YOU!!

ABRAHAM GRATEFULLY TOLD THE SERVANT TO **NAME HIS OWN REWARD...** THE MAN ASKED FOR THE SO-CALLED "LORD'S RIGHT"— THAT IS, THE RIGHT TO **LIE WITH EVERY BRIDE** ON HER **WEDDING NIGHT** BEFORE HER HUSBAND. ABRAHAM **HAD TO SAY YES...**

I'M A MAN OF MY WORD!

AFTER PUSHING HIS WAY INTO A FEW MARRIAGE BEDS, THE SERVANT WAS **MURDERED** BY AN ANGRY HUSBAND, WHO THEN CAME BEFORE ABRAHAM FOR JUDGMENT. THE SPLIT-FACED ONE LET HIM OFF AND **APOLOGIZED...**

I SHOULD HAVE KNOWN THIS WOULD HAPPEN... IT'S **MY** FAULT... SORRY...

MECCA

MECCA, A STONY PLACE WITH JUST ENOUGH WELL WATER TO SUPPLY A SMALL TOWN, LAY AT THE HALFWAY POINT ON THE CARAVAN ROUTE BETWEEN YEMEN AND SYRIA.

DESPITE THE REMOTE LOCATION, PLENTY OF MERCHANDISE PASSED THROUGH MECCA: IN-CENSE, SLAVES, AND RAISINS TRAVELED NORTH, WHILE HOUSE-WARES, CLOTH, AND BIBLES HEADED SOUTH.

MECCA ALSO SOLD GOODS TO MUCH OF CEN-TRAL ARABIA... EVERY YEAR, THE TOWN HOSTED A TRADE FAIR WHERE PEOPLE GATHERED FROM FAR AND WIDE TO BUY, SELL, AND MINGLE.

TO SERVE THE VISITORS SPIRITUALLY, MECCA MAINTAINED A LARGE SHRINE, THE **KABA**, HOUSING HUNDREDS OF DIFFERENT GODS, SO MECCA WAS ALSO A **HOLY CITY**.

FOR THE PAST CENTURY A SINGLE TRIBE, THE **KURAISH,** HAD CONTROLLED MECCA, ITS WATER, AND THE KABA. BY THE MID-500s, THIS TRIBE NUMBERED SEVERAL HUNDRED PEOPLE, DIVIDED INTO A DOZEN CLANS.

THE KURAISH RAN MECCA AS A FAMILY BUSINESS, WITH NO **MAYOR, CITY COUNCIL,** OR **LAWS.** THE TRIBE SOLVED PROBLEMS IN A FAMILY WAY, THAT IS, BY NEGOTIATION AMONG THE ELDERS.

ONCE A YEAR, THE MERCHANTS OF KURAISH POOLED THEIR STUFF AND PACKED IT OFF ON CAMELS HEADING UP THE TRAIL TO SYRIA.

AS WITH MOST BUSINESSES, SOME GREW WHILE OTHERS SHRANK... AND NOW THE TRIBE HAD RICH AND POOR LIVING SIDE-BY-SIDE.

SO HERE IS MECCA IN THE YEAR 570: A DUSTY, DESERT DEPOT... HOME TO A FEW THOUSAND PEOPLE, INCLUDING SLAVES AND OTHERS... A LARGE FAMILY OF UNEQUALS... AND A SYSTEM OF GOVERNMENT ILL-EQUIPPED TO HANDLE THE CHALLENGE THAT CAME NEXT...

AMONG THOSE MECCANS BORN AROUND THE YEAR OF THE ELEPHANT, HERE IS ONE FROM A RICH FAMILY: **ABU SUFYAN**, SON OF HARB, WHO BEGAN GOING WITH THE CARAVAN TO SYRIA AS A YOUNG MAN AND SAW SOMETHING OF THE WORLD.

KNOWN AS AN EASYGOING BUT SKILLFUL BUSINESSMAN, ABU SUFYAN PROSPERED.

AHH... GO AHEAD! DRAW MY PICTURE... I DON'T MIND...

ARE YOU BUYING OR SELLING?

HE MARRIED AN APPROPRIATE BUT FAMOUSLY SARCASTIC WOMAN NAMED HIND, DAUGHTER OF UTBA, AND THEY HAD SEVERAL CHILDREN.

THEN, IN THE YEAR 613, WHEN ABU SUFYAN AND UTBA WERE AROUND 40 YEARS OLD, CAME A **FAMILY CRISIS**...

HONEY? WHERE ARE YOU GOING?

YOU WOULDN'T UNDERSTAND, YOU... YOU...

THEIR DAUGHTER **UMM HABIBA** HAD BEEN GOING TO A **PRAYER MEETING** AND WAS NOW ABOUT TO MARRY SOMEONE IN THE GROUP!

IDOLATER!!

SLAM!

THE MEETINGS WERE LED BY ABU SUFYAN'S THIRD COUSIN **MUHAMMAD**, SON OF ABDULLAH— ONE OF THE POOR KURAISH OF MECCA. HIS STORY IS MORE COMPLICATED.

ORPHANED EARLY IN CHILDHOOD, MUHAMMAD WAS RAISED BY A POOR UNCLE WITH MANY CHILDREN OF HIS OWN—AN ACT OF CHARITY THAT MUHAMMAD NEVER FORGOT.

WHERE'S COUSIN MUHAMMAD?

IN THIS BOOK, PERMANENTLY OFF-CAMERA!

MARRIAGE WAS NOT SO EASY FOR A POOR BOY WITH NO PARENTS.

THE YOUNG MAN TOOK A JOB AS ESTATE MANAGER FOR A YOUNGISH WIDOW, **KHADIJA**. UNDER MUHAMMAD'S MANAGEMENT, SHE PROSPERED... THEY FELL IN LOVE... MARRIED... AND HAD SEVERAL CHILDREN, OF WHOM ONLY TWO DAUGHTERS SURVIVED INTO ADULTHOOD.

KHADIJA, BY THE WAY, HAD A COUSIN, A CHRISTIAN, WHO HAD TRANSLATED SOME SCRIPTURE INTO ARABIC... THERE WAS PROBABLY RELIGIOUS TALK IN THE HOUSEHOLD.

ONE DAY IN 610, WHILE MEDITATING IN THE DESERT, MUHAMMAD HEARD A **VOICE**... IT IDENTIFIED ITSELF AS THE ANGEL **GABRIEL** AND SAID ITS MESSAGES CAME DIRECTLY FROM **GOD!**

WHAT?

AT FIRST, MUHAMMAD THOUGHT HE WAS LOSING HIS MIND, BUT KHADIJA ASSURED HIM THE VOICE WAS **REAL**... SOON MORE REVELATIONS CAME... BUT FOR THREE YEARS THEY REMAINED A FAMILY SECRET... UNTIL IN 613 THE VOICE ORDERED MUHAMMAD TO **SPREAD THE WORD.**

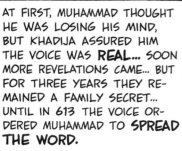

COME IN! COME IN!

HE INVITED ALL HIS UNCLES TO DINNER AND ANNOUNCED HE WAS A PROPHET. THEY ROLLED THEIR EYES POLITELY.

COFF COFF

AHEM!

NICE DINNER!

BUT WHEN MUHAMMAD CHANTED HIS REVELATIONS IN PUBLIC (THEY WERE ALWAYS IN VERSE), **YOUNG PEOPLE** RESPONDED. WITHIN A YEAR, HE HAD 150 FOLLOWERS!

YOUNG PEOPLE! THEY'LL DO ANYTHING!

WHEN I WAS YOUNG, I POOPED IN A CHURCH...

IN MECCA, HE TAUGHT:

THERE IS ONLY ONE GOD, THE BIBLICAL GOD OF ABRAHAM, MOSES, AND JESUS. GOD IS COMPASSIONATE AND MERCIFUL.

MUHAMMAD WAS A PROPHET IN THE BIBLICAL TRADITION.

BELIEVERS, OR **MUSLIMS** (MEANING THOSE WHO SUBMIT TO GOD), WOULD ATTAIN PARADISE... UNBELIEVERS WERE HEADED FOR HELL.

MUSLIMS MUST PRAY FIVE TIMES A DAY, PROSTRATING THEMSELVES FACING **JERUSALEM.**

MUSLIMS SHOULD BE MODEST, SOBER, FRUGAL, AND CHARITABLE TOWARD WIDOWS AND ORPHANS. MUSLIMS SHOULD TREAT EACH OTHER AS BROTHERS AND SISTERS.

THAT IS **NOT** WHAT I POINT TOWARD GOD!

ONE OF MUHAMMAD'S UNCLES IS SUPPOSED TO HAVE SAID.

SOME OF THESE IDEAS MADE MECCA UNCOMFORTABLE!

FOR ONE THING, THERE WAS THAT BUSINESS ABOUT HELL...

HONEY, WE UNDERSTAND THAT YOU MAY NOT WANT TO SEE US **RIGHT NOW**... BUT FOR **ALL ETERNITY?**

OH, TOASTY WARM YOU'LL BE!

FOR ANOTHER, MUHAMMAD PREACHED TO VISITORS AT MECCA'S ANNUAL FAIR, TRYING TO TURN THEM AGAINST THEIR OWN GODS...

HELL, NO!

THIS CAN'T BE GOOD FOR BUSINESS!

AND ANOTHER: MUSLIMS POOLED THEIR RESOURCES TO START THEIR OWN BUSINESS VENTURES—OUTSIDE THEIR FAMILIES' CONTROL.

ABU SUFYAN! **COME ON!!**

SIGH... I SUPPOSE I'D BE REALLY PISSED IF I WERE THAT SORT OF PERSON...

AND ANOTHER: MUHAMMAD ARRANGED MARRIAGES BETWEEN MUSLIMS—ABU SUFYAN'S DAUGHTER, FOR EXAMPLE—AGAIN OUTSIDE THE FAMILIES' CONTROL.

DO SOMETHING!

GOOD IDEA... BUT WHAT?*

FROM THE START, THERE WERE HOTHEADS IN MECCA WHO WANTED TO **KILL** MUHAMMAD... AND WITH NO LAW AGAINST MURDER AND NO POLICE FORCE, WHAT HELD THEM BACK?

WHOA, THERE!

IN SHORT, THEIR **RELATIVES.** AFTER A MURDER, BY ANCIENT CUSTOM, THE VICTIM'S **CLAN** TOOK REVENGE ON **ANYONE** IN THE MURDERER'S CLAN... WHICH THEN RETALIATED... AND SO ON, IN A POTENTIALLY ENDLESS CYCLE OF VIOLENCE. VERY UNDESIRABLE!

DON'T **START,** SON! HIS UNCLE IS MY BUSINESS PARTNER...

HIS MOTHER WAS MY MOTHER'S COUSIN...

FAMILIES CAN BE SO **STIFLING**...

WHEN THIS **LAW OF RETALIATION** FAILS TO KEEP THE PEACE, THE RESULT IS THE KIND OF **BLOOD FEUD** FOUND ACROSS THE WORLD WHEREVER LAW ENFORCEMENT IS WEAK.

EE-HAW! WINGED ME A HATFIELD, BOY!

WHEN IN DOUBT, TRY ECONOMIC SANCTIONS!

IN THIS SOOTHING ENVIRONMENT, THE KURAISH IMPOSED A **BOYCOTT** ON ALL MUSLIM BUSINESSES.

TENSIONS ROSE: MASTERS TORTURED MUSLIM SLAVES... PARENTS BEAT MUSLIM CHILDREN... MUSLIMS LOST THEIR HOMES AND PROPERTY...

BY ALL THE SACRED STONES OF ARABIA, GIVE IT UP!

WHAT, AND BE LIKE **YOU?**

IN 618, MUHAMMAD'S WIFE KHADIJA DIED.

MUHAMMAD KEPT INSISTING THAT ALL MECCA MUST BECOME MUSLIM... THE KURAISH DEMANDED THAT MUHAMMAD KEEP QUIET... NEITHER SIDE WOULD BACK DOWN...

WE'VE REDUCED THEM TO BEGGARY—WHY WON'T THEY BE **REASONABLE?**

BY 622, FEELINGS HAD RISEN SO HIGH THAT THE ELDERS OF ALL THE CLANS BUT MUHAMMAD'S AGREED TO **MURDER** THEIR COUSIN, THE PROPHET.

WHAT ELSE CAN WE DO, REALLY?

THEN, QUIETLY, A FEW AT A TIME, THE MUSLIMS BEGAN TO **LEAVE MECCA**, SLIPPING AWAY BY FOOT OR CAMELBACK INTO THE DESERT.

LATE ONE NIGHT, ELEVEN ASSASSINS GATHERED TO COMMIT THE CRIME... NATURALLY, COORDINATING ELEVEN PEOPLE SLOWED THINGS DOWN A BIT...

BY THE TIME THEY REACHED MUHAMMAD'S HOUSE IT WAS DAWN, AND HE WAS GONE!

I'M KIND OF RELIEVED, ACTUALLY.

OUT OF SIGHT, OUT OF MIND!

LAST WE'LL SEE OF HIM, I RECKON...

MEDINA

BEFORE LEAVING MECCA, MUHAMMAD HAD A REVELATION THAT CHANGED EVERYTHING: **IT IS PERMITTED TO FIGHT AGAINST THOSE WHO OPPRESS YOU.** (BEFORE THIS, HE HAD PREACHED FORBEARANCE.)

NOW, AS HE AND THE OTHER MUSLIMS TOOK REFUGE IN THE OASIS OF **MEDINA**, A GREEN SPOT 150 MILES NORTHEAST OF MECCA, THE PROPHET MAY HAVE BEEN PLANNING TO MAKE WAR ON MECCA—BUT FIRST HE AND HIS COMPANIONS HAD TO GET SETTLED!

WOW... ARE WE IN PARADISE ALREADY?

NOT YET, ABU BAKR!

MEDINA HAD TWO TRIBES OF ARABS, UNTIL RECENTLY INVOLVED IN A BLOOD FEUD.

MANY OF THESE HAD CONVERTED TO ISLAM AS A WAY OF BRIDGING THEIR DIFFERENCES.

MUSLIMS ARE ONE COMMUNITY TO THE EXCLUSION OF OTHERS...

SAID MUHAMMAD.

ALONGSIDE THE ARABS LIVED THREE TRIBES OF **JEWS.** TWO TRIBES FARMED, WHILE THE THIRD ONE MADE ARMOR AND JEWELRY.

UH-OH!

WHAT'S WRONG?

HAVEN'T YOU READ **THE BOOK?** PROPHETS ARE TROUBLE!

THE LOCAL MUSLIMS WELCOMED THE REFUGEES AS SPIRITUAL BROTHERS AND SISTERS...

COME IN... COME IN... WHAT'S *OURS* IS *YOURS*... ER... EVEN THOUGH WE OWN QUITE A LOT, AND YOU SEEM TO HAVE LOST, UM, EVERYTHING...

BUT AFTER A FEW MONTHS OF LIVING OFF CHARITY IN TIGHT QUARTERS, THEY BEGAN TO ACT LIKE *REAL* BROTHERS AND SISTERS!

GET OFF MY SIDE OF THE RUG!

HANDS OFF MY SHIRT!

WHO STOLE MY SPECIAL PILLOW?

MUHAMMAD HOPED TO EASE THE PAIN BY CONVERTING MEDINA'S *JEWS.* IF ONLY THE JEWS WOULD BECOME MUSLIMS AND SHARE THEIR PROPERTY...

HMMM? COME ON... HOW ABOUT IT...?

FOR SOME REASON, THE JEWS WERE NOT KEEN ON THIS SCHEME!

UM... WE ALREADY HAVE A PERFECTLY GOOD ONE-GOD TYPE THING GOING...

WHAT DO WE NEED WITH YOURS?

COCKAMAMIE AS IT SOUNDS TO US, ESPECIALLY...

PIQUED, MUHAMMAD CHANGED THE DIRECTION OF PRAYER FROM *JERUSALEM* TO *MECCA* AND CHANGED THE SABBATH FROM SATURDAY TO FRIDAY.

ABOUT FACE!

UM... I THINK WE JUST MADE 300 ENEMIES...

SO THE PROBLEM RE-MAINED: THE MECCAN REFUGEES HAD LOST THEIR HOMES, THEIR CAMELS, THEIR STUFF BACK IN MECCA...

GRR...

THE TIME HAD COME AT LAST... MUHAMMAD TOLD THE MUSLIMS TO PREPARE FOR WAR.

EXCUSE ME, I'D LIKE TO BUY A SWORD, SOME ARMOR, AND THOSE EARRINGS FOR THE WIFE...

WILL THAT BE ON CREDIT AGAIN?

IN THE EARLY SPRING OF 624, THE MUSLIMS RODE OUT UNDER MUHAMMAD'S GREEN BANNER TO ATTACK THE KURAISH.

THEY AIMED TO LOOT MECCA'S GREAT CARAVAN, JUST THEN SETTING OFF WITH **ABU SUFYAN** IN THE LEAD.

HO!

SOMEHOW, WORD OF THE RAID LEAKED OUT AND REACHED ABU SUFYAN.

NEAR SOME WELLS, HE SPOTTED FRESH **CAMEL DUNG**. PINCHING IT BETWEEN HIS FINGERS, HE FOUND **DATE PITS**... THESE MUST HAVE BEEN **OASIS CAMELS**...

THEY'RE NEARBY...

HE IMMEDIATELY TURNED BACK AND SENT A MESSENGER AHEAD TO MECCA.

BAW BAW BAW!

WHEN THE WORD ARRIVED, MECCA SPRANG INTO ACTION—IF "SPRANG" IS REALLY THE RIGHT WORD...

OOF... I'M A CLOTH DEALER, NOT A SOLDIER!!

A **MECCAN WAR PARTY** RODE OUT TO FACE THE MUSLIMS. ABU SUFYAN MET THEM, POINTED THE WAY, AND TOOK THE CARAVAN HOME.

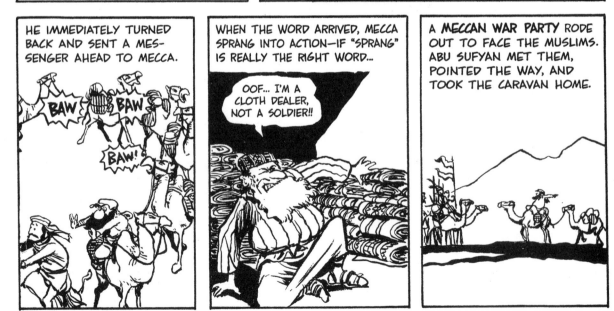

SO THE MUSLIMS MISSED THE CARAVAN, AND ABU SUFYAN MISSED THE BATTLE, WHICH TOOK PLACE ON MARCH 15, 624.

BY THE MOON GOD, THE SUN GOD, AND THE GOD OF LITTLE PEBBLES, I FEEL STRANGELY **INHIBITED** FROM **KILLING** YOU, MY KINSMAN...

BY GOD, I DON'T!!

THIS FIGHT, AT THE WELLS OF **BADR**, KILLED MANY OF MECCA'S OLD LEADERS, INCLUDING SOME OF THE MUSLIMS' WORST ENEMIES.

NOW THE MUSLIMS FELT BETTER! THEY HAD THE SPOILS OF BATTLE AND, LET'S FACE IT, A **SENSE OF ACCOMPLISHMENT!** WHY STOP NOW?

TEN YEARS THOSE DOGS PUSHED US AROUND!

YOU SHOWED 'EM!

MORE! **MORE!! MORE!!!**

SO THEY TURNED AGAINST THE JEWS...

YEAH!

HEY! I **MADE** THOSE WEAPONS!

MEDINA'S JEWS, AFTER ALL, RESISTED ISLAM... THEY MUST HAVE HOPED FOR MUHAMMAD'S DEFEAT... THEY MAY EVEN HAVE WARNED **ABU SUFYAN**... SO, IN SHORT ORDER, THE MUSLIMS ATTACKED AND OVERWHELMED THE METALWORKING TRIBE, THE **BANU QAINUQA**...

QAINUQA? ARE THESE MY ANCESTORS?

AFTER CONSIDERING A DEATH SENTENCE, MUHAMMAD SPARED THE BANU QAINUQA... WHAT BECAME OF THEM IS UNCLEAR... MOST MUST HAVE LEFT TOWN...

NOW SEVERAL JEWS WERE MURDERED IN THE STREETS... THE OTHER TWO TRIBES BARRICADED THEMSELVES IN THEIR FORTS...

BACK IN MECCA, WITH SO MANY ELDERS DEAD, ABU SUFYAN WAS NOW IN COMMAND. HE VOWED TO **GIVE UP FRIED FOOD** UNTIL THE DEFEAT AT BADR WAS AVENGED.

WITH ABU SUFYAN, THAT'S A SERIOUS THREAT!

THE NEXT YEAR, ABU SUFYAN LED THE KURAISH TO VICTORY OVER THE MUSLIMS AT **UHUD.**

FALAFEL AND HOME!

ABU SUFYAN FOLLOWED UP BY ATTACKING MEDINA ITSELF.

DEEP-FRIED CHICKPEAS!!

BUT THE MUSLIMS HAD DUG A TRENCH AROUND THE TOWN... THE KURAISH, HAVING NEVER SEEN SUCH A THING, GAVE UP AND WENT HOME.

HMM... NO FAIR... MAYBE I'LL HAVE THOSE CHICKPEAS ANYWAY...

WIN, LOSE, OR DRAW, AFTER EACH BATTLE THE MUSLIMS ALWAYS DID THE SAME THING: **ATTACK THE JEWS.** AFTER UHUD, MUHAMMAD BANISHED MEDINA'S SECOND TRIBE OF JEWS, THE BANU* AL-NADHIR.

*BANU = SONS OF

AFTER THE "TRENCH," THE MUSLIMS ROUNDED UP THE LAST JEWISH TRIBE, THE **BANU QURAIZA,** ENSLAVED THE WOMEN AND CHILDREN, AND MASSACRED ITS 700 MEN. MEDINA WAS NOW 100% MUSLIM, MORE OR LESS.

NOW, ONCE MORE, THE BACK-GROUND COMES TO THE FORE... IN THE LATE 620s, A NEW "ROMAN" EMPEROR, **HERA-CLIUS,** MOBILIZED HIS ARMIES, ATTACKED PERSIA, AND WON BACK MOST OF HIS EMPIRE.

IN 628, THE ROMANS CAPPED THEIR VICTORIES BY RETAKING **JERUSALEM,** WITH THE USUAL SLAUGHTER OF JEWS...

MAN, WHAT IS IT ABOUT THIS PLACE...?

AND MUHAMMAD QUICKLY CHANGED HIS STRATEGY. HE MADE A TRUCE WITH MECCA AND STEPPED UP HIS WAR AGAINST THE JEWS OF ARA-BIA, WHO HAD LOST THEIR PERSIAN PROTECTORS.

FIRST HE **ENLARGED HIS ARMY** WITH THE HELP OF VARIOUS ARAB TRIBES.

THEN THEY ASSAULTED **KAIBAR,** A MAINLY JEWISH CITY OF SOME 50,000 PEOPLE IN NORTHERN ARABIA.

WOA!

TAKING THE TOWN, THE MUSLIMS SET THESE TERMS: THE KAIBAR JEWS MUST PAY **HALF THEIR ANNUAL INCOME** TO MEDINA.

DID YOU **HAVE** TO SAY, "STARTING WHEN?"

SUDDENLY, THE MUSLIMS SAW **REAL WEALTH** FLOWING IN... AND MECCA TOOK NOTE!

JINGLE JINGLE

!

ALSO IN 628, MUHAMMAD MADE ANOTHER BRILLIANT MOVE: HE SUMMONED ABU SUFYAN'S DAUGHTER **UMM HABIBA** BACK FROM **ETHIOPIA** (SEE P. 14) AND **MARRIED** HER!*

I NOW PRONOUNCE US MAN AND WIFE.

ABU SUFYAN WAS NOW **FAMILY!**

WHAT? WHAT?

ABU SUFYAN WAS COMPLETELY DEFANGED... HIS ENEMY HAD BECOME HIS **SON-IN-LAW**... AND BESIDES, HIS FIGHTING MEN WERE GOING OVER TO THE MUSLIMS IN DROVES. WHAT COULD HE DO?

NEGOTIATE THE BEST DEAL I CAN GET...

SHARING A DONKEY WITH ONE OF MUHAMMAD'S UNCLES, AL ABBAS, FOR PROTECTION, ABU SUFYAN RODE TO MEDINA.

THERE UMM HABIBA GAVE HER FATHER A RUDE RECEPTION.

AH-AH! CAN'T SIT THERE!

I SEE YOUR MANNERS HAVEN'T IMPROVED SINCE YOU LEFT HOME...

AT LAST HE CONVERTED TO ISLAM, GRUMBLING ALL THE WAY.

SAY "THERE IS NO GOD BUT GOD AND MUHAMMAD IS HIS PROPHET!"

UM... CAN I LEAVE OUT THE SECOND PART?

SAY IT!

SIGH... THERE IS NO GOD BUT GOD, AND MUMBLE MUMBLE...

GOOD ENOUGH!

MUHAMMAD WED 19 WOMEN, EACH OF THEM (EXCEPT FOR KHADIJA, HIS FIRST WIFE) CHOSEN TO MAKE AN ALLIANCE WITH HER FAMILY OR TRIBE.

HALF OF ARABIA'S HIS IN-LAW!

ONE WIFE (AISHA, DAUGHTER OF HIS FRIEND ABU BAKR—AND ONLY 9 YEARS OLD AT THE TIME OF THE WEDDING) WAS SUSPECTED OF CHEATING ON HIM, BUT THE ONLY RESPONSE WAS THE PROPHET'S REVELATION THAT HIS WIVES SHOULD BE MODEST AND **COVER THEIR HEADS.**

YOU'LL BE UNDER COVER AND ABOVE SUSPICION!

THIS INCIDENT IS SUPPOSED TO HAVE STARTED THE **VEILING** OF MUSLIM WOMEN... BUT IN FACT, ARAB WOMEN HAVE BEEN VEILED, ON AND OFF, SINCE BABYLONIAN TIMES. MUSLIMS NOW DISAGREE ABOUT WHETHER THE "VEIL" SHOULD BE A SIMPLE SCARF OR A TOTAL BODY TENT.

AN OUNCE OF PREVENTION IS WORTH A POUND OF CURE!

ESPECIALLY WHEN THE **CURE** IS A **POUNDING**...

22

ABU SUFYAN, AL ABBAS, AND MUHAMMAD THEN NEGOTIATED THE TERMS OF MECCA'S SURRENDER. THE MECCANS PROMISED THAT **ALL KURAISH** WOULD EMBRACE ISLAM, WHILE MUHAMMAD PROMISED TO ENTER MECCA PEACEFULLY.

'BYE! SEE YOU SOON!

MAN, NOW WE HAVE TO SELL THIS DEAL TO THE HOME FOLKS...

ABU SUFYAN ANNOUNCED THE DEAL TO THE PEOPLE OF MECCA, WHILE HIS WIFE **HIND** BERATED HIM.

UM... YOU CAN STAY IN MY HOUSE AND NOBODY WILL GET HURT!

DON'T LISTEN TO THIS TUB OF LARD!!

IN JANUARY 630, THE MUSLIMS MARCHED INTO MECCA, AND THEIR ENEMIES CROWDED INTO ABU SUFYAN'S HOUSE.

ALL THE IDOLS IN THE KABA WERE SMASHED... EVERYONE ASSEMBLED BEFORE MUHAMMAD (MEN AND WOMEN SEPARATELY!), AND MADE THEIR CONVERSION—THOUGH **HIND** ARGUED ALL THE WAY...*

DO NOT STEAL.

DO NOT KILL YOUR CHILDREN...

DO NOT DISOBEY ME...

I USED TO TAKE A LITTLE FROM ABU SUFYAN, O.K.?

BY GOD, **YOU** KILLED MY CHILDREN AT BADR!

BY GOD, WOULD WE HAVE **SAT HERE** ALL THIS TIME IF WE MEANT TO DISOBEY YOU??!!

MEANWHILE, THE PAGANS WERE TRYING TO FIX THE ARABIAN **CALENDAR.** PURELY **LUNAR,** ITS TWELVE MONTHS FELL NEARLY **TWO WEEKS SHORT** OF A 365-DAY SOLAR YEAR.

WHAT A MESS... THE MOON GOD WON'T COOPERATE WITH THE SUN GOD...

WE NEED A BABYLONIAN CONSULTANT...

IN 631, THE PROPHET HAD A REVELATION THAT THE OLD CALENDAR WAS **SACRED** AND MUST **NEVER BE CHANGED**— SO THE ISLAMIC CALENDAR STAYED LUNAR AND HAS NEVER BEEN ADJUSTED TO THIS DAY.

WHY NOT LENGTHEN THE YEAR?

WHAT? AND PUT OFF TAX COLLECTIONS?

AND SO IT "DRIFTS" THROUGH THE SEASONS: THE MONTH OF **RAMADAN,** FOR INSTANCE, WHEN MUSLIMS **FAST** DURING **DAYLIGHT HOURS,** CAN COME IN WINTER OR SUMMER. THIS MAY EXPLAIN WHY THERE ARE SO FEW MUSLIMS NORTH OF THE **ARCTIC CIRCLE...**

GO **DOWN,** WON'T YOU? I'M **STARVING** UP HERE!

AND NOW, TO EVERYONE'S SURPRISE, MUHAMMAD MADE HUGE GIFTS FROM HIS TREASURY TO **ABU SUFYAN** AND HIS FAMILY, PUT HIM AND THE OTHER NEW CONVERTS IN CHARGE OF MECCA, AND WENT HOME TO MEDINA!

FOR ABU SUFYAN, 400 CAMELS...

MAN, THIS ISN'T SO BAD, IS IT?

GROWL...

FOR THE NEXT TWO YEARS, MUSLIM ARMIES RANGED OVER ARABIA, SMASHING IDOLS AND ENFORCING A NEW REVELATION: IDOLATERS MUST **CONVERT** OR **DIE.**

IN THAT CASE, WE **CONVERT!**

AND WE MEAN THAT SINCERELY...

AFTER A FINAL PILGRIMAGE TO MECCA, THE PROPHET AGAIN RETURNED TO MEDINA, WHERE HE FELL ILL AND DIED IN THE SPRING OF 632 AT THE HEIGHT OF HIS POWER.

TRULY A DIVINE BEING, WAS HE NOT?

NO. HE WAS A MAN.

AND ABU SUFYAN? HE LIVED ON, FAT AND HAPPY, FOR ANOTHER TWENTY YEARS.

WELL, **SOMEBODY** HAS TO TAKE CARE OF BUSINESS!

24

HAS **ANY PROPHET** EVER HAD **MORE SUCCESS** IN HIS OWN LIFETIME? MANY HAVE GAINED FAME AND FOLLOWERS, BUT WHO CAN MATCH MUHAMMAD FOR SHEER **ACREAGE**? HE WAS **POLITICIAN, GENERAL,** AND **SPIRITUAL GUIDE** ALL IN ONE!

NOW THE MOVEMENT HAD TO FIND A NEW LEADER, A **CALIPH** ("SUCCESSOR") WHO COULD PLAY ALL THOSE ROLES.

BUT A PROPHET, **NO!** MUHAMMAD WAS THE LAST OF THE PROPHETS!

AFTER A NOISY ELECTION (ONE CANDIDATE FROM MEDINA WAS BEATEN HALF TO DEATH) THE LEADERS CHOSE **ABU BAKR,** MUHAMMAD'S MOST TRUSTED COMPANION.

AYE

AYE

AYE

OW!

ON HEARING THE NEWS, TRIBES ACROSS ARABIA STOPPED SENDING THEIR TAXES TO MEDINA.

HEY, OUR DEAL WAS WITH ONE GUY...

AND **NEW PROPHETS** STARTED POPPING UP!

THERE IS NO GOD BUT **LALA,** AND I AM HIS PROPHET! **FORWARD!**

MAYBE.

WHATEVER.

WORKED ONCE, MIGHT WORK TWICE.

ABU BAKR REIGNED FOR TWO YEARS, THE WHOLE TIME SPENT PUTTING DOWN REBELLIOUS ARABIANS.

O.K.! I WAS **WRONG!!** WHO KNEW?

BY THE TIME HE DIED, ALL ARABIA WAS MUSLIM AGAIN... THE "FALSE PROPHETS" WERE GONE... AND IN 634, ANOTHER OF THE "COMPANIONS" BECAME CALIPH: **UMAR,** WHO DIRECTED THE GREAT ARAB CONQUESTS TO COME.

LET'S THINK BIG...

PLEASE RECALL (FROM P. 21) THAT CONSTANTINOPLE HAD REGAINED ITS EASTERN EMPIRE AFTER A LONG, WEARYING WAR WITH PERSIA... NOW THE EMPEROR **HERACLIUS** LOOKED FORWARD TO A GLORIOUS NEW "ROMAN" ERA!

WHO KNOWS? MAYBE WE CAN EVEN TAKE THE QUOTES OFF!

BUT CALIPH UMAR, WHO LED A LARGE ARMY WITH AN ANNOYING HABIT OF DIVIDING AND SQUABBLING ALONG TRIBAL LINES, HAD ANOTHER IDEA...

WHY NOT SEND THEIR AGGRESSIVE ENERGY **OUTWARD** AND ENLARGE THE "HOUSE OF ISLAM" AS MUCH AS POSSIBLE?

ROMAN, SCHMOMAN!

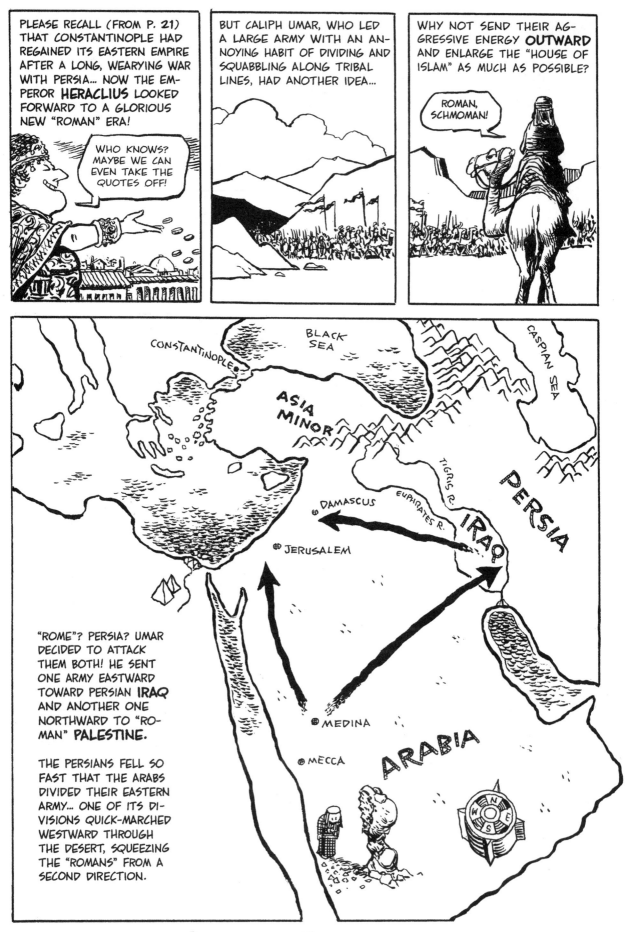

"ROME"? PERSIA? UMAR DECIDED TO ATTACK THEM BOTH! HE SENT ONE ARMY EASTWARD TOWARD PERSIAN **IRAQ** AND ANOTHER ONE NORTHWARD TO "ROMAN" **PALESTINE.**

THE PERSIANS FELL SO FAST THAT THE ARABS DIVIDED THEIR EASTERN ARMY... ONE OF ITS DIVISIONS QUICK-MARCHED WESTWARD THROUGH THE DESERT, SQUEEZING THE "ROMANS" FROM A SECOND DIRECTION.

LIKE PERSIA, THE "ROMANS" WERE WEAKENED BY WAR... THE EMPEROR RUSHED TO EQUIP AND MOVE MEN TO PALESTINE, AND BY THE SUMMER OF 636, HE HAD **50,000** MEN ON THE SCENE... ON AUGUST 20, THEY STAKED EVERYTHING ON A SINGLE BATTLE WITH THE ARABS—AND LOST. NO PRISONERS WERE TAKEN, AND "ROMAN" POWER FELL TO NOTHING IN A SINGLE DAY.

ALL PALESTINE AND SYRIA NOW SURRENDERED. IN 638, CALIPH UMAR QUIETLY ENTERED JERUSALEM.

WITHIN SIX YEARS, THIS ARMY WENT ON TO CONQUER **EGYPT,** WHILE THE EASTERN FORCE TOOK MOST OF **PERSIA.**

IN CONSTANTINOPLE, HERACLIUS DIED IN A STATE OF NEAR INSANE DISBELIEF.

IN THE CONQUERED LANDS, UMAR FOLLOWED THE PROPHET'S OWN POLICY: **NO FORCED CONVERSIONS** OF **CHRISTIANS** AND **JEWS**. THESE "PEOPLE OF THE BOOK"—NEARLY EVERYONE IN EGYPT, PALESTINE, AND SYRIA—WERE FREE TO KEEP THEIR RELIGION.*

WELL, NOT **EXACTLY** FREE... YOU **DO** HAVE TO LOAD THIS DONKEY WITH **MONEY**...

IN FACT, THE CALIPH **NEEDED** THOSE CHRISTIANS AND JEWS— THEY WERE THE TAXPAYERS! MUSLIMS WERE TAXED AT A **MUCH LOWER RATE** THAN NON-BELIEVERS.

THEY GREET US WITH OPEN ARMS!

EVEN SO, MOST PEOPLE'S TAXES WENT **DOWN**, SINCE NOW THEY WERE SUPPORTING A **NOMAD ARMY IN TENTS** INSTEAD OF BYZANTINE LUXURY.

THE *&%$#% "ROMANS" USED TO TAKE **TWO** DONKEY-LOADS!

THE ARABS HAD NEVER SEEN SO MUCH MONEY! WHEN **500,000** GOLD COINS ARRIVED IN MEDINA, THE CALIPH NEEDED THE NUMBER EXPLAINED...

IT'S LIKE FIVE THOUSAND A **HUNDRED** TIMES...

NO!

UP TO THIS TIME SYRIA, EGYPT, AND PALESTINE ALL HAD THEIR OWN INDEPENDENT CHRISTIAN CHURCHES SUCH AS THE **ARIANS, NESTORIANS, MONOPHYSITES,** AND MORE— WHOSE DISAGREEMENTS WITH THE ORTHODOX WERE FEW BUT LOUD.

PAGE 2,736, PARAGRAPH 48, SUBPARAGRAPH 9 SAYS THE LORD'S ENEMY **(NAMELY YOU)** SMELLS LIKE ROTTEN EGGS!

STRANGELY, I AGREE VERBATIM...

THE "ROMAN" (I.E., GREEK) CHURCH AND THE LOCALS TOOK TURNS PERSECUTING EACH OTHER, DEPENDING ON WHO WAS IN CHARGE OF THE GOVERMENT AT THE MOMENT.

ANATHEMA!

OH, THE OTHER CHEEK'S GONNA TURN SO SOON YOU WON'T KNOW WHAT HIT IT...

THE MUSLIMS, BY STOPPING THESE CHURCHES FROM ATTACKING EACH OTHER, CAME AS A **RELIEF** TO MANY CHRISTIANS!

WOULD YOU LIKE ME TO EXPLAIN THEIR FOUL HERESIES NOW?

NO! NO! ANYTHING BUT THAT!!!

IN 644, AFTER A TEN-YEAR REIGN, UMAR WAS MURDERED BY A DISGRUNTLED SERVANT... AND WHO WOULD SUCCEED HIM AS CALIPH?

NOW WE MEET ONE MORE FROM THE FIRST GENERATION: **ALI**, A YOUNG COUSIN RAISED BY MUHAMMAD AND KHADIJA AS AN **ADOPTED SON**, WHO HAD BEEN IN THE HOUSEHOLD WHEN THE REVELATIONS BEGAN. ALI WAS THE **THIRD MUSLIM!**

AND NO PICTURES, PLEASE!

NOT ONLY THAT, BUT ALI WAS **MARRIED** TO MUHAMMAD'S FAVORITE DAUGHTER **FATIMA** (BY SPECIAL PERMISSION, SINCE THEY WERE SEEN AS BROTHER AND SISTER)..

A GREAT FIGHTER, ALI LED THE ARAB ARMY AGAINST PERSIA... YET HE HAD BEEN TWICE **PASSED OVER** AS CALIPH... AND NOW HE WAS PASSED OVER FOR A **THIRD TIME**— IT'S HARD TO SAY WHY!

IS ALI NOT PIOUS?

IS ALI NOT MIGHTY?

IS ALI NOT IN IRAQ, FAR FROM WHERE DECISIONS ARE MADE?

INSTEAD, MUSLIM LEADERS PICKED A SCHOLARLY OLD GENT NAMED **UTHMAN**—WHO HAPPENED TO BE MARRIED TO MUHAMMAD'S OTHER DAUGHTER RUQAIYAH.

SO THE SUCCESSION HAS TO PASS THROUGH THE **DAUGHTER?**

DON'T EVEN SUGGEST IT...

UTHMAN WAS ALSO FIRST COUSIN ONCE REMOVED TO THAT MUSLIM-COME-LATELY **ABU SUFYAN**. THIS MADE ALI'S BACKERS FUME...

FUME FUME FUME

FOR **TWELVE YEARS** THEY FUMED AT WHAT THEY SAW: THE GOVERNOR OF SYRIA WAS **ABU SUFYAN'S SON**... THE GOVERNOR OF EGYPT WAS SOMEONE MARKED FOR DEATH BY MUHAMMAD, BUT STILL ALIVE THROUGH ABU SUFYAN'S PROTECTION.

WAS NOT ABU SUFYAN A DOOFUS?

IN 656, A CROWD OF ALI'S ALLIES ASSASSINATED THE THIRD CALIPH IN THE MEDINA MOSQUE, ACCIDENTALLY CHOPPING OFF HIS WIFE'S* FINGERS AS SHE TRIED TO PROTECT HIM.

*A SECOND WIFE, NOT MUHAMMAD'S DAUGHTER, WHO HAD SINCE DIED.

SO ALI BECAME CALIPH AT LAST...

BUT ALI UNDERESTIMATED ABU SUFYAN'S SON **MUAWIYA**, THE GOVERNOR OF SYRIA. LIKE HIS FATHER, MUAWIYA KNEW HOW TO TURN A SITUATION TO HIS OWN ADVANTAGE!

JUST LOOK AT HIM WITH HIS CHRISTIAN WIFE AND HIS SWIMMING POOL...

FUME FUME

SHOWING OFF THE WIDOW'S FINGERS IN THE MOSQUE, MUAWIYA CHALLENGED ALI TO BRING UTHMAN'S MURDERERS TO JUSTICE.

GASP

ALI WAFFLED... MUAWIYA RAISED TROOPS... AND AS THEY FACED ALI'S ARMY, MUAWIYA TOLD HIS LANCERS TO WRAP COPIES OF THE **KORAN*** AROUND THEIR SPEARS.

WATCH THIS...

*THE KORAN IS THE COMPILATION OF THE PROPHET'S POETIC REVELATIONS.

THIS MEANT: BETTER FOR MUSLIMS TO SETTLE THEIR PROBLEMS BY THE **WORD** THAN BY THE **SWORD**... AND ALI TOOK THE BAIT.

SIGH... IT'S ONLY REASONABLE...

EACH SIDE CHOSE SEVERAL LEARNED JUDGES, WHO BEGAN DISCUSSING THE LEGALITY OF ALI'S ELECTION...

BLAH BLAH
BLAH BLAH BLAH
BLAH BLAH BLAH
BLAH BLAH BLAH
BLAH BLAH BLAH
BLAH BLAH BLAH...

THE LONGER THIS WENT ON, THE BETTER, FROM MUAWIYA'S POINT OF VIEW!

BLAH BLAH
BLAH BLAH BLAH
BLAH BLAH BLAH
BLAH BLAH BLAH
BLAH BLAH BLAH
BLAH BLAH BLAH...

BECAUSE AT LAST, IN 661, SOME OF ALI'S **OWN BACKERS** LOST PATIENCE AND ASSASSINATED THIS SON, SON-IN-LAW, AND COUSIN OF THE PROPHET.

AND SO **MUAWIYA**, SON OF ABU SUFYAN, BECAME CALIPH!

I JUST **KNEW** THEY'D EAT EACH OTHER ALIVE!

A GIFTED "PEOPLE PERSON" LIKE HIS DAD, MUAWIYA SAT AS CALIPH IN DAMASCUS* FOR 20 YEARS... AND AFTER HIM HIS SON... AND SO ON, INCLUDING SOME COUSINS, FOR **90 YEARS** (661-750). THIS FAMILY OF CALIPHS IS KNOWN AS THE **UMAYYAD DYNASTY** (AFTER ABU SUFYAN'S UNCLE UMAYYA). IF ABU SUFYAN LIVED ON IN PARADISE, HE MUST HAVE HAD A GOOD, LONG LAUGH!!

"I NEVER APPLY THE SWORD WHEN THE LASH SUFFICES, NOR THE LASH WHEN MY TONGUE IS ENOUGH. IF THERE IS EVEN ONE THREAD BINDING ME TO MY FELLOW MAN, I DO NOT LET IT BREAK. IF HE PULLS, I LOOSEN, IF HE LOOSENS, I PULL."

—MUAWIYA

UMAYYAD MOSQUE, DAMASCUS — NOTE ROMAN INFLUENCE!

MUAWIYA CERTAINLY DID APPLY THE SWORD TO **ALI'S SUPPORTERS.** AS THE CALIPH'S MEN HUNTED THEM DOWN, PRO-ALI ACTIVISTS WENT UNDERGROUND AND CARRIED ON SECRETLY, MAINLY IN IRAN AND SOUTHERN IRAQ. THIS SECT OR POLITICAL PARTY, THE **SHIITES** (SHIA = PARTY) SURVIVES TO THIS DAY BELIEVING THAT ISLAM MUST BE RULED BY A DESCENDANT OF FATIMA AND ALI.

USING THE SEA-GOING SMARTS OF THE SYRIANS, MUAWIYA OUTFITTED THE FIRST **ARAB NAVY** AND LAUNCHED IT AGAINST THE COAST AND ISLANDS OF ASIA MINOR.

BY GOD, THIS **ROLLING** IS WORSE THAN A **CAMEL!**

MOAN... AND YOU CAN TELL A CAMEL TO **STOP...**

WHAT'S THAT?

THERE THEY FOUND THE **CO-LOSSUS OF RHODES,** A THOUSAND-YEAR-OLD **GIANT BRONZE ZEUS** AND ONE OF THE **SEVEN WON-DERS** OF THE ANCIENT WORLD—BUT TO THE MUSLIMS, JUST ANOTHER IDOL.

GRRR...

GRRRR...

THEY SMASHED IT IN PIECES AND SOLD THE METAL TO A JEWISH SCRAP DEALER, WHO NEEDED **900 DONKEYS** TO HAUL IT AWAY...

IT'S GOOD TO RECYCLE!

MUAWIYA ALSO SWUNG THE SWORD BEYOND HIS BORDERS... HE AND THE LATER UMAYYADS SENT THEIR ARMIES BEYOND IRAN, INTO ASIA MINOR, AND ALL THE WAY ACROSS NORTH AFRICA... UNTIL BY 690 THEY CONTROLLED A **VERY WIDE** EMPIRE.

IN 711, THE NORTH AFRICANS CROSSED INTO **SPAIN** AND QUICKLY SWEPT OVER MOST OF IT.

MUSLIM NAVIES ATTACKED EUROPEAN SHIPS IN PORT OR AT SEA. THE MEDITERRANEAN, WHICH ONCE **CONNECTED** EUROPE AND AFRICA, NOW **DIVIDED** THEM.

MUSLIM TRADERS CROSSED THE SAHARA DESERT, REACHING **GHANA**.

STILL, THERE WERE LIMITS. AS EARLY AS 652, THE ARABS GAVE UP ON **NUBIA**, UPRIVER FROM EGYPT, MAKING A TREATY CALLED THE **BAKT** WITH THE NUBIANS (FROM WHICH COMES THE ENGLISH WORD "PACT").

SEND SLAVES!

SEND WHEAT!

DONE DEAL!

AGAIN AND AGAIN, ARAB ARMIES BASHED AGAINST THE WALLS OF **CONSTANTINOPLE**, UNTIL AT LAST THEY QUIT TRYING IN 718.

THEY'RE JUST SO ⚡#& **BIG!**

FROM SPAIN THEY INVADED **FRANCE**, LOST A BIG FIGHT AT **TOURS** IN 732, AND LIMPED BACK TO SPAIN.

NOT **AGAIN!**

32

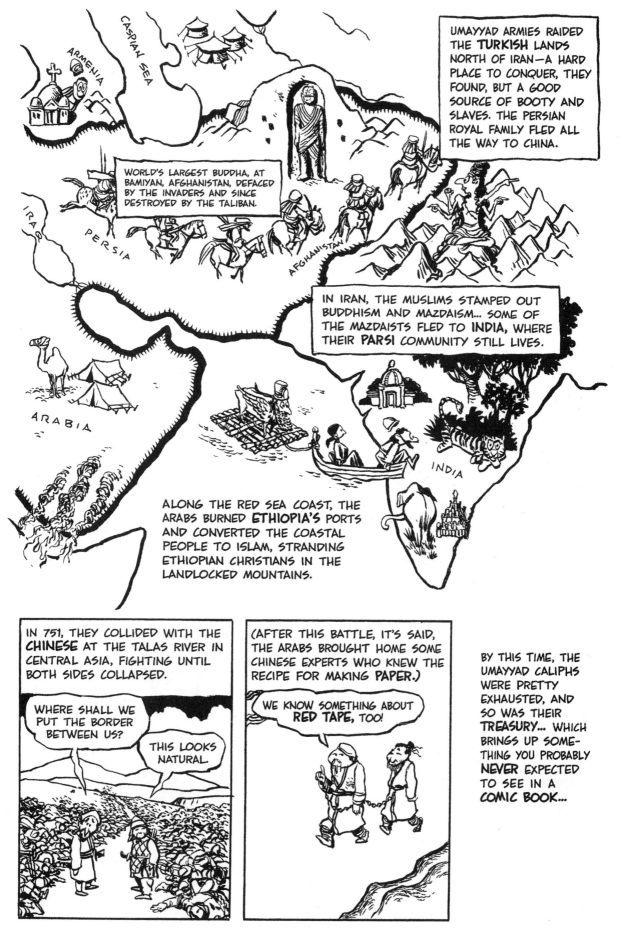

UMAYYAD ARMIES RAIDED THE **TURKISH** LANDS NORTH OF IRAN—A HARD PLACE TO CONQUER, THEY FOUND, BUT A GOOD SOURCE OF BOOTY AND SLAVES. THE PERSIAN ROYAL FAMILY FLED ALL THE WAY TO CHINA.

WORLD'S LARGEST BUDDHA, AT BAMIYAN, AFGHANISTAN, DEFACED BY THE INVADERS AND SINCE DESTROYED BY THE TALIBAN.

IN IRAN, THE MUSLIMS STAMPED OUT BUDDHISM AND MAZDAISM... SOME OF THE MAZDAISTS FLED TO **INDIA**, WHERE THEIR **PARSI** COMMUNITY STILL LIVES.

ALONG THE RED SEA COAST, THE ARABS BURNED **ETHIOPIA'S** PORTS AND CONVERTED THE COASTAL PEOPLE TO ISLAM, STRANDING ETHIOPIAN CHRISTIANS IN THE LANDLOCKED MOUNTAINS.

ARMENIA

CASPIAN SEA

IRAQ

PERSIA

AFGHANISTAN

ARABIA

INDIA

IN 751, THEY COLLIDED WITH THE **CHINESE** AT THE TALAS RIVER IN CENTRAL ASIA, FIGHTING UNTIL BOTH SIDES COLLAPSED.

WHERE SHALL WE PUT THE BORDER BETWEEN US?

THIS LOOKS NATURAL

(AFTER THIS BATTLE, IT'S SAID, THE ARABS BROUGHT HOME SOME CHINESE EXPERTS WHO KNEW THE RECIPE FOR MAKING **PAPER**.)

WE KNOW SOMETHING ABOUT **RED TAPE**, TOO!

BY THIS TIME, THE UMAYYAD CALIPHS WERE PRETTY EXHAUSTED, AND SO WAS THEIR **TREASURY**... WHICH BRINGS UP SOME-THING YOU PROBABLY **NEVER** EXPECTED TO SEE IN A **COMIC BOOK**...

UMAYYAD TAX POLICY

AND NOW, LET'S THRILL TO THE SHORT AND SORRY SAGA OF

IN THE BEGINNING, THE ARABS SPENT LITTLE ON GOVERNMENT. THE ARMY CAMPED IN TENTS, AND LEADERS LIKE UMAR LIVED SIMPLY.

HOW LONG COULD THE CALIPHS RESIST THE LURE OF **LUXURY?** NOT VERY LONG, IT TURNED OUT... THE UMAYYADS' PEOPLE, AFTER ALL, HAD BEEN **MERCHANTS!**

WE LOVE STUFF!

GLITTERING MOSQUES AND MANSIONS ROSE... BACK IN MEDINA, THE FOUNDERS' GRANDCHILDREN COLLECTED **GOVERNMENT PENSIONS** AND LIVED A LIFE OF MUSIC, POETRY, DINNER PARTIES, AND MULTIPLE MARRIAGES.

CITY OF PEACE

THE NEW CALIPH, ABU AL-ABBAS, CLAIMING TO BE A **BETTER MUSLIM** THAN THE UMAYYADS, SET ABOUT WIPING OUT THE ENTIRE FAMILY. HE NICKNAMED HIMSELF THE **BLOODSPILLER.**

IT'S GOOD TO BE HONEST!

ONE OF HIS MEN INVITED 80 UMAYYAD PRINCES TO A BANQUET, HAD THEM **STABBED**, COVERED THE QUIVERING BODIES WITH LEATHER RUGS, AND BADE THE OTHER GUESTS SIT DOWN AND DINE.

AMAZING MEAL!

YES... I FELT THE EARTH MOVE...

FAMILY MEMBERS LUCKY ENOUGH TO MISS THE PARTY NOW SCATTERED LIKE PIGEONS STARTLED BY A LOUD SOUND. TWO TEENAGE UMAYYAD PRINCES TRIED TO ESCAPE BY LEAPING INTO THE EUPHRATES RIVER... ONE TURNED BACK AND WAS KILLED... THE OTHER SWAM ON... HE WILL RESURFACE LATER...

GO! GO!

ABU AL-ABBAS SOON SICKENED AND DIED, LEAVING HIS BROTHER **AL-MANSUR**, WHO SHARED HIS TASTE FOR ODD EXECUTIONS, TO BE CALIPH. AL-MANSUR JAILED ONE REBEL IN A HOUSE OF **SALT BLOCKS** BUILT IN A **POND**, SO THE DISSOLVING BUILDING SLOWLY SANK, CRUSHING THE PRISONER.

COULDN'T HE **LICK** HIS WAY OUT?

WHAT? AND DIE OF HIGH BLOOD PRESSURE?

36

TO A THOUGHTFUL MAN LIKE AL-MANSUR, SQUASHING PEOPLE WAS A CRUSHING BORE... HE WANTED **MORE**... HE WANTED TO BUILD A PROPER **CIVILIZATION**, SOMETHING TO LAST A WHILE... AND AFTER CONSULTING THE WISE MEN OF **PERSIA**—POETS, SCHOLARS,* LAWYERS, EVEN FORMER **BUDDHIST MONKS**—THE CALIPH DECIDED TO START BY BUILDING A NEW **CAPITAL CITY**...

SOLID FOUNDATIONS, GENTLEMEN! SOLID FOUNDATIONS!!

IN 768, MUHAMMAD'S BRILLIANT BIOGRAPHER **MUHAMMAD IBN ISHAQ** DIED. THIS SCHOLAR DEVOTED HIS LIFE TO COLLECTING, COMPARING, AND EVALUATING TRADITIONAL STORIES ABOUT THE PROPHET, WHICH HE CRAFTED INTO A DETAILED, THOUGHTFUL BOOK.

ALTHOUGH CALIPH AL-MANSUR'S PEOPLE TRIED TO **REWRITE HISTORY** TO DOWNPLAY ABU SUFYAN'S ROLE, IBN ISHAQ DID HIS BEST TO BE FAIR.

PUT ABU SUFYAN ON THE **BACK** END OF THE DONKEY! MAKE HIS WIFE A SHREW! OR ELSE NO FUNDING!

SIGH...

IBN ISHAQ ALSO AUTHORED ONE OF HISTORY'S GREAT **SCHOLARLY PUT-DOWNS** WHEN HE MARKED UP A STUDENT'S PAPER BY SAYING, "IT COULD USE SOME VETERINARY SURGERY."

IN OTHER WORDS, IT'S A **DOG!** GET IT?

CONNECTED BY THE TIGRIS RIVER TO THE ARABIAN SEA, BAGHDAD SAW BOATLOADS OF IVORY, GOLD, SLAVES, SILKS, SPICES, PEARLS, AND GEMSTONES COME IN FROM AFRICA, INDIA, AND THE FAR EAST...

MONEY WAS MADE SO FAST IT SEEMED LIKE **MAGIC!**

HOW **DID** YOU GET SO RICH?

AHHH... IT'S A WONDERFUL TALE... ONE DAY, A LAMPSELLER CAME TO BAGHDAD CRYING **"NEW LAMPS FOR OLD!"** I TRADED IN MY OLD LAMP FOR A NEW ONE...

SUDDENLY, AS I POLISHED THAT LAMP, A **GENIE** EMERGED... "THANK YOU, MASTER," QUOTH THE GENIE IN A THUNDEROUS VOICE, "FOR FREEING ME FROM MY PRISON! IN GRATITUDE, I WILL GRANT THEE **THREE WISHES!**" NATURALLY, I...

Y'KNOW, I SELL **MORE LAMPS** WITH THAT STORY...

AL-MANSUR SURROUNDED HIMSELF WITH **PERSIAN ADVISERS**—A PERSIAN **VIZIER**, OR PRIME MINISTER, RAN THE STATE—AND THEY TOLD THE CALIPH ABOUT **ANOTHER** GREAT TREASURE: THE PERSIAN **LIBRARIES**.

WE PERSIANS PAY PEOPLE TO SIT AND THINK!

WHAT A DEEPLY AMUSING IDEA!

THESE LIBRARIES, FULL OF THE LORE OF THE HINDUS, PERSIANS, GREEKS, AND ROMANS, HAD ONE **PROBLEM** FROM THE CALIPH'S POINT OF VIEW: NOTHING WAS IN **ARABIC**.

A PERFECTLY GOOD LANGUAGE, AND IT'S MINE!

AL-MANSUR, WHO WANTED TO SPREAD THIS KNOWLEDGE TO THE WHOLE MUSLIM WORLD, ORDERED **EVERYTHING** TRANSLATED INTO ARABIC.

EVERYTHING?

SURE... OTHERWISE HOW DO I KNOW WHAT TO BURN?

THIS JOB TOOK **ONE HUNDRED YEARS**...

MORE ELIXIR OF KOLA NUTS?

SCRITCH SCRITCH SCRITCH

AND SO, IN THE 800s, THE STUDY OF SCIENCE, MATH, AND MEDICINE BEGAN TO FLOURISH IN BAGHDAD'S PART OF THE WORLD...

SCRITCH SCRITCH SCRITCH

THE PERSIAN CHEMIST **JABIR** STANDARDIZED LAB WORK AND MESSED WITH EXPLOSIVES...

WOW!

BOOM

THE MATHEMATICIAN **AL-KHWARISMI** (FROM KHWARISM, OR KHIVA, NORTH OF PERSIA), PRODUCED THE FIRST BOOK OF **ALGEBRA.**

THANKS, AL, THANKS AL-OT...

OTHERS WROTE ABOUT AGRICULTURE, MEDICINE, OPTICS, MINERALOGY, METEOROLOGY, ASTRONOMY, ETC. ETC. ETC....

SCRITCH SCRITCH SCRITCH SCRITCH SCRITCH

AND SO, BESIDES PALACES AND MOSQUES, A TRAVELER IN THOSE DAYS MIGHT ALSO FIND PUBLIC HOSPITALS, PARKS AND GARDENS, PLACES FOR TRAVELERS, BATHS, UNIVERSITIES, ASTRONOMICAL OBSERVATORIES—IN SHORT, THE INGREDIENTS OF A GREAT CIVILIZATION...*

WHICH WAY DO WE GO FROM HERE?

UM...

NO WONDER AL-MANSUR'S FAMILY RULED ISLAM FOR A FULL **FIVE CENTURIES** (750–1258). THEY ARE KNOWN AS THE **ABBASID** DYNASTY, AFTER THEIR REMOTE ANCESTOR IN MECCA, MUHAMMAD'S UNCLE AL-ABBAS.

SOME ENGLISH WORDS THAT COME FROM MEDIEVAL ARABIC: ALCOHOL, ALCHEMY, ALEMBIC, ALKALI, ALGEBRA, AMBER, ALGORITHM, ARSENAL, ADMIRAL, ALCOVE—NOT TO MENTION **SUGAR** AND **SYRUP**!

AH, THE INGREDIENT OF A GREAT CIVILIZATION!

MANY OF THESE "ARABIC" WORDS THEMSELVES CAME ORIGINALLY FROM SOMEWHERE ELSE. FOR EXAMPLE, THE WORD "SINE" IN TRIGONOMETRY, ACCORDING TO MANY HISTORIES, COMES FROM AN ARABIC WORD MEANING "BAY." BUT THE SINE HAS NOTHING TO DO WITH A BAY.

$$\text{SINE OF } A = \frac{y}{r}$$

IN FACT, THE ARABS JUST COPIED THE WORD "SINE" FROM HINDU GEOMETRY, WHERE IT CAME FROM A SANSKRIT WORD MEANING **BOWSTRING**.

WHEN RADIUS = 1, "BOWSTRING" = TWICE THE SINE OF A

SOURCE: A CARTOON HISTORY OF MATH PUBLISHED IN INDIA!

ALTHOUGH THE ARAB CONQUESTS HAD ENDED, ISLAM'S INFLUENCE STILL SPREAD. MUSLIM PREACHERS AND JUDGES, TRAVELING WITH MERCHANTS, MADE CONVERTS IN AFRICA, INDIA, THE SPICE ISLANDS, AND CHINA.

CHRISTIAN EUROPE ALSO NOTICED ISLAM'S SUCCESS...

GOD'S WOUNDS!

IN CONSTANTINOPLE, THE EMPEROR LEO DECIDED THE MUSLIMS WERE RIGHT ABOUT ONE THING: **IMAGES** WERE **BAD.** HE STARTED A CENTURY OF PICTURE- AND STATUE-SMASHING, OFFICIALLY KNOWN AS **ICONOCLASM.**

THE MUSLIMS ARE DOING **SOMETHING** RIGHT—MAYBE **THIS** IS IT!

THE GERMAN EMPEROR KARL (A.K.A. **CHARLE-MAGNE**), SENT DIPLOMATS TO BAGHDAD TO MAKE AN ALLIANCE AGAINST CONSTANTINOPLE. (HE PREFERRED ROME TO "ROME.")

DON'T FORGET THE JEWISH TRANSLATOR!

CHARLEMAGNE'S PEOPLE MUST HAVE REACHED BAGHDAD, THOUGH NO MUSLIM RECORD OF THE VISIT HAS SURVIVED...

BECAUSE THE GERMANS WROTE ABOUT THE AMAZING STUFF THAT **CAME BACK** FROM THE CALIPH!

HE SENT CHARLEMAGNE A **CLOCK**, A **CHESS SET**, AND AN **ELEPHANT**... GERMANY HAD NEVER SEEN THE LIKE... THE KING ORDERED HIMSELF A **BURIAL SHROUD** EMBROIDERED WITH ELEPHANTS...

I WANT TO BE WITH YOUR IMAGE ALWAYS!

THIS, IN TURN, WOKE UP THE **SWEDES**.

BY ODIN'S WHISKERS!

A FEW DECADES AFTER THE ELEPHANT EPISODE, THEY PUSHED SOUTH, FOUNDED **RUSSIA**, AND BEGAN SHIPPING AMBER AND SLAVES TO BAGHDAD.

SWEDEN

RUSSIA

SLAVES OR SLAVS?

SAME TO US.

AND THEN, JUST WHEN EVERYTHING LOOKED ROSY, BAGHDAD'S EMPIRE BEGAN TO FALL APART...

43

BREKDOWN

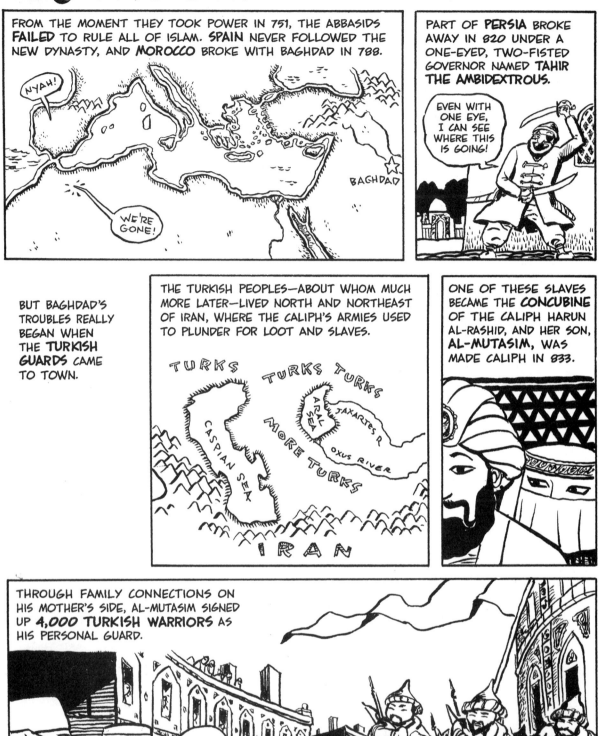

FROM THE MOMENT THEY TOOK POWER IN 751, THE ABBASIDS **FAILED** TO RULE ALL OF ISLAM. **SPAIN** NEVER FOLLOWED THE NEW DYNASTY, AND **MOROCCO** BROKE WITH BAGHDAD IN 788.

NYAH!

WE'RE GONE!

BAGHDAD

PART OF **PERSIA** BROKE AWAY IN 820 UNDER A ONE-EYED, TWO-FISTED GOVERNOR NAMED **TAHIR THE AMBIDEXTROUS.**

EVEN WITH ONE EYE, I CAN SEE WHERE THIS IS GOING!

BUT BAGHDAD'S TROUBLES REALLY BEGAN WHEN THE **TURKISH GUARDS** CAME TO TOWN.

THE TURKISH PEOPLES—ABOUT WHOM MUCH MORE LATER—LIVED NORTH AND NORTHEAST OF IRAN, WHERE THE CALIPH'S ARMIES USED TO PLUNDER FOR LOOT AND SLAVES.

TURKS

TURKS TURKS

ARAL SEA

JAXARTES R

OXUS RIVER

CASPIAN SEA

MORE TURKS

IRAN

ONE OF THESE SLAVES BECAME THE **CONCUBINE** OF THE CALIPH HARUN AL-RASHID, AND HER SON, **AL-MUTASIM,** WAS MADE CALIPH IN 833.

THROUGH FAMILY CONNECTIONS ON HIS MOTHER'S SIDE, AL-MUTASIM SIGNED UP **4,000 TURKISH WARRIORS** AS HIS PERSONAL GUARD.

GROWING CANE HAS ALWAYS BEEN **HARD WORK,** BUT ESPECIALLY SO IN SOUTHERN IRAQ. MILLENNIA OF **IRRIGATION** (THIS WAS ANCIENT SUMER, REMEMBER!) HAD BADLY **SALTED** THE **SOIL**... SO BEFORE PLANTING, WORKERS HAD TO **HACK AWAY** TWO OR THREE FEET OF SALTY EARTH*... THEN CAME THE GROWING SEASON, AND FINALLY THE BLISTERY, BACKBREAKING LABOR OF CUTTING... ALL PERFORMED BY THOUSANDS OF **EAST AFRICAN SLAVES,** KNOWN IN ARABIC AS THE **ZANJ** (AS IN "ZANZIBAR").

*APPARENTLY, CHEMISTS EXTRACTED NITRATES FROM THIS SOIL AND USED IT FOR VARIOUS PURPOSES, INCLUDING POSSIBLY FIREWORKS.

IN 868, A FIGHT BROKE OUT ON ONE OF THE PLANTATIONS... SOME OF THE ZANJ SLAVES TURNED ON THEIR OVERSEERS AND HACKED THEM TO DEATH... THE SELF-FREED SLAVES TOOK TO THE SWAMPS... THE REBELLION SPREAD...

50

THE CARTOON HISTORY OF THE UNIVERSE

Volume 15

DIVERSITY

TEN THOUSAND YEARS AGO, AFRICA LOOKED A LITTLE DIFFERENT THAN IT DOES TODAY... THE MOUNTAINS AND JUNGLES AND PLAINS WERE THERE, OF COURSE, BUT IN THE NORTH, WHERE A VAST DESERT NOW SPANS THE WIDEST PART OF THE CONTINENT, THERE WERE **LAKES**, AND **GRASS**, AND HERDS OF **ANIMALS**...

DRY SPELL

PEOPLE NATURALLY FOLLOWED THESE HERDS OF WILD GAME... AND AS TIME WENT BY, THE HUNTERS NOTICED SOMETHING: UNLIKE MOST ANIMALS, LIKE ZEBRAS AND GIRAFFES, WHICH WISELY TOOK TO THEIR HEELS WHEN THEY SAW HUMANS COMING, CERTAIN **OBSEQUIOUS BOVINES** WERE COMFORTABLE WITH PEOPLE... NEVER COMPLAINED WHEN BOSSED AROUND... AND SO, GRADUALLY, THE AFRICAN HUNTERS BECAME **LORDS OF THE COWS...**

PEOPLE WHO OWN COWS USUALLY WANT EVEN MORE COWS—MORE COWS THAN THEIR NEIGHBOR OWNS, THAT IS... SO INSTEAD OF KILLING THEIR COWS, THEY MILK THEM OR (IN HARD TIMES) BLEED THEM... HERDS GROW LARGER... AND SO, UNDER HUMAN MANAGEMENT, COWS TEND TO OUTGROW THE SUPPLY OF **COW-FOOD**...

WHEN CATTLE GOBBLE UP GRASS AND TRAMPLE DOWN SOIL, THE EARTH GROWS HARDER, LESS SPONGY AND POROUS... RAIN RUNS OFF INSTEAD OF SOAKING IN... GRASSES DIE BACK... SCRUBS AND THORNBUSHES SPROUT...

AS THE LAND DRIES, SO DOES THE AIR... LESS RAIN FALLS... RIVERS SHRINK TO A TRICKLE... LAKES EVAPORATE, LEAVING BEDS OF SALT... CATTLE, LED BY THEIR BRAINY OWNERS, FIND THE LAST BITS OF GRASS... AND SO ON...

UNTIL, CUT BY GULCHES AND DOTTED WITH SALT FLATS, THIS FORMER GRASSLAND BECOMES THE **SAHARA DESERT,** COVERING ONE QUARTER OF AFRICA AND STILL GROWING!!*

UH... NOW THIS WAY...

WHY DO WE STILL TRUST THEM?

DID OVERGRAZING ALONE DRY UP THE SAHARA, OR DID THE CATTLE HAVE HELP FROM OTHER CLIMATIC FACTORS? THIS IS A SUBJECT SCHOLARS LOVE TO DEBATE...

CHANGING OCEAN CURRENTS... WIND PATTERNS... CLOUD FORMATIONS....

BUT SURELY THE AFRICANS BEAR **SOME** RESPONSIBILITY?

BLAMING THE VICTIM IS SO RACIST!!

ONE THING IS CERTAIN: CATTLE AND SHEEP, UNDER HUMAN GUIDANCE, HAVE TURNED (OR HELPED TURN) PRAIRIE INTO DESERT IN ASIA AND AMERICA, TOO...

WHITE FOLKS HAVE RUINED LAND! CAN'T BLACK FOLKS RUIN LAND TOO?

WHITE PEOPLE RUIN WORSE! COUGH.

SUBTLE SUNSPOT CYCLES? COFF COFF...

AND THESE DESERTS HAVE AN UNSETTLING WAY OF ALWAYS GETTING BIGGER, NOT SMALLER!

UM... DID ANYONE REMEMBER TO BRING WATER?

LIBERAL!

HERDERS AND CATTLE SQUEEZED SOUTHWARD, CROWDING AND JOSTLING THEIR NEIGHBORS. HUNDREDS OF DIFFERENT CULTURES CONVERGED ON **LAKE CHAD**, SHRUNKEN BUT STILL WET.

LAST ONE IN IS A BLADDER OF SOUR MILK!

MEANWHILE, NOMADS FROM THE FAR NORTH SPREAD INTO THE SAHARA, BRINGING SHEEP, GOATS, AND DONKEYS—ANIMALS THAT COULD LIVE ON WHATEVER SCRUBBY VEGETATION WAS LEFT. BESIDES RAISING LIVESTOCK, THE NOMADS ALSO CARRIED ON A TRADE IN SLAVES AND SALT.

WHAT HAPPENED WHEN SAHARAN HUNTERS AND HERDERS WENT SOUTH AND RAN INTO THE PEOPLE ALREADY THERE? WARS, NO DOUBT... BUT SURELY ALSO ALLIANCES, INTERMARRIAGE, EXCHANGES OF IDEAS AND THINGS... IN OTHER WORDS, HISTORY... TOO BAD WE DON'T KNOW THE DETAILS, BUT ONLY SOME OF THE RESULTS...

IN THE WEST, THE COWHERDS MADE LITTLE HEADWAY. THESE GRASSLANDS WERE TURNING INTO FARM COUNTRY, WITH PLENTY OF FARMERS DEFENDING IT...

#*&*!$% VICIOUS VEGETARIANS!

PELTED BY OKRA! HOW RUDE!

BUT IN THE SOUTHEAST, THE CATTLE-KEEPERS FOUND WIDE-OPEN PLAINS TEEMING WITH BEASTS—JUST LIKE HOME!

OH, THAT FINE, FAMILIAR SMELL...

EXCEPT FOR ONE LITTLE THING: A BITING INSECT, THE TSETSE FLY.

GAH!

TSETSE FLIES INFECT CATTLE WITH SLEEPING SICKNESS. IT'S BAD!

I DON'T GET IT... SHE'S ALWAYS BEEN A MORNING COW...

AND SO, THE HERDERS HAD TO STAY IN SELECTED FLY-FREE ZONES, LEAVING THE PLAINS TO THE WILDLIFE.

ZZZZ

WE'RE IMMUNE! I SAID, "WE'RE IMMUNE!" HEY! PSST! YOO-HOO...

HAVE YOU NOTICED THAT WE'RE A LITTLE **VAGUE** ABOUT **TIMING** HERE? THAT'S BECAUSE NOBODY KNOWS EXACTLY WHEN ALL THIS HAPPENED...

IT'S 2:30 RIGHT NOW...

THE SAHARA PROBABLY BEGAN DRYING UP AROUND **4000 BCE**. THE LAST SAHARAN GIRAFFE MUST HAVE LIVED AROUND 2500 YEARS LATER.

SAHARAN ROCK CARVING

WHEN DID WEST AFRICANS BEGIN TO FARM? ESTIMATES RANGE FROM 2000 TO 1000 BCE. *

WHEN DO YOU START FARMING?

FIRST THING EVERY MORNING.

THEN, A LITTLE LATER (WE THINK!), PEOPLE SOUTH OF THE SAHARA LEARNED HOW TO SMELT AND WORK **IRON**.

BY 500 BCE, THE OPEN COUNTRY OF WEST AFRICA WAS SOWN WITH FIELDS OF GRAIN AND WORKED BY PEOPLE WITH IRON TOOLS.

HOE! HOE! HOE!

HEH HEH HEH...

WHEN AND HOW DID WEST AFRICA DEVELOP AGRICULTURE? SCHOLARS HAVE SEVERAL IDEAS. SCENARIO #1: WEST AFRICANS GOT THE IDEA FROM VISITING EGYPTIANS.

LIKE THIS—

GHASP! THROWING AWAY FOOD?

SCENARIO #2: THEY FIGURED IT OUT ON THEIR OWN.

SCENARIO #3 (VERY DEBATABLE): THEY FIGURED IT OUT ON THEIR OWN A **LONG TIME AGO** AND TAUGHT IT TO THE ANCIENT EGYPTIANS!

GHASP! THROWING AWAY FOOD?

THE WANDERING BANTU

SOUTH OF THE OPEN FARM COUNTRY LOOMS THE **EQUATORIAL FOREST**, DENSE WITH LIFE... HOT, HUMID, DRAINED BY COUNTLESS STREAMS AND IMMENSE RIVERS, THE JUNGLE HAS SUPPORTED PEOPLE FOR AGES.

LONG AGO, THE FOREST-DWELLERS FOUND **GOLD**... SOMEDAY THIS GOLD WOULD CHANGE THE WORLD, BUT FOR NOW IT WAS ONLY A NOVELTY ITEM.

WHAT USE IS IT, REALLY?

SOME WONDERFUL ARTISTS LIVED IN THE FOREST TOO.

NIGERIAN STATUETTE, NOK PERIOD, C. 500 BCE

AROUND 2,300 YEARS AGO, SOME WEST AFRICAN FARMERS BEGAN LEAVING THEIR HOMES AND MOVING SOUTH. WE KNOW THEM TODAY AS THE **BANTU.**

ORIGINAL HOMELAND OF THE BANTU

FARMERS LIKE TO HAVE **LARGE FAMILIES,** SO THEY ALWAYS NEED **MORE LAND**... AND BESIDES, THE SQUEEZE OF PEOPLE FROM THE DRYING NORTH NEVER LET UP... SO BUNCHES OF BANTU HIT THE ROAD.

YOU'RE SURE YOU WON'T STAY?

SOME OF THEM PLUNGED RIGHT INTO THE FOREST AND HEADED SOUTH.

OTHERS, CARRYING SEEDS AND EQUIPMENT, HIKED **AROUND** THE FOREST, KEEPING THE TREES TO THEIR RIGHT.

LIKE THE CATTLE KEEPERS, THE BANTU FARMERS ALSO CAME TO THE PLAINS AND HILLS OF EAST AFRICA.

THEY BROKE GROUND, SOWED THEIR SEEDS, AND PRAYED FOR RAIN.

MAYBE A RAIN DANCE WILL HELP!

AND WAITED... BECAUSE, UNFORTUNATELY, THE RAINS COME TO EAST AFRICA ON A **DIFFERENT SCHEDULE** FROM THE RAINS OF WEST AFRICA... SO THE BANTUS' FAVORITE GRAINS FAILED TO SPROUT. NOW WHAT?

I'M HUNGRY...

THE TRICK TO RAIN DANCES IS TO DO THEM **IN SEASON**...

THE ANSWER TO THE BANTU PRAYERS CAME FROM FAR AWAY, FROM **EASTERN ASIA**, TO BE EXACT, WHERE SEAFARING FOLK CALLED THE **MALAY** HAD BEGUN TO EXPLORE THE OPEN OCEAN AROUND THEM.

THE MALAY AND THEIR COUSINS THE **POLYNESIANS** SAILED THEIR DOUBLE-HULLED BOATS TO THE WORLD'S **REMOTEST ISLANDS...*** AND THEY ALWAYS TOOK THEIR **FARM GEAR** WHEN THEY WENT: PIGS, BANANAS, EDIBLE RATS, ASIAN YAMS, AND TARO (A PLANT WITH BIG, STARCHY, EDIBLE ROOTS).

THE REMOTEST POLYNESIAN SETTLEMENT WAS **EASTER ISLAND**, 2000 MILES FROM ANYWHERE. THERE RIVAL TRIBES TRIED TO IMPRESS EACH OTHER BY SETTING UP GREAT **STONE STATUES** MOVED INTO PLACE WITH LOGS FROM THE ISLAND'S FORESTS.

AS THEY CUT DOWN TREES, SOIL BEGAN TO ERODE... FARMLAND DETERIORATED... AND RAINFALL EVEN GREW SCARCE. (TREES PUMP WATER UP INTO THE AIR.)

DESPERATELY TRYING TO CONQUER EACH OTHER, THE CLANS PUT UP EVEN **MORE STATUES**—UNTIL, IN THE END, NOT A TREE WAS LEFT, AND THE ISLANDERS WERE TRAPPED IN A RUINED ECOSYSTEM.

LET'S BUILD SOME BOATS AND GO!

OUT OF WHAT?

WHILE MOST BOATLOADS OF MALAYS WENT EAST, SOME HEADED WEST, CROSSED THE INDIAN OCEAN (4,000 MILES!), AND LANDED IN **MADAGASCAR** MORE THAN 2,000 YEARS AGO.

IN MADAGASCAR THEY FOUND AN UNINHABITED TROPICAL PARADISE.

LET'S DESPOIL IT A LITTLE!

BEST OF ALL, BANANAS AND TARO **THRIVED** THERE: SAME WEATHER AS HOME!

YUP... LOOKS FAMILIAR...

SOON THE MALAYS SEEM TO HAVE SENT OUT COLONISTS TO SETTLE THE MAINLAND.

AND THERE THEY MET THE FAMISHED **BANTU**.

SUDDENLY THE BANTU HAD FOOD CROPS THAT WOULD GROW IN **EAST AFRICA**... THEY TOOK THOSE YAMS AND TARO AND **RAN WITH THEM**... RAN ALL OVER THE SOUTHERN PART OF THE CONTINENT, THAT IS...

OH, WELL... BACK TO MADAGASCAR...

WHEN THE BANTU CAME TO EAST AFRICA, PEOPLE ALREADY LIVED THERE. IN FACT, PEOPLE—MODERN, HOMO SAPIENS-TYPE PEOPLE—HAVE LIVED IN EAST AFRICA FOR SOMETHING LIKE

150,000 YEARS.

MY PEOPLE WERE HERE BEFORE THEY WERE PEOPLE!

THESE FOLKS, WHO STILL ROAMED THE LAND HUNTING AND GATHERING, MUST HAVE BEEN SURPRISED BY WHAT THEY SAW!

THEY'RE CLEARING THE GROUND...

AND CHOPPING IT UP!

AND PLANTING FUNNY LITTLE TREES...

IN FACT, THEY MUST NOT HAVE LIKED IT AT ALL, BECAUSE THE BANTU WERE OBVIOUSLY TAKING THE LAND—AND SO...

FORWARD!!!

BUT THE BANTU HAD BETTER TECHNOLOGY, BETTER ORGANIZATION, MORE FOOD, MORE PEOPLE—A WINNING COMBINATION, ALL ELSE BEING EQUAL.

WHOA, THERE'S A LOT OF THEM!

HOW CAN ANYONE BREED SO FAST AND STILL FOLLOW THE WANDERING VEGETABLES?

AND SO, OVER MANY CENTURIES, BANTU FARMERS TOOK OVER MOST OF SOUTHERN AFRICA, WHILE THE EARLIER INHABITANTS RETREATED TO THE BADLANDS.

ARE THEY STILL AT IT?

AFRAID SO...

THE BANTU HAD LESS SUCCESS WITH THOSE OTHER NEWCOMERS, THE COW-KEEPERS, BUT THAT'S A STORY FOR LATER...

"KING SOLOMON'S MINE!"

UPRIVER FROM EGYPT, IN ANCIENT TIMES, LAY TWO HIGHLAND KINGDOMS, **NUBIA** AND **ETHIOPIA**. THE EGYPTIANS USED TO TRADE AND SQUABBLE WITH NUBIA, BUT COULD NEVER CONQUER MUCH OF IT FOR LONG, AND ETHIOPIA WAS... WELL, IT WAS BEYOND NUBIA.

YOU CAN'T REALLY GET THERE FROM HERE!

LIKE SO MANY NEIGHBORS IN HISTORY, NUBIA AND ETHIOPIA WERE OFTEN **ENEMIES**. WHEN ONE WAS STRONG, THE OTHER WAS WEAK, FOR THEY THRIVED AT EACH OTHER'S EXPENSE.

AS FAR AS I'M CONCERNED, THE BORDER IS RIGHT OVER **THERE**...

NUBIA'S WEALTH CAME FROM **GOLD MINES, CATTLE,** AND **SLAVES...** THE NUBIANS OFTEN RAIDED THEIR WESTERN NEIGHBORS, KIDNAPPED THEM, AND SHIPPED THE SLAVES DOWNRIVER TO EGYPT.

NUBIAN PRINCESS AND ENTOURAGE VISIT EGYPT.

"NUBIAN SLAVE" BECAME A STOCK PHRASE, A CLICHÉ OF ANCIENT HISTORY... BUT IN FACT, MOST OF THESE "NUBIAN" SLAVES CAME FROM SOMEWHERE ELSE.

NUBIA IS JUST THE LOCATION OF THE DEALERSHIP!

SILENCE!

WHEN EGYPT DECLINED, NUBIA'S FORTUNES ROSE. IN THE 700s BCE, A NUBIAN KING CONQUERED EGYPT, AND EGYPTIAN-STYLE TEMPLES AND PYRAMIDS ROSE ALONG THE UPPER NILE.

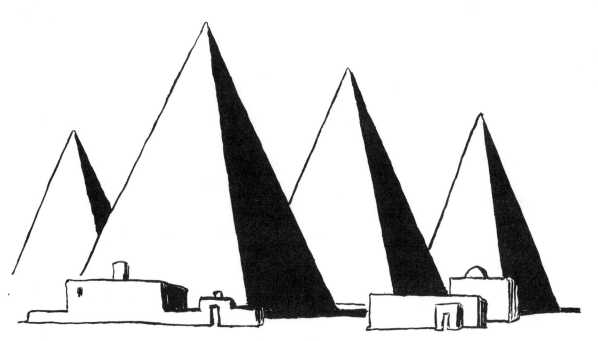

UPHILL FROM NUBIA, ETHIOPIA'S **MOUNTAINS** HAD THEIR ADVANTAGES: FOR ONE, THEY MADE THE PLACE HARD TO **CONQUER**... FOR ANOTHER, THEY CREATED A CLIMATE IDEAL FOR GROWING A CERTAIN **WONDERFUL SHRUB**, A PLANT THAT REALLY DOES HAVE **MAGIC BEANS**, A BOTANICAL CRAVED BY HALF THE WORLD...

THE WORLD DISCOVERED COFFEE FAIRLY LATE IN HISTORY. FOR THE LONGEST TIME, IT WAS ETHIOPIA'S SECRET.

WHUZZAT? HM? HAH?

NEVER MIND!

SO, FOR INSTANCE, THE GREEK HERODOTUS WROTE THAT ETHIOPIANS WERE THE MOST **BEAUTIFUL** PEOPLE IN THE WORLD—BUT HE FAILED TO NOTICE THAT THEY WERE ALSO THE MOST **ALERT!**

I WONDER WHY THEY'RE SO TALKATIVE...

YAWN... WILL YOU EXCUSE ME FOR A SECOND? I NEED MY THIRD CUP OF THE MORNING TO GET THROUGH THE REST OF THIS...

CLINK

WHIRRRRR

TINK TINK TINK

FWUMP

BUP BUP BUP BUP

BUP **GUSHH**

GLUG GLUG GLUG

AAAAH! ASIWASSAYING, **ETHIOPIA**ISJUSTACROSSA NARROWWATERWAYFROM **YEMEN**ANDPEOPLEHAVEGONE BACKANDFORTHANDMINGLED FORCENTURIESANDNOWETHIOPIA'S HISTORYREALLY**BEGINS!**

MOMMY! THE HISTORIAN IS SCARY!

66

THE ETHIOPIANS TRACE THEIR NATIONAL ROOTS BACK TO THE 900s BCE, WHEN THE **QUEEN OF SHEBA** VISITED **KING SOLOMON** IN JERUSALEM (1 KINGS 10: 1-10). SHEBA IS IN YEMEN, BUT THE ETHIOPIANS CLAIM THE QUEEN AS ONE OF THEIR OWN.

THE QUEEN, GOES THE STORY, WENT TO JERUSALEM TO SEE HOW SPLENDID SOLOMON HAD MADE IT.

AFTER A LONG JOURNEY, SHE MET THE KING, FAMED FOR HIS WISDOM, HIS SPENDING, AND HIS **HUNDREDS** OF WOMEN...

FROM THE MOMENT SHE ARRIVED, THE QUEEN WAS STIFF-ARMING THE KING'S ADVANCES...

LISTEN! A SONG I WROTE JUST FOR YOU!

YOUR EYES ARE LIKE DOVES... YOUR HAIR IS LIKE A FLOCK OF GOATS... YOUR TEETH ARE LIKE SHEEP...

FRUSTRATED BUT RESOURCEFUL, SOLOMON TOLD HIS **CHEF** TO LOAD SHEBA'S DINNER WITH **SALT**.

IN THE MIDDLE OF THE NIGHT, THE QUEEN WOKE UP BURNING WITH THIRST.

OVER HEE-ERE!

THE ONLY WATER, OF COURSE, WAS IN SOLOMON'S ROOM...

THE QUEEN, SAY THE ETHIOPIANS, WENT HOME **PREGNANT**... HER SON BECAME **ETHIOPIA'S FIRST KING**... HIS LINE LASTED NEARLY **3,000 YEARS** INTO THE MID-TWENTIETH CENTURY... AND ETHIOPIAN CULTURE HAS HAD SOME **JUDAIC CUSTOMS** THE WHOLE TIME!

CHRISTIAN KINGS

AFTER **ALEXANDER THE GREAT** CONQUERED EGYPT IN THE LATE 300s BCE, THE PTOLEMIES WHO FOLLOWED HIM BEFRIENDED ETHIOPIA AS AN ALLY AGAINST THEIR COMMON ENEMY, NUBIA.

THE GREEKS ALSO KNEW THAT ETHIOPIA COMMANDED THE MOUTH OF THE **RED SEA**, A KEY WATERWAY ON THE ROUTE TO **INDIA**. IT **PAID** TO BE FRIENDS!

WINE AND GEWGAWS FROM FAR AWAY, O NEGUS!*

IT'S GOOD TO HAVE FRIENDS!

*THE ETHIOPIAN MONARCH'S TITLE

AROUND 200 BCE, GREEK MERCHANTS SET UP SHOP AT AN ETHIOPIAN SEAPORT, ADULIS, AND THERE, SOME THREE CENTURIES LATER, CHRISTIAN PREACHERS BEGAN TO ARRIVE.

MAN, WITH THIS STUFF OUR WORK SHOULD GO TWICE AS FAST!

IN THE EARLY 300s OF OUR ERA, A GREEK CHRISTIAN TUTORED THE ETHIOPIAN CROWN PRINCE **EZAMA**.

JESUS LOVES YOU!

WELL, HE MUST HAVE VERY GOOD TASTE THEN...

EZAMA BECAME KING, HAD HIMSELF BAPTIZED IN 333, AND MADE CHRISTIANITY THE **OFFICIAL RELIGION** OF THE STATE!

ALL RIGHT... **ONE MORE TIME**... HOW CAN I WORSHIP A PRINCE OF **PEACE** AND STILL RUN A **GOVERNMENT**?

IT'S A MIRACLE!

IT MAY SOUND PARADOXICAL—OR IT MAY HAVE SOUNDED PARADOXICAL ONCE—BUT EZAMA WAS ONE OF THE FIRST **AGGRESSIVE CHRISTIANS.** HE FLUNG HIS ARMIES AGAINST NUBIA AND IN 350 SACKED ITS CAPITAL MEROE.

WOW! GOD IS GOOD!

ETHIOPIAN POWER EXPANDED... AXUM, THE CAPITAL, GREW GREAT... EMBASSIES FROM CONSTANTINOPLE CAME AND WENT, BABBLING DOCTRINE...

I SAY GOD HAS ONE NATURE...

I SAY GOD HAS THREE...

WELL, WHO SENT YOU?

THE EMPEROR. WHO SENT YOU?

THE EMPEROR'S WIFE...

AS WE SAW ON P. 4, ETHIOPIA INVADED YEMEN IN 525,* DRIVING THE LAST JEWISH KING INTO THE SEA.

THEN CAME THE FAILED MARCH ON MECCA... PERSIA'S INVASION OF YEMEN... AND BY THE EARLY 600s, ETHIOPIA'S STRENGTH WAS DWINDLING...

OH, MANNNN!

AFTER INVADING YEMEN, HISTORIANS SUSPECT, THE KING OF ETHIOPIA TURNED AGAINST THE JEWS OF HIS OWN COUNTRY, WHO TOOK TO THE MOUNTAINS TO ESCAPE PERSECUTION.

THERE THEY LIVED, NEARLY CUT OFF FROM THE OUTSIDE WORLD, FOR THE NEXT **1,400 YEARS.**

ARE YOU SURE WE GOT ALL THE **BOOKS**?

WHO AM I SUPPOSED TO ASK?

IN 1948, THE NEW STATE OF **ISRAEL** WELCOMED "ALL JEWS" AS CITIZENS—BUT WERE THESE ETHIOPIANS "REAL" JEWS? RABBIS AND POLITICIANS ARGUED FOR **25 YEARS** BEFORE DECIDING TO ANSWER **YES!**

ARE!

AREN'T!

LET'S ASK A HISTORIAN!

WHAT DO I KNOW?

ISLAM ARRIVES

ISLAM, WHICH HAS PLAYED A HUGE ROLE IN AFRICAN HISTORY, FIRST CAME TO THE CONTINENT **PEACEFULLY.** IN 618, YOU MAY RECALL, MUHAMMAD SENT MISSIONARIES TO ETHIOPIA.

THEY MET WITH THE NEGUS, OR KING, AND TOLD HIM THEY WORSHIPPED THE GOD OF THE ETHIOPIANS... AND UNLIKE MECCA'S **PAGANS,** THEY SAID, THE MUSLIMS WERE **ETHIOPIA'S FRIENDS.** THE NEGUS WAS HAPPY TO HEAR IT.

&*%$# PAGANS POOPED IN MY CHURCH!

HE WELCOMED THE GROUP TO HIS COUNTRY... BUT NEITHER HE NOR HIS PEOPLE SHOWED MUCH INTEREST IN ISLAM...

SEE? WOULDN'T **YOU** LIKE TO TRY **THIS?**

LIKE TO WATCH, MAYBE...

EVENTUALLY, MOST OF THE MUSLIMS WENT HOME.

AND ANOTHER THING—HAVE YOU REALLY THOUGHT THROUGH THE **SEQUESTRATION OF WOMEN** THING?

IN THE MEANTIME, ISLAM HAD GROWN MILITANT, AND THE NEXT MUSLIM "VISIT" WAS THE **INVASION OF EGYPT** IN 640.

NEGUS, THEY'VE CONQUERED ARABIA! THEY'VE BEATEN THE "ROMANS"! THE EGYPTIANS! THE PERSIANS! THE SYRIANS!

UM... CAN CAMELS CLIMB MOUNTAINS?

FROM EGYPT THEY MOVED UPRIVER AND ATTACKED NUBIA, OR TRIED TO...

HELL, NO!!

THE FORCE WAS WITH THE NUBIANS—THE FORCE OF GRAVITY, THAT IS... THEY HELD OFF THE ARABS AND ANNOYED THEM WITH CROSS-BORDER RAIDS...

WHY DON'T YOU GIVE UP AND GO AWAY?

BECAUSE WE HAVE THE **MORAL** HIGH GROUND!!

UNTIL BOTH SIDES AGREED TO TALK.

ALL RIGHT. **WHAT** IN GOD'S NAME* DO YOU **WANT** WITH US?

UM... LET ME ASK YOU THE SAME QUESTION...

*THE NUBIANS WERE CHRISTIAN BY THIS TIME.

IN 652, THEY AGREED TO A TREATY (SEE P. 32), IN WHICH THE MUSLIMS PROMISED TO LEAVE NUBIA ALONE: THE ONLY COUNTRY TO GET THIS PROMISE FROM THE ADVANCING ARAB ARMIES.

AND YOU PROMISE TO SEND US A YEARLY SHIPMENT OF WHEAT, DON'T FORGET!

YEH YEH... DON'T REMIND US...

FARTHER SOUTH, ETHIOPIA AND ARABIA BATTLED ON AND ON... IN 702, THE ETHIOPIAN NAVY ATTACKED **JIDDA,** NEAR MECCA.

THIS IS **OUTRAGEOUS!** HASN'T ANYONE HEARD THIS IS **OUR CENTURY?**

THE ARABS RETURNED THE FAVOR BY DESTROYING ETHIOPIA'S MAIN PORT, ADULIS.

SORRY!

SORRY!

AN ARAB ARMY OCCUPIED THE ETHIOPIAN COASTLINE AND "PERSUADED" THE PEOPLE THERE TO CONVERT TO ISLAM.

MOSTLY MUSLIMS

IN THIS WAY, ETHIOPIA BECAME **LANDLOCKED,** AN ISOLATED MOUNTAIN KINGDOM CUT OFF FROM ROME, CONSTANTINOPLE, AND OTHER CHRISTIAN CENTERS... AND SO IT REMAINED FOR THE NEXT **1,200 YEARS,** ALMOST TO THE PRESENT DAY.

MEANWHILE, THE ARABS HAD "SWEPT OVER" NORTH AFRICA (AS HISTORIANS LIKE TO SAY). THIS BIT OF HOUSEKEEPING TOOK NEARLY **70 YEARS**— AND NOT JUST BECAUSE THERE WAS SO MUCH SAND ON THE FLOOR.

Constantinople

Rome

Carthage

Alexandria

THE FIRST OBSTACLE SOUNDED MIGHTY BUT FELL FAST: THE "ROMANS," WHO RULED CARTHAGE, AND THE GERMANIC **VANDALS** WHO LORDED OVER THE REST OF THE COAST, COLLAPSED IN A GREAT BATTLE NEAR CARTHAGE IN 647.

THE NEXT OBSTACLE TURNED OUT TO BE MORE **DIFFICULT**: NAMELY, **EVERYONE ELSE** WHO LIVED THERE, IN OTHER WORDS, THE **BERBER TRIBES**.

WHAT DO **YOU** WANT?

UM... CAN WE TALK TO THE MEN?

THE ARABS SAW THESE FIERCELY INDEPENDENT DESERT DWELLERS AS **KINDRED SPIRITS**, SO THEY MADE AN EFFORT TO TALK TO THEM.

LOOK HOW **ALIKE** WE ARE... EXCEPT WITH YOU, THE **GUYS** WEAR THE VEILS, THE **GODS** ARE FALSE AND THE **WOMEN** ARE MOUTHY... BUT WE CAN **FIX** THAT!

IF THE BERBERS ACCEPTED ISLAM, IT WAS SAID, THEY WOULD BE **TREATED AS EQUALS**: THEIR MEN WOULD JOIN THE GREAT ARMY, WIN NEW LANDS, SHARE IN THE SPOILS, DOMINATE WOMEN, AND BE **LORDS OF THE LAND.** THAT'S WHAT THE ARABS SAID!

OR ELSE WE KILL YOU! NOW— HOW DOES **THAT** SOUND?

WE'LL GET BACK TO YOU!

AFTER PLENTY OF THIS PALAVER, A BERBER CHIEFTAIN TOOK THE BAIT: **KUSAILA**, HEAD OF THE **AWRABA** PEOPLE, BROUGHT HIS ENTIRE TRIBE TO ISLAM IN THE YEAR 678.

AS PROMISED, THE COMBINED ARAB-AWRABA ARMY WON BATTLE AFTER BATTLE.

TO SAVE THEMSELVES, MORE BERBERS RUSHED TO JOIN UP AND CONVERT!

AND WE MEAN IT!!

TOO BAD... NOW THE **ARAB** SOLDIERS WERE COMPLAINING ABOUT **TOO LITTLE BOOTY!** WHOM COULD THEY **PLUNDER** IF EVERYONE WAS THEIR **FRIEND?**

IT'S THE ERA BEFORE CANNED FOOD... WE **EAT** PLUNDER!

TRUE... TRUE...

THEIR GENERAL SAW THE POINT... GO AHEAD, HE SAID, AND PILLAGE **KUSAILA'S** PROPERTY. BIG MISTAKE!

KUSAILA SAID NOTHING... HE WENT ON WITH THE ARMY ALL THE WAY TO THE ATLANTIC OCEAN.

THERE THE AWRABA TURNED ON THE ARABS.

AFTER A SLAUGHTER, THE BERBERS MARCHED IN TRIUMPH BACK TO THE ARAB BASE AT CARTHAGE.

FOR **TEN YEARS** KUSAILA RULED NORTH AFRICA, BUT AT LAST A NEW ARAB ARMY ARRIVED, AND IN 690 THE BERBER CHIEF FELL IN BATTLE.

IN THE TURMOIL THAT FOLLOWED, A NEW BERBER LEADER EMERGED. HISTORY, HAVING FORGOTTEN HER REAL NAME, REMEMBERS HER ONLY AS **AL-KAHINA,** THE PROPHET.

THE GODDESS OF **FIRE** WILL PROTECT US!

I DON'T LIKE THE SOUND OF THIS...

IN 696, AL-KAHINA TOLD HER PEOPLE TO **SCORCH** THE **EARTH**—BURNING THEIR OWN CROPS TO STARVE THE ARABS.

UM... PROPHET... ARE YOU **SURE?**

HAVE YOU EVER MET A PROPHET WHO **WASN'T?**

OF COURSE, THIS POLICY ALSO STARVED AL-KAHINA'S FRIENDS, WHO SOON BECAME HER **FORMER** FRIENDS.

I SEE A GREAT VICTORY!

ALL I CAN SEE ARE **KABABS...** COUS-COUS...

EGGPLANT STUFFED WITH SPICED ONIONS...

STILL, WITH A FEW FOLLOWERS, SHE FOUGHT ON FOR YEARS.

MAN, THESE BERBER WOMEN JUST WON'T STAY INVISIBLE!

IN 704 THE ARABS LAUNCHED A LAST, RUTHLESS, SEVEN-YEAR CAMPAIGN AGAINST THE WESTERN BERBERS, SLAUGHTERING EVERY RESISTER, AND BY 711, ALL NORTH AFRICA WAS ISLAMIC. FROM KUSAILA'S CONVERSION, THE CONQUEST HAD TAKEN **33 YEARS.**

"THE BERBERS APOSTATIZED 70 TIMES," WROTE THE HISTORIAN IBN KHALDUN.

A PRO-ARAB BERBER, **TARIK** IBN **ZIYAD** IBN **ABDULLAH** IBN **WALGHU,** WAS NAMED GOVERNOR OF THE FAR WEST, BASED IN TANGIER.

TARIK SOON WENT OFF TO HELP INVADE **SPAIN,** YET ANOTHER PLACE FOR ARABS AND BERBERS TO SQUABBLE, BUT THAT IS A STORY FOR LATER...

MINE!

MINE!

SUDDENLY, SUDAN

CAMELS, HISTORIANS SEEM TO AGREE,* FIRST CAME TO AFRICA FROM ARABIA IN ROMAN TIMES. LONG BEFORE THE ARABS ARRIVED, SAHARAN PEOPLE WERE PUTTING THEMSELVES AND THEIR FREIGHT ON CAMELBACK.

YOU'RE &%$# WELCOME!

*POSSIBLY THE ONLY TIME THEY HAVE EVER DONE SO.

WITH CAMELS ONE COULD STILL CROSS THE SAHARA, BY NOW HORRENDOUSLY DRY, IN A JOURNEY OF OVER A MONTH.

THE LAST REST STOP ON THE WAY, ABOUT A WEEK FROM THE END, WAS A BLEAK OASIS TOWN BUILT ALL OUT OF SALT. FROM THERE A LONE MESSENGER WOULD SPEED SOUTH FOR SUPPLIES—AND WOE TO THE CARAVAN IF HE FAILED TO MAKE IT.

HOW DO YOU LIKE LIVING HERE?

THE JOB IS O.K., BUT MY BLOOD PRESSURE IS OFF THE CHART.

AND SO, AROUND THE YEAR 700, THE FIRST MUSLIMS DRAGGED THEIR PARCHED TONGUES ACROSS THE DESERT WASTES TO THE **SUDAN** ("LAND OF THE BLACKS" IN ARABIC).

YOU WANNA TUCK THAT THING IN?

YETH... THORRY...

GHANA RISES

THE TRAVELERS CAME TO **KUMBI SALEH**, BETWEEN THE SENEGAL AND NIGER RIVERS, WHERE A PEOPLE CALLED THE **SONINKE** HAD TAKEN CHARGE AND ESTABLISHED THE KINGDOM OF **GHANA**. ALL THE SUDAN'S GOLD PASSED THROUGH GHANA AS IT HEADED NORTH...

Senegal R. — *KUMBI SALEH* — *Niger R.* — GOLD MINES — GOLD MINES

SINCE THE KING TOOK A CUT OF EVERY GOLDEN OUNCE, HE TENDED TO BE DAZZLINGLY ACCESSORIZED.

OW! MY EYES!

DETAILS ARE SKETCHY, BUT IT SEEMS THAT THE KING'S SUBJECTS FLOPPED ON THEIR FACES IN HIS PRESENCE AND THAT A **DRUM*** FORMED A SPECIAL PART OF THE OFFICIAL REGALIA.

IT'S AGAINST MY RELIGION TO BOW TO ANYONE BUT GOD!

THAT'S NICE! NOW ADJUST OR DIE.

HEARING AFRICANS USE DRUMMING FOR **LONG-DISTANCE COMMUNICATION**, LATER EUROPEANS WOULD CALL IT THE "JUNGLE TELEGRAPH." BUT **SOUND** CARRIES POORLY IN THE JUNGLE.

BUMBA BUMBA

IT'S SO QUIET, YOU CAN HEAR A GNAT SNORE!!

IN FACT, THE WESTERN SUDANESE KINGDOMS OF **GHANA, MALI, SONGHAY,** AND **KANEM** WERE ALL IN **OPEN COUNTRY**, WHERE DRUMBEATS CARRY A LONG WAY.

BUPPA BUPPA BUP BOP BUM BUM BUM BOPPA BUM BOOOM BOPPA BUM BOPPA BUB BUB TAKKA BOM BOM TAK TAK BOM BOM

WHAT? WHAT?

OH, AHEM... NOTHING!

IN SOME OF THESE AFRICAN SOCIETIES, THE KING OR CHIEF OWNED **ALL** THE DRUMS—GIVING HIM AN EFFECTIVE **MONOPOLY** ON **INFORMATION TECHNOLOGY**.

EUROPEANS DIDN'T EVEN **HAVE** A TELEGRAPH UNTIL 1850!

BESIDES FLOPPING FOR THE KING, ANOTHER CUSTOM UNNERVED THE MUSLIMS: MOST SUDANESE WORE FEW **CLOTHES**...

SO? IT'S HOT HERE, AND OUR DARK SKIN PROTECTS US FROM **SOLAR RADIATION**...

GOD HELP ME!

THE VISITORS TRIED TO EXPLAIN THE ADVANTAGE OF **MODESTY**...

GOD SAYS TO **COVER** WOMEN FROM TOP TO TOE... THIS KEEPS MEN **CALM**...

WHO ISN'T CALM?

LOOK AT HIM SWEAT...

THEY ALSO EXPLAINED THAT THEY HAD **BUSINESS CONTACTS** ON THREE CONTINENTS.

GOD BROUGHT WEALTH TO **US**, AND HE CAN BRING IT TO **YOU**, TOO!

AM I DOING SO BADLY?

AFTER THINKING THINGS OVER, THE KING OFFERED THEM SOME LAND **OUTSIDE TOWN**... A PLACE TO LIVE AND DO BUSINESS WITHOUT ALWAYS BEING UNDERFOOT.

LET GOD BRING WEALTH TO **YOU**, AND **YOU** BRING IT TO **ME**!

AND IF THEY WANTED TO MEET SOME GHANAIAN **WOMEN**, THAT COULD BE ARRANGED TOO!

YOU WANT THEM ALL **DRAPED UP**? TO HELP YOU **RELAX**?

UM... MAYBE WE **CAN** LEARN TO LIVE WITH **SOME** OF YOUR CUSTOMS...

SO GHANA KEPT ITS OLD RELIGION, BUT A **MUS-LIM TOWN** GREW UP ALONGSIDE KUMBI SALEH.

WE ARE FLEXIBLE WHEN WE NEED TO BE...

THE CARAVANS OF GHANA GOLD,* AFTER CROSSING THE SAHARA, ALL CAME TO A PLACE CALLED **SIJILMASA**—ROMANTIC NAME!—A REMOTE, FLYBLOWN OUTPOST ON THE DESERT'S NORTHERN EDGE. FROM SIJILMASA THE PRECIOUS STUFF MOVED ON TO TANGIER, KAIROWAN, CORDOBA, DAMASCUS, AND THE REST OF THE MUSLIM WORLD...

I SMELL GOLD!

I SMELL WATER!

BESIDES GOLD, THESE CARAVANS CARRIED ANOTHER VALUABLE ITEM FROM THE SOUTHERN FOREST: A KIND OF NUT CALLED **KOLA.**

1000 MLES ACROSS A TRACKLESS WASTE, YOU'RE CARRYING **NUTS?**

NORTH AFRICANS LOVED TO BREW UP THE DRIED NUTS, NOT FOR NOURISHMENT BUT FOR THE **BUZZ.** KOLA NUTS CONTAIN **CAFFEINE!**

OOO!

SEE THE POINT NOW?

THE NUTS MAY HAVE GONE OUT OF FASHION, BUT THEIR **NAME** IS STILL EVERYWHERE, OFTEN LINKED BY A HYPHEN TO SOME OTHER STIMULATING NAME...

METH COLA

Kokaine Kola

DRECKOLA

78

NOW WE COME AGAIN TO THE DREARY DECADE OF THE

A REVOLTING TIME IN THE MUSLIM WORLD...

I'M REVOLTING!

NO, I'M REVOLTING. YOU'RE DISGUSTING.

REMEMBER UMAYYAD **TAX POLICY?** THE ONE THAT PUSHED PEOPLE TO **CONVERT** BY CUTTING THEIR TAXES? IN THE 720s, THE GOVERNOR OF NORTH AFRICA RAISED TAXES ON **RECENT CONVERTS.** THE BERBERS—ALL RECENT CONVERTS—CRIED FOUL!

FOUL!

THEY HAD A FEW OTHER COMPLAINTS TOO: BERBER TROOPS ALWAYS WENT IN FRONT, WHILE ARABS BROUGHT UP THE REAR... ARABS HOGGED THE BEST BOOTY, WHILE BERBERS GOT LITTLE OR NONE... ARABS STOLE BERBER SHEEP AND GOATS AND KIDNAPPED BERBER WOMEN... AND SO, IN 740, THE BERBERS MUTINIED AGAIN, TURNING ON THEIR ARAB OFFICERS...

AFTER THIS "BATTLE OF THE NOBLES" CAME A MELEE, AS THE BERBER TRIBES TURNED AGAINST **EACH OTHER...**

AND NORTH AFRICA SPLINTERED INTO LITTLE CHIEFDOMS... ONE OF THEM, THE "BANK VAULT OF THE DESERT" SIJILMASA, STAYED INDEPENDENT FOR THE NEXT TWO CENTURIES.

'EY! SIJILMASA! WOULDN'T IT BE BETTER IF WE ALL JOINED FORCES? GOT TOGETHER? HELPED EACH OTHER OUT? COME ON... WHAT DO YOU SAY...?

I SAY: YOU'RE OUT THERE, AND THE GOLD IS IN HERE...

WHILE ALL THIS WAS GOING ON, ISLAM WAS CHANGING... THE UMAYYADS FELL... THE ABBASID DYNASTY BEGAN... BAGHDAD WAS FOUNDED... THE NEW CALIPHS AND THEIR PERSIAN VIZIERS TRIED HARD TO TREAT ALL MUSLIMS EQUALLY... BUT IT WAS TOO LATE, AND AFRICA WAS SO FAR AWAY...

I KNOW IT'S OUT THERE SOMEWHERE...

IN 788, THE GOVERNOR OF **MOROCCO** REFUSED TO SEND ANY MORE MONEY TO BAGHDAD.

I LOVE EVERYTHING ABOUT THE CALIPH BUT HIS TAX COLLECTORS!

IN THE EARLY 800s, CIVIL WAR BROKE OUT IN **EGYPT**... FOR DECADES, BAGHDAD KEPT TRYING TO COLLECT, BUT PAYMENT WAS SPOTTY.

YEH... JUST A MINUTE...

WITH EGYPT WEAK, **NUBIA** DECIDED TO ASSERT ITSELF. IN 836, THE NUBIANS STOPPED SENDING BAGHDAD THE GOLD AND SLAVES PROMISED LONG AGO IN THE BAKT.

WHY GIVE 'EM AWAY WHEN WE CAN SELL 'EM?

"'TIS MORE BLESSED TO SELL THAN TO GIVE..." OR SOMETHING LIKE THAT...

FOR THE NEXT CENTURY AND A HALF, NUBIA THRIVED BY SENDING GOLD AND SLAVES DOWN THE NILE... RICH NUBIANS BUILT MANSIONS WITH HOT AND COLD RUNNING WATER...

YEAH... YOU WASH THOSE HANDS!

WITH NO MONEY RUNNING OFF TO BAGHDAD, THE **FAR WEST** ALSO DID WELL. TRADE FLOURISHED BETWEEN MOROCCO AND GHANA (WITH LUCKY SIJILMASA IN THE MIDDLE)... AND **MORE MOSQUES** ROSE SOUTH OF THE SAHARA.

OF COURSE, NONE OF THIS DID BAGHDAD ONE BIT OF GOOD...

WHERE DOES THIS LEAVE US, SON?

HOLDING THE BAG, DAD.

INSTEAD, BAGHDAD'S BUSINESS MOVED INTO **EAST AFRICA**... ARABS AND PERSIANS OPENED SHOPS ALONG THE COAST SELLING CARPETS, CLOTH, SPICES, BRASS-WARE, AND CHEAP CHINESE POTTERY...

BECAUSE **FREE TRADE** IS GOOD FOR YOU!

WHY SHOULD WE LET YOU LAND?

MOGADISHU

PEMBA
ZANZIBAR
DAR ES SALAAM

IN EXCHANGE, THEY TOOK AWAY IVORY, GOLD, AND, INEVITABLY, **HUMAN BEINGS.**

UM... WHY DO THEY CALL IT "FREE" TRADE AGAIN?

BY THE MID-800s, THE EAST AFRICAN **SLAVE TRADE** WAS BOOMING. MASSES OF AFRICANS WERE SHIPPED FROM THE LAND OF THE "ZANJ" (TANZANIA, ZANZIBAR)* TO THE MARSHES OF **SOUTHERN IRAQ**...

*FROM PERSIAN ZANG=ETHIOPIA

AND SO CAME THE YEAR **869** AND A **HISTORICAL TURNING POINT**...

ZANJ REVOLT

IN BAGHDAD AT THIS TIME, YOU MAY RECALL (SEE P. 45), TURKISH GUARDS WERE BUSILY SETTING UP AND KNOCKING DOWN CALIPHS AT A WHIM.

OO! I FEEL AN ATTACK OF WHIMSY COMING ON!

LOOK OUT!

THE REVOLT, WHICH CRIPPLED THE CALIPHATE, BEGAN AMONG THE SLAVES IN THE SUGAR PLANTATIONS OF SOUTHERN IRAQ.

IN 869, ONE **ALI IBN MUHAMMAD** APPROACHED THE RUNAWAYS AND OFFERED TO LEAD THEM... HE CLAIMED TO BE THE **RIGHTFUL CALIPH**... HE CLAIMED TO BE A **MAGICIAN**... HE MADE ALL SORTS OF CLAIMS!

I CAN TURN THE ZANJ INTO A MIGHTY FIGHTING FORCE! I CAN TURN SLAVES INTO PRINCES! I CAN VAPORIZE FROGS! I'M A WIZARD! WATCH ME!

GASP!

POF

WE CAN ONLY GUESS WHAT THE ZANJ SAID TO EACH OTHER ABOUT ALI IBN MUHAMMAD...

CLEARLY A STARK, RAVING LUNATIC!

BUT HE DOES KNOW THE COUNTRYSIDE...

WHY NOT GIVE HIM A CHANCE?

I WANT TO KNOW HOW TO DO THAT "POF" THING...

SOME OF THE ESCAPEES FOLLOWED HIM... THEY MUST HAVE WON BATTLES AND COLLECTED WEAPONS... FOR SOON SLAVES FROM ALL OVER THE NEIGHBORHOOD ROSE UP AND JOINED IBN MUHAMMAD'S ARMY.

THE CALIPH'S ARMY CAME DOWN AND FELL TO A ZANJ AMBUSH IN THE SWAMPS.

BOO!

LATER, DOWNSTREAM AT BASRA, PEOPLE NOTICED THE SOLDIERS' HEADS FLOATING BY...

FOR FOURTEEN YEARS, THE ZANJ HELD SOUTHERN IRAQ... NOTHING COULD TOUCH THEM... AND OF COURSE THEY ALWAYS HAD **SUGAR** TO EAT...

THIS REBELLION IS HARD ON THE TEETH...

THEY FOUGHT WITH DESPERATE BRAVERY AND WITHOUT MERCY— AS EX-SLAVES HAVE FOUGHT EVER SINCE MOSES AND SPARTACUS.

LIBERTY OR DEATH!!

YOU LACK SOPHISTICATION, MY DEAR FELLOW! HAVE YOU NEVER CONSIDERED THE IDEA THAT NO ONE IS EVER COMPLETELY FREE?

BUT COMPLETELY DEAD, YES!

BUT IN THE END, THEY FELL. IN 883, THE CALIPH MADE THE ZANJ PRIORITY #1 AND SENT DOWN A POWERFUL FORCE THAT TOOK THE ZANJ FORT, KILLED ALI IBN MUHAMMAD, AND MASSACRED HIS FOLLOWERS.

THIS SHOULD TEACH YOU TO THINK TWICE ABOUT REBELLION...

AND YOU TO THINK TWICE ABOUT SLAVERY.

AND THAT IS THE END OF THAT... ISN'T IT?

THE EFFECTS OF THE ZANJ REVOLT WERE FELT IN ASIA, EUROPE, AND AFRICA...

CALIPH, CALIPH, CALIPH

FIRST AFRICAN EFFECT OF THE ZANJ REVOLT: **EGYPTIAN INDEPENDENCE.** WHEN THE REVOLT BEGAN, THE CALIPH BEGGED THE GOVERNOR OF EGYPT FOR MONEY... THE GOV' REFUSED, AND EGYPT NEVER OBEYED BAGHDAD AGAIN.

YEAH!

SECOND EFFECT: THE EAST AFRICAN TRADE WITH THE PERSIAN GULF SLUMPED FOR CENTURIES.

WHAT HAPPENED TO THE BRASSWARE, THE CROCKERY, THE WILD SAILOR BOYS?

THIRD EFFECT: ASSORTED MUSLIM REVOLUTIONARIES, FLEEING THE CALIPH, CAME TO AFRICA.

GOOD NEWS! I BRING HOLY BOOKS!

OH, MAAAANNN...

FOR EXAMPLE, A SHIITE PREACHER CALLED **ABU ABDULLAH** SHOWED UP AMONG THE **KUTAMA BERBERS**, A POOR TRIBE IN THE NORTH-CENTRAL SAHARA.

HIS LEADER, HE SAID, WAS THE **MAHDI**, THE ENLIGHTENED ONE, A RIGHTEOUS MAN WHO WOULD OUST CORRUPTION AND BRING PURITY AND JUSTICE TO THE MUSLIM WORLD—A MAN DESCENDED, INCIDENTALLY, FROM THE SAINTED ALI AND FATIMA.

THIS "MAHDI"— IT ISN'T REALLY **YOU,** IS IT?

OH, NONO- NONO!

THE MAHDI WOULD BE COMING OUT OF HIDING SOON, HE SAID, AND THEY BELIEVED...

COME ON, ADMIT IT! IT'S YOU!

OH HA HA HA HA NO!

BEHIND ABU ABDULLAH, THE KUTAMA CONQUERED MOST OF TUNISIA IN A SINGLE YEAR, 903.

WELL, IF IT **ISN'T** YOU, IT **SHOULD** BE, SHOULDN'T IT?

SIGH...

TO MAKE A LONG STORY SHORT, THE SLAVS AND ZAWILA PUT DOWN THE BERBERS, AND FROM THAT POINT ON, THE MAHDI'S POWER DEPENDED ON AN **ARMY OF SLAVES.**

WHATEVER WORKS—TO PROMOTE RIGHTEOUSNESS, THAT IS!

TWENTY YEARS LATER, THE MAHDI STILL RULED... NORTH AFRICAN SHIITES NOW CALLED HIM THE LEADER OF **ALL ISLAM,** THE TRUE CALIPH (OR IMAM, AS SHIITES SAY), A TITLE THAT CARRIED EXTRA MORAL AUTHORITY.

IT'S NICE TO KNOW WE'RE SLAVES TO A GOOD CAUSE...

(MEANWHILE, JUST TO KEEP UP, SPAIN'S RULER WAS CALLING HIMSELF CALIPH, TOO, MAKING A TOTAL OF THREE!)

AFTER THE MAHDI DIED, HIS SON TOOK OVER... THEIR SHIITE DYNASTY IS KNOWN AS THE **FATIMIDS** AFTER THEIR ANCESTOR, MUHAMMAD'S DAUGHTER FATIMA... AT LEAST, THEY SAID SHE WAS THEIR ANCESTOR, THOUGH SOME PEOPLE SAID OTHERWISE!

I HEAR THEY'RE JEWISH ON THE MAHDI'S MOTHER'S SIDE...

THE FATIMID CALIPHS FOLLOWED THE MAHDI'S PLAN: THEIR ARMIES CONQUERED **SICILY** (948), **EGYPT** (969), AND **SIJILMASA** (978), WHICH THEY RULED WITH **50,000** "NUBIAN" SLAVE SOLDIERS,* ASSORTED SLAVS, AND A POWERFUL NAVY.

RIGHTEOUS!

NORMALLY, WE THINK OF SLAVES AS PEOPLE WHO HAVE TO BE **DISARMED** AND GUARDED, SO THE IDEA OF PUTTING **WEAPONS** INTO THEIR HANDS BY THE THOUSAND BOGGLES THE MIND.

I'M A CREATIVE GENIUS!

STILL—YOU CAN SEE HOW IT HAPPENED. THE MAHDI WANTED AN ARMY... HE HAD NO ROOTS IN THE COUNTRY... NOBODY OWED HIM ANYTHING!

SO IT'S SLAVES, ALL THE WAY UP TO THE GENERAL STAFF!

AMAZINGLY, IT WORKED... THE FATIMID SLAVE ARMY LASTED FOR **CENTURIES** AND WAS COPIED BY MANY LATER EMIRS, CALIPHS, AND SULTANS... BUT STILL, IT CAN'T HAVE BEEN THE MOST **RELAXING** ARRANGEMENT IN THE WORLD...

YOU GOING TO KEEP US HAPPY, MAHDI?

ULP! WHATEVER YOU WANT!

TO CELEBRATE THE CONQUESTS, A FATIMID CALIPH ORDERED UP A NEW CAPITAL CITY, **CAIRO.** THE FIRST STONES WERE LAID BY THE VICTORIOUS GENERAL, **JAWHAR** THE **ROMAN,** A GREEK SICILIAN, REALLY, AND A SLAVE LIKE THE REST OF HIS ARMY.

I'M A SLAVE, MY OFFICERS ARE SLAVES, MY PRIVATES ARE SLAVES...

YOU'RE LUCKY TO HAVE PRIVATES! THIS WAY, LADIES...

YES, OH HAREM EUNUCH...

AND SO THEY MOVED TO EGYPT, WHERE AS SHIITES THE FATIMIDS WERE IN A MINORITY.

WHISPER

WHISPER

WHISPER

WHISPER

THIS HELPS EXPLAIN WHY THESE CALIPHS CONTINUED TO USE SLAVE ARMIES...

WHO ELSE CAN WE TRUST?

WHOM?

AND WHY THEY MADE LIFE FAIRLY EASY FOR CHRISTIANS AND JEWS.*

HERE... TAKE THIS... AND **DO** TELL ME IF YOU HEAR ANY MUTTERING!

ONE FATIMID, THE BLUE-EYED LUNATIC **AL-HAKIM** (RULED 996-1021), TURNED AGAINST CHRISTIANS AND JEWS. HE TAXED THEM, JAILED THEM, MADE THEM WEAR FUNNY CLOTHES... WHICH WAS ODD, BECAUSE AL-HAKIM'S **MOTHER** WAS A CHRISTIAN. BUT THEN, AL-HAKIM ALSO MURDERED HIS OWN TUTOR... STRANGE BOY...

IT'S ALL MOM'S FAULT!

AL-HAKIM USED TO ROAM CAIRO'S MARKETS WITH HIS BURLY SLAVE **MASOUD**... DISHONEST MERCHANTS WOULD BE SODOMIZED ON THE SPOT BY MASOUD... EVEN TODAY, CAIRENES STILL SAY, "DON'T GIVE ME A HARD TIME, OR I'LL BRING MASOUD!"

I DON'T GET IT, MASOUD! IT'S THE **FOURTH TIME** FOR THAT ONE... HE MUST BE ADDICTED TO CHEATING...

AFTER AL-HAKIM DIED (MURDERED, PERHAPS BY HIS SISTER), HIS FOLLOWERS WORSHIPPED HIS MEMORY. THEY FOUNDED A SECT, THE **DRUZE,** SO SCORNED BY OTHER MUSLIMS THAT SOME MODERN-DAY DRUZES HAVE EVEN JOINED THE **ISRAELI ARMY**...

HUT HUT HUT! THEY THINK OUR FOUNDER'S A NUT!

THROUGH UP AND DOWN, ONE PLACE PROSPERED: **SIJILMASA.**

UNDER THE FATIMIDS, SIJILMASA'S MINT STAMPED OUT THE PUREST GOLDEN DINARS IN THE WORLD... AH, SIJILMASA... CITY OF DEALS, AND DEALERS, AND GUIDES, AND MULLAHS HEADING SOUTH... CITY OF SLAVES, CITY OF WEALTH... WHERE ARE YOU NOW, SIJILMASA?

SIJILMASA TODAY:

ISLAM GOES SOUTH

WHILE THE MAHDI & CO. SPREAD SHIISM UP NORTH, MUSLIM PREACHERS ALSO HEADED SOUTH. SOME OF THEM ACTED AS FATIMID AGENTS... OTHERS WERE FLEEING ONE CALIPH OR ANOTHER... ALL OF THEM SOUGHT CONVERTS IN THE SUDAN... AND NONE OF THEM HAD MUCH SUCCESS, AT FIRST...

YOU'RE GOING TO **HELL!!**

YEAH, WELL, I'M DRESSED FOR IT...

IN FACT, ISLAM SUFFERED A SEEMING SETBACK: IN 970, JUST AS THE FATIMIDS WERE CONQUERING EGYPT, THE KING OF **GHANA** LAUNCHED AN INVASION OF THE SOUTHERN SAHARA.

BY THE GODS OF ALL THAT'S GREEN, WHAT A COUNTRY THESE MUSLIMS LIVE IN!

THE GHANAIANS—STILL ENTHUSIASTIC PAGANS—CONQUERED AN IMPORTANT BERBER TRADE CENTER CALLED AWDAGHUST.

BY THE GODS OF ALL THAT'S GREEN, WHY—?

THEY FOUND A TRIBE OF BERBERS WILLING TO DO THINGS GHANA'S WAY, AND TURNED ALL AWDAGHUST'S BUSINESS OVER TO THEM.

REMEMBER: YOU SEND US A HIGHER CUT OF THE PROFIT—AND **STOP** PREACHING AT US!!

YES, BY THE GOD OF ALL THAT'S GOLD...

FOR THE NEXT FEW DECADES, GHANA'S EMPIRE WAS AT ITS HEIGHT. STABILITY PREVAILED NORTH AND SOUTH.

FATIMID CALIPHATE
• SIJILMASA
• AWDAGHUST
KUMBI
• SALEH
GHANA
Senegal R.
TAKRUR
Niger R.
LAKE CHAD
KANEM
BORNU

STILL, EVEN IN PAGAN GHANA, ISLAM SPREAD... MORE MUSLIM TRADERS AND CLERICS ARRIVED, MARRIED LOCAL WOMEN, HAD FAMILIES... AND THE NEXT THING YOU KNEW, MORE MOSQUES HAD POPPED UP!

THEY LOOK MORE LIKE US NOW, ANYWAY...

BUT THEY STILL HAVEN'T MASTERED THE TROPICAL DRESS CODE!

MEANWHILE, MUSLIM PREACHERS KEPT WORKING ON THE LEADERS OF TRIBES AND TOWNS IN AND AROUND GHANA.

OUR PROPHET, GOD BLESS HIM, TEACHES THAT WOMEN MUST BE KEPT IN THEIR PLACE, YOUR MAJESTY! ACCEPT ISLAM, AND YOUR PEOPLE CAN CONFINE THEIR WIVES! SOUND GOOD?

OH, I DON'T THINK SO...

SUCCESS WAS LIMITED!

MAYBE YOU SHOULD TRY CONVERTING A TRIBE WITH A MALE LEADER... ONLY A SUGGESTION...

AND A VERY GOOD ONE TO BE SURE...

THE FIRST AFRICAN KING TO CONVERT TO ISLAM WAS THE RULER OF TAKRUR, ON THE SENEGAL RIVER, IN 1030.

MANY ELITE FAMILIES IN AFRICA TRACE THEIR ANCESTRY BACK TO AN ARAB, A PERSIAN, OR SOME OTHER "WHITE" PERSON, EVEN THOUGH THE FAMILY LOOKS JUST LIKE THE NEIGHBORS.

I AM MUSA, SON OF ABDULLAH, SON OF AHMED, SON OF ISMAIL, SON OF IBRAHIM THE BUM OF BAGHDAD!

YOU ARE SO VERY SPECIAL.

MODERN HISTORIANS SUGGEST THE FAMILIES MADE UP THESE STORIES RECENTLY AS A WAY OF PUFFING UP THEIR STATUS IN AN ERA OF WHITE SUPREMACY. THIS IS HOW HISTORIANS THINK WHEN THEY LACK DOCUMENTATION.

IF IT COMES TO US BY MOUTH, I DON'T BELIEVE IT, BECAUSE I'M A SKEPTIC!

IF IT COMES FROM AN ELITE, I DON'T BELIEVE IT, BECAUSE I'M ANTI-ELITIST!

IF IT COMES STRAIGHT FROM MY OWN BRAIN, I BELIEVE IT, BECAUSE I'M HIGHLY INTELLIGENT!

GENETICS TO THE RESCUE: IN 1999, SCIENTISTS STUDIED THE DNA OF THE SOUTH AFRICAN LEMBA PEOPLE, WHO CLAIM DESCENT FROM JEWS WHO LEFT YEMEN IN THE 500s. TURNS OUT THE LEMBA'S STORY IS TRUE...

BELIEVE US NOW?

THAT'S NOT PAPER!!

SHORTER HOUSES

THE SOUTHERNERS FOLLOWED A MILITANT MUSLIM PREACHER, **ABDULLAH IBN YASIN**... FROM HIS BASE DEEP IN THE SAHARA, THE PREACHER DENOUNCED THE GAP BETWEEN **RICH** AND **POOR** HE SAW IN THE AGING EMPIRES OF GHANA AND EGYPT.

THIS IS WHAT HAPPENS WHEN EMPIRES AGE!

IBN YASIN BELIEVED THAT ALL HOUSES SHOULD BE THE **SAME HEIGHT!**

DOWN WITH UP!

THOUGH NOT POPULAR AMONG PEOPLE WITH TALL HOUSES, HIS MESSAGE ROUSED THE POOR BERBERS WHO LIVED IN HOVELS AND TENTS!

DEMOLISH! DEMOLISH!

AROUND 1055, HIS FOLLOWERS SEIZED AWDAGHUST, DROVE OUT THE GHANAIANS, AND SHORTENED THE HOUSES OF THE BERBERS WHO DEALT WITH THEM.

THESE PEOPLE ARE CRAZY!

WHY STOP THERE? IBN YASIN NOW LED AN EXPEDITION NORTH, ACROSS THE SAHARA.

THAT DUNE THERE IS TOO TALL!

MAN, AREN'T THEY ALL...

JUST AS THE FATIMID'S SHEPHERDS WERE NIBBLING AWAY TUNISIA, IBN YASIN'S BERBERS SWOOPED DOWN ON **SIJILMASA** AND GOT HOLD OF THE GOLD.

NOW HERE'S SOMETHING THAT CAN **NEVER** BE TOO TALL...

IN ALMOST NO TIME, THE LEVELING ZEALOTS HELD BOTH ENDS OF THE SAHARAN TRADE ROUTE AND WEAKENED GHANA BESIDES.

UM, AH, ER, EH, PANT, PUFF, PANT, PUFF!

OH, I DON'T LIKE THE SOUND OF THAT...

IN 1059, IBN YASIN DIED IN BATTLE... TWO BROTHERS STEPPED FORWARD TO LEAD HIS LEVELERS, WHO ARE KNOWN TO HISTORY AS THE

ALMORAVIDS,

PROBABLY BECAUSE OF THE FORTS (AL-MURABIT) THEY BUILT.

TALL ENOUGH, I'NIT?

BY 1070, THE ALMORAVIDS HAD TAKEN MOROCCO... IN 1090, THEY CROSSED TO GIBRALTAR... WITHIN FOUR YEARS, THEY CONTROLLED MOST OF SPAIN.

BY SANTIAGO'S BLUE, BLISTERING BEARD! WHO ARE THESE MASKED MEN?

MEANWHILE, IN THE SOUTH, THE ALMORAVIDS WENT AFTER THE PAGANS OF GHANA. AROUND 1075, THEY SACKED AND BURNED KUMBI SALEH (OR ELSE THEY DIDN'T! HISTORIANS DISAGREE). THE ROYAL FAMILY AND THEIR SONINKE PEOPLE FLED.

NO, IT'S **NOT** BURNING, AND WE WERE JUST LEAVING ANYWAY...

IN THE END, THE ALMORAVID EMPIRE STRETCHED 2,000 MILES NORTH TO SOUTH, AN ALL-TIME LATITUDE-SPANNER UNTIL SPANISH AMERICA.

WHEN GHANA FELL, A NEIGHBORING KING, **UMME JILME** OF **KANEM** AND **BORNU** (BIG, CENTRAL, AND WE HAVEN'T MENTIONED IT YET), TOOK AN INTEREST IN ISLAM.

AN INTEREST? IT SCARES THE HELL OUT OF ME!

APPARENTLY, KANEM'S TRADITIONAL PRIESTS DISLIKED THE MUSLIMS. THERE SEEM TO HAVE BEEN FIGHTS...

BURN IN HELL, DEVIL-WOSHIPPERS!

CRUNCH

GO AWAY!

EEK!

THUD!

EVEN SO, THE KING HIRED A TEACHER AND SECRETLY TOOK LESSONS IN ISLAM...

AIEEEE

RIPP

CRACKLE CRACKLE CRACKLE

NEVER MIND THAT! CARRY ON...

AROUND 1090, HE WENT PUBLIC WITH HIS FAITH.

IT'S A **PERSONAL** DECISION... IT DOESN'T AFFECT ANY OF **YOU**... YOU'RE **ABSOLUTELY FREE** TO WORSHIP THE OLD GODS...

THAT IS, IF YOU DON'T MIND YOUR **KING** THINKING YOU'RE AN **IDIOT**...

OR THAT I'LL BE **TAXING** YOU TO BUILD **MOSQUES**...

AND, BY THE WAY, ANYBODY SO MUCH AS **TOUCHES** A MUSLIM, I'LL **KILL** YOU...

UMME JILME RULED LONG... SO DID HIS SON, **DUNAMA,** A PIOUS MUSLIM WHO WENT TO MECCA THREE TIMES (BUT RETURNED ONLY TWICE—HE DROWNED ON THE WAY HOME). UNDER FATHER, SON, AND GRANDSON, KANEM AND BORNU GREW GREAT IN THE 1100s.

NEXT DOOR, IN THE WESTERN WRECKAGE OF GHANA, ANOTHER LEADER, **SUNDIATTA,** CHIEF OF THE **MALINKE** PEOPLE, BECAME A MUSLIM AND RAISED AN ARMY.

A WINNING COMBINATION, OBVIOUSLY!

HE UNIFIED THE OLD GHANAIAN EMPIRE AND ADDED LAND ALL THE WAY TO THE ATLANTIC. HIS KINGDOM OF **MALI** WAS WEST AFRICA'S GREAT POWER OF THE 1200s AND 1300s.

MALI

TIMBUKTU

MALI'S WEALTH IN GOLD WAS LEGENDARY. ITS GREATEST KING, **MANSA MUSA** (KING MOSES), LEFT SO MUCH MONEY IN CAIRO ON HIS WAY TO MECCA THAT HE CHANGED WESTERN HISTORY FOREVER.

A STORY FOR LATER!

MANSA MUSA ALSO BUILT UP A UNIVERSITY TOWN TO HELP KEEP SUDANESE ISLAM PROPER AND PURE: **TIMBUKTU,** HOPELESSLY REMOTE FOR EUROPEANS, CENTRALLY LOCATED FOR AFRICANS!!

WE MIGHT ALSO MENTION A WEST AFRICAN TRADITION THAT MALI SENT A FLEET TO BRAZIL IN THE 1300s!

NOT ALL SUDANESE LIKED THEIR ISLAM PURE. SOME IGNORED THE NEW THING COMPLETELY... OTHERS MIXED IT IN WITH THEIR OLD-TIME RELIGION...

I'LL BE RIGHT WITH YOU, GOD... JUST AFTER I SPRINKLE CHICKEN BLOOD ON THE FETISH...

AND SOME STOOD UP TO IT, LIKE THE PRINCE **ODUDWA**, WHOSE FATHER, A HALF-IRAQI* CHIEF, WAS A MUSLIM.

WHAT ABOUT **MOM'S** GODS?

AND WHAT'S UP WITH ALL THIS **DRAPERY**?

*ACCORDING TO ONE VERSION OF THE STORY

ODUDWA WANTED TO FOLLOW THE FAITH OF HIS AFRICAN ANCESTORS. HE SET UP AN IDOL...

HIS BROTHER, A MUSLIM, BURNED IT DOWN.

AFTER SOME FIGHTING, ODUDWA STOLE HIS BROTHER'S **KORAN**...

AND PLUNGED INTO THE JUNGLE WITH A FEW OF HIS FRIENDS, MOVING SOUTH ALL THE WAY TO **IFE**, ON THE NIGERIAN COAST.

THERE ODUDWA FOUNDED THE **YORUBA** NATION, WHICH GAINED POWER IN THE REGION AND LATER INFLUENCED THE MUSIC, MEDICINE, AND MAGIC OF THE AMERICAS.

IFE

YORUBA COUNTRY

THROUGHOUT HIS REIGN, GOES THE STORY, ODUDWA KEPT THE PILFERED KORAN TIED UP WITH ROPE UNDER HIS THRONE.

GUESS THAT SHOWS WHO'S ON TOP...

ISLAM ALSO FAILED TO APPEAL TO THE **ETHIOPIAN HIGH-LANDERS,** WHO MOSTLY CLUNG TO CHRISTIANITY, EXCEPT FOR A SMALL JEWISH MINORITY.

THE ALTITUDE IS AFFECTING THEIR JUDGMENT...

FOR CENTURIES AFTER LOSING ITS SEAPORT IN 702, ETHIOPIA WAS MIRED IN POVERTY. THE ROYAL FAMILY SURVIVED, BUT CENTRAL GOVERNMENT DID NOT EXIST, AND EACH TRIBE FENDED FOR ITSELF.

AROUND 950, IT APPEARS, A GIFTED MILITARY LEADER AROSE AMONG THE JEWS: A WOMAN CALLED

JUDITH "THE FIRE."

SHE'S HOT!

BIT BY BIT, HER LITTLE ARMY CONQUERED THE COUNTRY, AND FOR SOME YEARS ETHIOPIA HAD A **JEWISH QUEEN.**

WHY DON'T YOU **WIN** MORE OFTEN? DON'T YOU **CARE** ABOUT **ME**?

GOD, I FEEL SO GUILTY...

NEXT DOOR, THE **NUBIANS** TOOK NOTE. THEY PREFERRED ETHIOPIA WEAK—AND CHRISTIAN!

WHAT **IS** THIS?

STRONG AND JEWISH? **NOT** IN THE PLAN...

UM... SHOULD WE HELP OUR **DEAR** FRIEND THE CHRISTIAN KING, WHOM WE'VE LEFT MIRED IN POVERTY ALL THESE YEARS?

YES! YES! YES!!

THEY SENT TROOPS TO SAVE THE OLD ROYAL FAMILY AND RESTORE IT TO POWER.

IT WAS DONE, AND SOON JUDITH THE FIRE WAS NO MORE THAN AN EMBER.

STILL, THE COUNTRY WAS TOO POOR TO SUPPORT A ROYAL COURT IN ANY ONE PLACE... SO FOR CENTURIES AFTERWARDS, KING AND RETINUE TRAMPED FROM CAMP TO CAMP, EATING EVERYTHING AND THEN MOVING ON.

OH, NO! HERE COMES THE KING!

MEANWHILE, BACK IN EGYPT, WE LAST SAW THE FATIMID CALIPH **AL-MUSTANSIR** (ON P. 91) AS HE SENT OFF THE NIBBLING HORDES TO PUNISH THE REBELS OUT WEST.

FOR YEARS, HIS ARABS AND SHEEP PILLAGED AND CHEWED... THE ALMORAVIDS JUMPED INTO THE MIX.... THE CALIPH'S HOPES ROSE AND FELL LIKE A CARTOONIST'S SALARY... AND THEN...

FROM ANOTHER DIRECTION ENTIRELY, **ASTONISHING NEWS:** IN 1058, A PRO-SHIITE ARMY OCCUPIED **BAGHDAD**—BAGHDAD! THE CALIPH—THE OFFICIAL, ABBASID CALIPH—SIGNED AWAY HIS RIGHTS AND SENT THE EMBLEMS OF OFFICE, INCLUDING THE PROPHET'S OWN SACRED CLOAK, TO AL-MUSTANSIR IN CAIRO. THE FATIMID AND HIS SHIITES WERE ON TOP OF THE WORLD—OR SO HE THOUGHT!

HOW WRONG HE WAS... MORE ASTONISHING NEWS WAS ON THE WAY... YOU CAN READ ALL ABOUT IT IN THE NEXT VOLUME!

THE CARTOON HISTORY OF THE UNIVERSE

Volume 16
THE MIDDLE OF SOMEWHERE

THE VERY, VERY VAST EXPANSE OF CENTRAL ASIA HAS ALWAYS SUPPORTED MANY WAYS OF LIFE. IN THE NORTHERN FORESTS, PEOPLE HUNTED AND FISHED... IN A FEW FERTILE SPOTS IN THE SOUTH, THEY FARMED AND RAN REST STOPS FOR CARAVANS... ON THE ARID, GRASSY PLAINS IN BETWEEN, NOMADS KEPT FLOCKS OF CATTLE OR CAMELS... AND HORSES, ALWAYS HORSES...

WHAT WAS LIFE LIKE FOR THESE WANDERING STEPPE-DWELLERS? AN OLD STORY CAPTURES SOME OF ITS FLAVOR: A MAN ON HORSEBACK, FAR FROM HOME ON A HUNTING TRIP, HAS FAILED TO BAG ANY GAME. HE SPIES A LONE FIRE ON THE PLAINS, APPROACHES IT, AND FINDS SOMEONE BUTCHERING A DEER.

THE RIDER "REQUESTS" SOME FOOD... THE OTHER HUNTER CUTS HIM A HAUNCH.

TRAVELING ON, STILL CARRYING THE MEAT, HE HAPPENS ON AN OLD MAN AND A BOY.

THE OLD MAN SAYS THE TWO OF THEM ARE STARVING.

THE HUNTER OFFERS TO TRADE THE DEER LEG FOR THE BOY. THE OLD MAN ACCEPTS.

AND SO THE HORSEMAN COMES HOME WITH A **SERVANT** FOR HIS WIFE **ALAN GOA** AND THEIR THREE SONS.

TIME PASSES... THE HUNTER DIES... THE SERVANT BOY IS NOW A YOUNG MAN.

AND **SOMEHOW** THERE ARE TWO MORE SMALL BOYS IN CAMP. THE FIRST THREE SONS CAN'T FIGURE IT OUT! WHERE DID **THEY** COME FROM?

WHERE ELSE IS THERE?

THEY CONFRONT THEIR MOTHER: WHO IS THE FATHER OF THE TWO NEW BOYS?

SHE TELLS THEM A STORY AND EXPECTS THEM TO BELIEVE IT.

AT NIGHT, THE LIGHT OF THE **MOON** COMES IN THROUGH THE SMOKEHOLE, TURNS INTO A WOLF-SPIRIT, AND SLIDES RIGHT UNDER MY COVERS!

ALAN GOA COMMANDS HER SONS TO BE LIKE THE FIVE FINGERS OF A SINGLE HAND— AND NO MORE QUESTIONS!

FROM THESE FIVE BOYS, GOES THE STORY, SPRANG THE **MONGOLS**... SON #5'S DESCENDANT, CENTURIES LATER, WAS

JENGHIS KHAN,

WHO CONQUERED ALL.

SO WHAT DID YOU TELL THEM, HONEY?

A BUNCH OF MOONSHINE!

ACROSS SUCH A WIDE AREA, YOU MIGHT EXPECT TO FIND ALL KINDS OF **RELIGIOUS** IDEAS, AND SO YOU WOULD... BUT HERE TOO THE STEPPE PEOPLE HAD SOMETHING IN COMMON: EVERY TRIBE HAD ITS **SHAMANS**—PEOPLE WHO COMMUNE WITH THE SPIRITS—AND ALL OF THEM WORSHIPPED THE BIGGEST THING IN THEIR LIVES: THE **SKY**.

AT TIMES, NOMADS MADE **WAR** ON EACH OTHER OVER THE STUFF OF LIFE ON THE STEPPE: WATER, PASTURE-LAND, AND LIVE-STOCK. THE STEPPE-DWELLERS WAGED **TWO KINDS** OF WARS:

FIRST, SIMPLE RAIDING AND HORSE-RUSTLING... THIS WENT ON BACK AND FORTH ALL THE TIME.

BUT SOMETIMES, PRESSED BY DROUGHT OR CROWDING, A TRIBE MIGHT **DRIVE THEIR NEIGH-BORS OFF THE LAND,** KILLING AND KIDNAPPING WITHOUT MERCY.

WHAT ABOUT THE ONES THAT GOT AWAY?

THEY'LL DO THE SAME TO THE NEXT PEOPLE.

AGAINST SETTLED PEOPLE, THE NOMADS FOUGHT THE SAME TWO WAYS: AT TIMES THEY RAIDED THE BORDER, TAKING WHATEVER THEY COULD.

BARBARIAN!

SLAVE!

THEY AVOIDED THE PITCHED BATTLES OF CIVILIZED WARFARE. WHEN IMPERIAL ARMIES MARCHED AGAINST THEM, THE NOMADS MELTED INTO THE LANDSCAPE!

CREAK CREAK RUMBLE CLATTER CLATTER

I'M THIRSTY!

AT OTHER TIMES THE NOMADS ATTACKED IN STYLE #2: **KILL EVERYONE** AND SEIZE THE **LAND...** THE DEATH TOLL WOULD BE IMMENSE, SINCE FARMERS, UNLIKE ENEMY NOMADS, HAD NOWHERE TO GO.

AND THERE ARE SO $%&# **MANY** OF THEM!

CIVILIZED PEOPLE DIDN'T GET IT... THEY CALLED IT **CRUELTY...** BUT IT WAS ONLY A **HABIT OF MIND,** REALLY...

DON'T YOU **REALIZE?** YOU COULD KILL JUST A **FEW,** TAKE OVER THE **GOVERNMENT,** TAX A WHOLE **NATION,** AND GET **REALLY RICH?**

GOSH... NO... REALLY?

HUNS AND TURKS AND SO FORTH

IN THE BEGINNING, HORSES RAN FREE... NO ONE COULD OUTRACE A HORSE... BUT SOMETIME BEFORE 2000 BCE, SOMEWHERE NEAR KURGAN, SOME CLEVER PEDESTRIANS CHASED HORSES INTO A CORRAL AND LEARNED HOW TO RIDE THEM.

NO ONE COULD STOP THESE PEOPLE ON HORSEBACK... THEY WENT WHEREVER THEY PLEASED: INDIA, IRAN, EUROPE. SOME, LIKE THE SCYTHIANS (SAKA, SHAKA) STAYED ON THE WESTERN PLAINS... OTHERS, THE YUEH-CHI, TOKHARIANS, AND WU-SUN (A-SOU, ASIANS) MOVED ALL THE WAY TO THE EDGE OF CHINA... AND ALL THESE PEOPLE SPOKE **INDO-EUROPEAN** LANGUAGES RELATED TO MODERN FRENCH, ENGLISH, GREEK, HINDI, FARSI, ETC...

108

WELL, SORT OF... EXCEPT THEY WERE NOT EXACTLY A RACE, SINCE THEY MARRIED THE LOCALS... AND BESIDES, THEY OWED THEIR MASTERY NOT TO ANYTHING **GENETIC** BUT RATHER TO THEIR OWNERSHIP OF **EQUINE** TECHNOLOGY.

SOME HUNDREDS OF YEARS BCE, THE **TURCO-MONGOL** PEOPLES NORTH OF CHINA GOT UP ON HORSEBACK. ONE OF THESE TRIBES, THE **HUNS**, INVADED CENTRAL ASIA (50 BCE), RUSSIA (300 CE), HUNGARY, AND FRANCE (450).

I'D HAVE STAYED, BUT I DIED YOUNG!

ATTILA

THE HUNS DROVE THEIR OLD INDO-EUROPEAN NEIGHBORS THE **YUEH-CHI** ALL THE WAY SOUTH TO AFGHANISTAN. FROM THERE ONE TRIBE OF YUEH-CHI WENT ON TO CONQUER **INDIA** AND BECOME FERVENT **BUDDHISTS**.

BUKHARA   SAMARKAND
OXUS R.   TIBET
                                    WHEN IN DOUBT,
                                    DRAW AN ELEPHANT!
                                        I'M ALWAYS
KABUL   IN DOUBT.
BAMIYAN
            PESHAWAR
INDUS R.   GANGES R.
            PATNA

FOR TWO CENTURIES (50-250) THESE KINGS (CALLED THE **KUSHAN DYNASTY** IN INDIA) RULED FROM CENTRAL INDIA TO BEYOND THE OXUS... AND SO BUDDHISM SPREAD TO CENTRAL ASIA AND FINALLY ON TO CHINA.

THREE HUNDRED YEARS LATER, BY THE EARLY 500s, SOME NEW TRIBES HAD EMERGED IN ASIA. ONE, THE **JUAN-JUAN,** HAD A VAST EMPIRE BASED IN MONGOLIA. ANOTHER, THE **TOBA,** RULED NORTH CHINA FOR SO LONG THAT THEY BLENDED WITH THE CHINESE. (SEE BOOK II, P. 273.)

AROUND 550, THE JUAN-JUAN KHAN ASKED FOR A CHINESE PRINCESS TO MARRY—TOO MUCH FOR THE CHINESE! THEY DECIDED TO WEAKEN THE JUAN-JUAN BY DIVIDING THEM...

LET US TURN ONE BARBARIAN AGAINST ANOTHER!

FIGHT FIRE WITH FIRE!

A DOG WITH A DOG!

A PIG WITH A DUCK!

WHATEVER.

CHINA SECRETLY ENCOURAGED A REVOLT BY ONE OF THE KHAN'S TOP GENERALS, **BUMIN,** CHIEF OF THE **TU-CHUEH** TRIBE.

WITH ANY LUCK, THEY'LL RIP EACH OTHER TO SHREDS!

I'D BE HAPPY!

BUMIN, YOU THE **MAN!**

YES, I AM!

SO BUMIN, NOT THE KHAN, GOT THE CHINESE PRINCESS-BRIDE...

OH, WE ARE SUBTLE!

SOPHISTICATED!

EVER SO CLEVER!

BUMIN GAVE CHINA MORE THAN IT WANTED! IN 552, HIS ARMY NEARLY WIPED THE JUAN-JUAN OFF THE FACE OF THE EARTH, DRIVING THE KHAN TO SUICIDE.

SUBTLETY ISN'T EVERYTHING!

AS CHINESE JAWS DROPPED IN SHOCK, THE WHOLE JUAN-JUAN EMPIRE FELL TO BUMIN'S TU-CHUEH—OTHERWISE KNOWN TO US AS THE **TURKS.**

WELL, AT LEAST THEY'RE **OUR** TURKS...

AREN'T THEY?

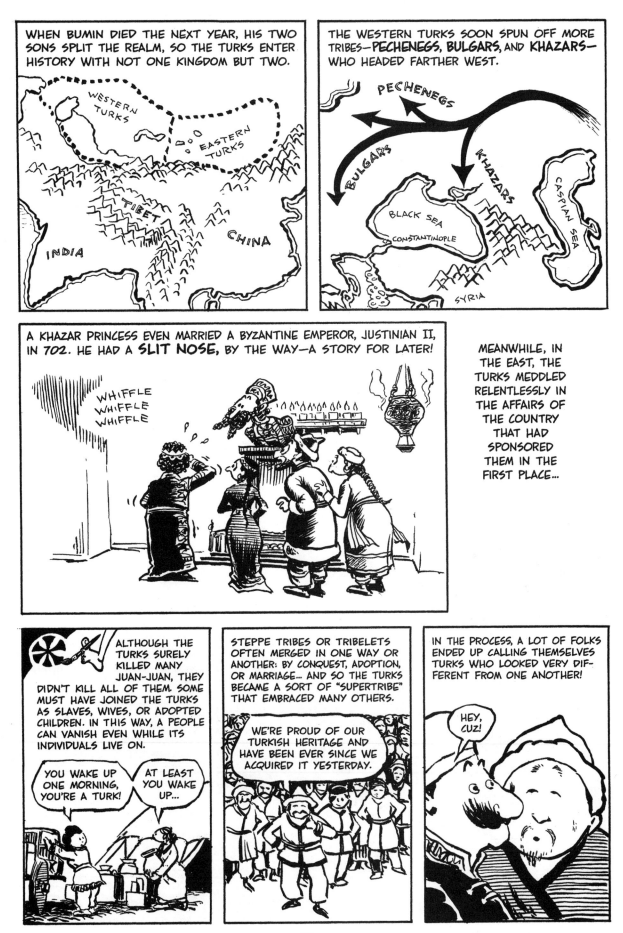

WHEN BUMIN DIED THE NEXT YEAR, HIS TWO SONS SPLIT THE REALM, SO THE TURKS ENTER HISTORY WITH NOT ONE KINGDOM BUT TWO.

WESTERN TURKS
EASTERN TURKS
TIBET
INDIA
CHINA

THE WESTERN TURKS SOON SPUN OFF MORE TRIBES—**PECHENEGS**, **BULGARS**, AND **KHAZARS**—WHO HEADED FARTHER WEST.

PECHENEGS
BULGARS
KHAZARS
BLACK SEA
CONSTANTINOPLE
CASPIAN SEA
SYRIA

A KHAZAR PRINCESS EVEN MARRIED A BYZANTINE EMPEROR, JUSTINIAN II, IN 702. HE HAD A **SLIT NOSE**, BY THE WAY—A STORY FOR LATER!

WHIFFLE WHIFFLE WHIFFLE

MEANWHILE, IN THE EAST, THE TURKS MEDDLED RELENTLESSLY IN THE AFFAIRS OF THE COUNTRY THAT HAD SPONSORED THEM IN THE FIRST PLACE...

ALTHOUGH THE TURKS SURELY KILLED MANY JUAN-JUAN, THEY DIDN'T KILL ALL OF THEM. SOME MUST HAVE JOINED THE TURKS AS SLAVES, WIVES, OR ADOPTED CHILDREN. IN THIS WAY, A PEOPLE CAN VANISH EVEN WHILE ITS INDIVIDUALS LIVE ON.

YOU WAKE UP ONE MORNING, YOU'RE A TURK!

AT LEAST YOU WAKE UP...

STEPPE TRIBES OR TRIBELETS OFTEN MERGED IN ONE WAY OR ANOTHER: BY CONQUEST, ADOPTION, OR MARRIAGE... AND SO THE TURKS BECAME A SORT OF "SUPERTRIBE" THAT EMBRACED MANY OTHERS.

WE'RE PROUD OF OUR TURKISH HERITAGE AND HAVE BEEN EVER SINCE WE ACQUIRED IT YESTERDAY.

IN THE PROCESS, A LOT OF FOLKS ENDED UP CALLING THEMSELVES TURKS WHO LOOKED VERY DIF-FERENT FROM ONE ANOTHER!

HEY, CUZ!

111

MULTICULTURAL CHINA

IN 552, EVERYONE MUST HAVE EXPECTED A TURKISH INVASION OF CHINA... BUT THEN THE TURKISH KINGDOM SPLIT IN TWO, AND ALL CHINA SIGHED WITH RELIEF.

AAAAAHHH...

EASTERN TURKISTAN SQUABBLED WITH WESTERN TURKISTAN... THE CHINESE EGGED THEM ON... AND IN 581, THE TURKS WENT TO WAR WITH EACH OTHER.

GOOD FOR ME!

SAFE FROM THE TURKS—FOR NOW—CHINESE WARLORDS BEGAN FIGHTING AMONG THEMSELVES... ONE CONQUERED ANOTHER... UNTIL AT LAST, IN 589, ONE OF THEM, FAMILY NAME **YANG**, RULED **ALL CHINA** AND FOUNDED THE SHORT-LIVED (BUT IMPORTANT) **SUI** DYNASTY.

Y'KNOW, THAT **GREAT WALL** WAS A POOR INVESTMENT...

CHINA ON THE EVE OF THE SUI CONQUEST

THE FIRST EMPEROR SUI, SEEING A RAVAGED LAND FULL OF PEOPLE RUINED BY WAR, CUT BACK ON LUXURY AND COMMANDED HIS NOBLES TO EASE UP ON THE PEASANTS.

WHAT?

SO THE NOBLES PROMPTLY KILLED HIM AND REPLACED HIM WITH HIS SON, A MORE **GENEROUS** PERSON.

SECOND EMPEROR SUI, A BIG SPENDER WITH BIG PLANS, SUITED THE NOBLES MUCH BETTER—AT FIRST.

YOU MAY NOW SQUEEZE THE PEASANTS!

OUR EMPEROR COMMANDS US!

SECOND EMPEROR'S FIRST PROJECT WAS TO GATHER ALL THE NOBLES' FIGHTING MEN AND FLING THEM AGAINST **KOREA**.

IT DOES GET THEM OUT OF THE COUNTRY...

THE KOREANS, WHO PIONEERED THE USE OF **IRON-PLATED SHIPS**, REPULSED THE CHINESE NAVY...

RINGS LIKE A DAMN BELL!

BONG BONG BONG BONG

WHILE THE CHINESE ARMY STARVED AND FROZE THROUGH A WINTER OUTSIDE KOREA'S WALLED CITIES.

THE IDEA, SEE, WAS TO BE **INSIDE** THE CITIES...

AT THE EXACT SAME TIME, THE EMPEROR WAS PLANNING A **GRAND CANAL** LINKING CHINA'S TWO MAJOR RIVERS. HE DRAFTED FIVE MILLION LABORERS TO DIG IT, TWO MILLION OF WHOM DIED IN THE PROCESS... BUT NEVER MIND! WHEN IT WAS DONE, SECOND EMPEROR SUI CRUISED DOWN THE WATERWAY IN A DRAGON BOAT, WHILE THE BARONS STOOD BY, AGHAST.

HE'S ROBBIN' US OF PEASANTS TO SQUEEZE!

IN 613, THE EMPEROR CALLED FOR A NEW WAR ON KOREA... THE BARONS RAISED THE MEN SOMEHOW—AND TURNED THEM AGAINST THE **EMPEROR** INSTEAD OF KOREA...

SQUEEZE THIS!

ONE WOULD-BE REBEL, **LI SHIH-MIN,** HAD A SPECIAL PROBLEM: HE WAS ONLY **SIXTEEN** YEARS OLD, AND HIS FATHER, THE GOVERNOR OF AN IMPORTANT PROVINCE, REMAINED LOYAL TO THE EMPEROR.

DAD! THE TIME IS **RIGHT!** THE EMPIRE CAN BE **OURS!** COME **ON!** WHY **WAIT?**

EVERYTHING ALWAYS GOES WRONG, SON... ONE DAY YOU'LL UNDERSTAND THIS...

NOT FAR FROM THE LI HOUSEHOLD WAS AN IMPERIAL LODGE LODGING IMPERIAL CONCUBINES. LI SHIH-MIN AND A FEW FRIENDS FORCED THEIR WAY IN.

THEY DISLODGED A CONCUBINE AND CARRIED HER HOME.

WHEN THEY PRESENTED HER TO FATHER LI, HE ACCEPTED HER AND ASKED NO QUESTIONS!

WHAT GOOD BOYS I HAVE...

THE NEXT MORNING, THE SON EXPLAINED THE SITUATION TO HIS DAD!

YOU JUST BOFFED THE **EMPEROR'S WOMAN.** YOU'RE A DEAD MAN!

UNLESS...

AND SO, THE **ENTIRE LI FAMILY** ROSE IN REVOLT—WITH LI SHIH-MIN NUDGING THEM ALONG!

RELAX, DAD! DON'T YOU WANT TO BE **EMPEROR?**

SIGH... DO I?

THE LI FAMILY, CHINESE ON THE FATHER'S SIDE, HAD MARRIED MANY **TURKISH WIVES**—LI SHIH-MIN'S MOTHER, FOR ONE... SO, THROUGH THE IN-LAWS, THE LI CALLED UP **TURKISH TROOPS** FOR THEIR ARMY.

TWO CENTURIES BEFORE BAGHDAD'S TURKISH GUARD!

THE TEENAGER ADVISED THEM TO STAY IN THE MOUNTAINS WHILE A DOZEN OTHER REBEL ARMIES WORE THEMSELVES OUT IN THE PLAINS. HE KNEW HISTORY!

THIS IS HOW THE HAN DYNASTY STARTED...

IN 618, THE BOY, NOW 21 YEARS OLD, GAVE THE WORD, AND OUT THEY CAME. WITHIN FIVE YEARS, THEY CONTROLLED CHINA, NORTH AND SOUTH.

SEE, DAD, ISN'T THIS **COOL**?

AND SO, THANKS TO LI SHIH-MIN'S STRATEGY AND DARING, BEGAN THE **TANG DYNASTY**. HIS FATHER WAS EMPEROR, AND HIS BROTHERS WERE FILLED WITH ENVY!

IS IT RIGHT THAT A YOUNGER BROTHER SHOULD HAVE MORE HONOR THAN THE ELDER?

NOT EVEN IF THE ELDER IS A MORON!

THE BROTHERS, IN FACT, RAISED AN ARMY TO ATTACK LI SHIH-MIN. BIG MISTAKE! HE KILLED **ALL** OF THEM, ALONG WITH THEIR FAMILIES.

BUT WHAT ABOUT **FAMILY FEELING**?

NOT ALWAYS POSITIVE, IS IT?

SOON AFTERWARD, HIS DESPONDENT DAD STEPPED DOWN... LI SHIH-MIN TOOK THE THRONE AND A NEW NAME, **TAI-TSUNG**, AND BECAME CHINA'S GREATEST EMPEROR.

TAKE IT, SON... YOU'VE EARNED IT... AND TAKE THESE **OFFICIALS** WHILE YOU'RE AT IT...

MY EMPEROR COMMANDS!

WOULD THIS BE A GOOD TIME TO CONSIDER THE HABITS OF HIGHLY EFFECTIVE PEOPLE?

A-HEM!

OH, WHY NOT?

THE HALF-TURKISH TAI-TSUNG BROUGHT A **MILLION TURKS** INTO CHINA, APPOINTED TURKISH OFFICIALS, RECRUITED TURKS FOR THE ARMY—AND USED THAT ARMY TO SMASH THE EASTERN TURKISH KINGDOM AND ATTACK THE WEST, PUSHING CHINESE POWER FAR INTO CENTRAL ASIA.

HEY! I THOUGHT WE WERE FRIENDS!

WELL, YOU'RE MY FRIEND...

YELLOW R.

TANG CHINA

YANGTZE R.

THE TANG RAN A **MULTICULTURAL EMPIRE**, WELCOMING NOT ONLY TURKS BUT ALSO COMMUNITIES OF KOREANS, INDIANS, PERSIANS, ARABS, AND JEWS TO CHINA... GOODS AND IDEAS MOVED BACK AND FORTH BY SHIP AND CAMEL.

WHAT'S A SHIP?

THE CAMEL OF THE SEA!

TAI-TSUNG IN IMPERIAL DRAGON ROBE, FROM A LARGER-THAN-LIFE-SIZED PORTRAIT

CHINESE WOMEN PLAYING POLO! HOW CENTRAL ASIAN CAN YOU GET?

116

WITHIN CHINA, TAI-TSUNG TOOK STEPS TO BREAK THE POWER OF THE GREAT LANDLORDS. HE KNEW THEY WERE TROUBLE—HE USED TO BE ONE HIMSELF!

LOOK WHAT WE DID TO THE SUI!

TO STAFF THE ADMINISTRATION WITH LOYAL, EDUCATED PUBLIC SERVANTS RATHER THAN SCHEMING WARLORDS' SONS, TAI-TSUNG BROUGHT BACK THE NATIONAL EXAMS. TO GET A GOVERNMENT JOB, YOU HAD TO ACE A **STANDARDIZED TEST** OPEN TO ALL.

TAI-TSUNG'S **LAND REFORM PROGRAM** BROKE UP GREAT ESTATES (ESPECIALLY THE ONES BELONGING TO HIS ENEMIES) AND PARCELED OUT THE LAND TO THE PEASANTS WHO WORKED IT. NOWADAYS, POLITICIANS OFTEN SAY THAT LAND REFORM "DOESN'T WORK," THAT THE NEW OWNERS JUST LOSE THEIR LAND ANYWAY, SO WHY BOTHER?* LET'S ASK THIS CHINESE PEASANT'S OPINION...

EXCUSE ME, DID LAND REFORM WORK FOR YOUR FAMILY?

ONLY FOR THE FIRST 150 YEARS!

BLOODTHIRSTY BARONS ALL BUT VANISHED... THE LAND WAS AT PEACE... THE ARMY ALMOST **INVISIBLE**, MAINLY POSTED TO THE FRONTIER TO INTIMIDATE FOREIGNERS...

LOOKS GOOD!

*THAT THESE POLITICIANS MIGHT BE IN THRALL TO THE CURRENT OWNERS OF PROPERTY IS A SCURRILOUS NOTION THAT WOULD PROBABLY NEVER OCCUR TO A PERSON WITH A GENEROUS VIEW OF HUMAN NATURE.

TAI-TSUNG'S POLICIES WENT ON SUCCESSFULLY UNDER TWO LONG-LIVED SUCCESSORS: FIRST, EMPRESS **WU,** THE ONLY OFFICIALLY RECOGNIZED WOMAN EMPEROR IN CHINESE HISTORY (REIGNED JOINTLY WITH HER HUSBAND 670–683 AND SOLO 690–705)...

THEN CAME EMPEROR **MING HUANG** (REIGNED 715–756), A PARTY ANIMAL, BUT A GOOD RULER MOST OF THE TIME, AND CHINA PROSPERED AS NEVER BEFORE.

AND DON'T FORGET US!!

OH, YES... CREDIT ALSO GOES TO THE THOUSANDS OF DEDICATED **CIVIL SERVANTS**— COMMISSIONERS, INSPECTORS, CANAL-KEEPERS, POSTAL WORKERS, JUDGES, TAX COLLECTORS— WHO ADMINISTERED THE LAWS FAIRLY TO THE BEST OF THEIR ABILITY!!

CHINESE HISTORIANS REFER TO THIS PERIOD, ESPECIALLY THE EARLY 700s, AS THE "FULLNESS OF TANG."

BUDDHISM GREW UNDER EMPRESS WU, AND SOON PEOPLE ALL ACROSS CHINA WERE MEDITATING, NOT ALWAYS ABOUT SPIRITUAL THINGS. IN 723, A BUDDHIST MONK DREAMED UP THE WORLD'S FIRST **CLOCK** (OR MORE PRECISELY, THE ESCAPEMENT MECHANISM THAT TURNS THE GEARS IN TICK-TOCK JUMPS).

THESE EARLY CHINESE CLOCKS WERE BUILT AS **ASTRONOMICAL TOOLS,** MODELS OF THE ROTATING SKY, COMPLETE WITH MECHANICAL FIGURES BEATING ALARM GONGS AT INTERVALS.

WATER FLOWED INTO BUCKETS MOUNTED ON THE RIM OF A LARGE WHEEL. AS EACH BUCKET FILLED IN TURN, THE WHEEL ADVANCED. (THE LOCKING MECHANISM IS NOT PICTURED.)

THE FULLNESS WAS FULL OF OTHER INVENTIONS AS WELL, SUCH AS MASS-MARKET **PORCELAIN,** THE FIRST SEAWORTHY **COMPASS,** AND THE FIRST **PRINTED BOOKS.**

PRINTED EXAMS, TOO!

THERE WAS CREATION AND **PROCREATION,** TOO... POPULATION DOUBLED FROM TAI-TSUNG'S DAY, REACHING A GRAND TOTAL OF EXACTLY **52,880,488,** ACCORDING TO THE OFFICIAL CENSUS COUNT OF 754.

HOLD STILL! HOLD STILL!

EVERYTHING WAS SO FINE, EMPEROR MING HUANG LEFT OFF GOVERNING AND PARTIED FULL-TIME WITH POETS, ACTORS, AND SOME ELEPHANTS THAT BOWED ONLY TO THE EMPEROR. BESIDE HIM ALWAYS WAS LADY **YANG GUEI-FEI** ("CONCUBINE YANG"), HIS FAVORITE.

YANG GUEI-FEI HAD A FAVORITE, TOO: **AN LU-SHAN**, A GENERAL FROM A CENTRAL ASIAN FAMILY.

SPEAKING OF CENTRAL ASIA... TROUBLE BEGAN THERE IN 750, WHEN A CHINESE GOVERNOR EXECUTED SOME TURKS IN FAR-OFF TASHKENT... THE TURKS, SEEKING REVENGE, ASKED THE MUSLIMS OF PERSIA FOR HELP, AND SOON...

ALL RIGHT! THE "HOUSE OF ISLAM" IS ABOUT TO ADD A ROOM!

IN 751, A CHINESE ARMY MET THE ARAB-PERSIAN-TURKISH FORCE IN THE BATTLE OF THE TALAS RIVER.

IN THAT ONE DAY, CHINA LOST ITS HOLD ON CENTRAL ASIA (AND THE MUSLIMS GOT THE RECIPE FOR PAPER-MAKING!).

BUT WHY WORRY? CHINA COULD ALWAYS WIN IT BACK! THE EMPEROR WAS RELAXED... **VERY RELAXED...**

THE EMPEROR DID SO LITTLE, IN FACT, THAT GENERAL **AN LU-SHAN** DECIDED TO SAVE THE EMPIRE HIMSELF! HE ATTACKED THE CAPITAL, PUTTING THE IMPERIAL FAMILY TO FLIGHT.

I'M STILL NOT WORRIED...

TAKING THE CITY IN 755, AN LU-SHAN MARCHED INTO THE PALACE AND ORDERED THE **DANCING ELEPHANTS** TO BOW DOWN TO HIM. THEY NERVOUSLY REFUSED.

D'OH!

WHILE AN LU-SHAN VENTED HIS IRE ON THE PITIFUL PACHYDERMS, THE EMPEROR'S SON RALLIED SUPPORT IN THE COUNTRYSIDE. HE TURNED FOR HELP TO ANOTHER TURKISH PEOPLE, THE MUSICALLY-NAMED **UIGHURS** ("WEE-GURS"), WHO HAD RECENTLY CONQUERED MONGOLIA.

WHATEVER WE CAN DO!

A UIGHUR ARMY CAME DOWN, CRUSHED AN LU-SHAN, AND MADE MING HUANG'S SON CHINA'S NEW RULER.

DON'T WORRY! WE'VE GOT YOUR BACK!

FOR HER RELATIONSHIP WITH THE REBEL, **YANG GUEI-FEI** LOST HER HEAD, WHICH INSPIRED NO END OF POEMS* AND DRAMAS.

THE TANG STILL HAD ITS DYNASTY, BUT THE FULLNESS HAD EMPTIED OUT IN ONE GREAT GUSH.

UM... ALL RIGHT THEN...

NICE THREADS!

UNDER PARTY BOY EMPEROR MING HUANG, **POETRY** FLOURISHED, MOST FAMOUSLY THE POET **LI PO** AND HIS MANY, MANY, MANY POEMS ABOUT BEING **DRUNK.**

CLEAR WINE WAS ONCE CALLED "A SAINT." THICK WINE WAS ONCE CALLED "A SAGE." OF SAGE AND SAINT I HAVE QUAFFED DEEP. WHAT NEED HAVE I TO STUDY THE SUTRAS? AT THE THIRD CUP I PENETRATE THE TAO. A FULL GALLON—NATURE AND I ARE ONE...

ONE PICKLED NIGHT IN 762, GOES THE STORY, LI PO SAW THE **MOON'S REFLECTION** IN A LAKE, TRIED TO EMBRACE IT, FELL IN, AND DROWNED.

HEY, CUTIE... GIVE US A HUG—OOP!

BUT WHO KNOWS? HIS DEATH CAME JUST AFTER THE AN LU-SHAN REBELLION... LI PO WAS A WESTERNER (HE ALSO SPOKE PERSIAN), WHO MAY HAVE BEEN FRIENDLY WITH THE **WRONG PEOPLE.** IS IT POSSIBLE THAT LI PO WAS **PUSHED?**

O.K.... HERE'S THE STORY...

121

SUDDENLY, POWER HAD SHIFTED IN CHINA: RATHER THAN CHINESE LORDING IT OVER THE TURKS, **UIGHURS** NOW LORDED OVER THE CHINESE.

SIGH...

THE CHINESE ARMY HAD ALWAYS DEPENDED ON CENTRAL ASIA FOR ITS SUPPLY OF HORSES. NOW CENTRAL ASIA WAS LOST... AND THE UIGHURS STEPPED IN.

MAY WE HELP?

EVERY YEAR THE UIGHUR KAGHAN SENT HORSES, TO BE PAID FOR IN VAST LOADS OF SILK... BUT THE CHINESE ECONOMY FALTERED... ONE YEAR THE UIGHURS SHIPPED 50,000 HORSES WHEN CHINA COULD AFFORD ONLY 6,000.

SIGH... SORRY...

THERE **WILL** BE A RESTOCKING FEE!

KHAGAN = KING; KHAN = KING OF KINGS

BUT THE UIGHURS NEVER INVADED CHINA... INSTEAD THEY ADOPTED FARMING, INVENTED AN ALPHABET, AND CONVERTED TO A "MODERN" RELIGION, IRANIAN **MANICHAEISM.**

GAH! WHAT HAPPENED TO THE UIGHURS?

VEGETABLES, SON. DON'T EVER EAT 'EM!

AND SO, IN 840, THEY FELL TO A LESS CIVILIZED TURKISH TRIBE, THE KIRGHIZ... BUT THE UIGHURS REMAINED IN WESTERN CHINA... AND LATER THEY WOULD BECOME SCRIBES AND TEACHERS TO SEVERAL ASIAN PEOPLES, INCLUDING THE MONGOLS...

MEANWHILE, CHINA HAD MONEY TROUBLE.

WELL, WE HAVE TROUBLE, ANYWAY...

IN TAI-TSUNG'S DAY, FARMERS PAID TAXES IN THE FORM OF GRAIN OR LABOR, BUT IN 780 THE GOVERNMENT SUDDENLY DEMANDED CASH ONLY, WHICH SEEMED MORE BUSINESSLIKE SOMEHOW.

PLEASE! TAKE THE PIG!

WE DON'T DO COMMODITIES.

COUNTLESS PENNILESS PEASANTS LOST THEIR LAND.

THE GOVERNMENT BLAMED THE MONEY SHORTAGE ON FOREIGNERS.

GRASPING MERCHANTS!

BUDDHISTS, WITH THEIR ALIEN IDEAS AND HUGE ASSETS...

GREEDY UIGHURS!

IT'S NOT OUR FAULT!

WHERE HAD THE MONEY GONE?

LET US PRAY FOR ENLIGHTENMENT BEFORE THIS LARGE, METALLIC STATUE OF— HEY... WAIT A MINUTE!!

IN 832, THE GOVERNMENT BEGAN SEIZING BUDDHIST BRONZES TO MELT DOWN FOR COINAGE.

IT'S O.K... IT WAS A COIN IN A PREVIOUS LIFE!

THERE WAS ENOUGH THERE TO KEEP THE NATION AFLOAT FOR ANOTHER 35 YEARS.

IT'S THE HALF-FULLNESS OF TANG!

OR THE HALF-EMPTINESS, IF YOU'RE LIKE ME...

THEN CAME DROUGHT, LOCUSTS, FAMINE, AND A PEASANT REVOLT IN 870 THAT CHASED TANG FROM ITS CAPITALS AND GAVE THE LAND BACK TO THE PEOPLE. IN 879, REBELS SACKED CANTON'S MERCHANT COLONY AND KILLED 100,000 FOREIGNERS.

THE TANG DYNASTY HUNG ON FOR A FEW MORE YEARS BEFORE EXPIRING IN CHAOS AND CIVIL WAR IN 906.

THE EMPEROR'S IN-LAWS

DURING TANG'S TROUBLES, MANY CHINESE LEFT THE COUNTRY IN SEARCH OF OPPORTUNITY.

THE OPPORTUNITY NOT TO STARVE, THAT IS...

THEY WENT BY LAND OR SEA TO KOREA... SOME SETTLED, AND SOME MOVED ON... TO AN ISLAND NATION THEY HAD BARELY HEARD OF BEFORE: **JAPAN.**

NO ONE KNOWS WHO FIRST PADDLED ACROSS TO JAPAN, BUT BY **4500 BCE**, A HUNTING, FISHING PEOPLE CALLED THE **AINU** HAD THE ISLANDS ALL TO THEMSELVES...

AND A FINE PLACE IT IS!

UNTIL AROUND **500 BCE**, WHEN A **KOREAN RELIGIOUS CULT** ARRIVED, LOOKING FOR THE PROMISED LAND. THEIR LEADER, THEY BELIEVED, WAS A **LIVING GOD.**

YOU'RE SURE THIS IS IT?

I'M NEVER WRONG.

← AINU LIP TATTOO

THESE PIONEERS FOUND A FERTILE PLAIN AND FARMED IT... THEIR NUMBERS GREW... AND THEY PUSHED BACK THE AINU IN A SERIES OF BORDER WARS THAT WENT ON FOR CENTURIES.

CALL IT THE AMERICAN PLAN!

UNLIKE SOME CULT LEADERS WE COULD NAME, THIS ONE HAD A SON, WHO SUCCEEDED HIS FATHER AS LEADER... HE TOO HAD A SON... AND SO ON, FROM THAT DAY TO THIS. FOR **2,500 YEARS**, THE **SAME FAMILY** HAS RULED JAPAN, AND THE NATION WORSHIPS ITS EMPEROR.

HE'S DESCENDED FROM THE SUN, YOU KNOW!

NO WONDER HE BURNS ME UP!

IN ALMOST EVERY KINGDOM KNOWN TO HISTORY, POWER-HUNGRY FAMILIES HAVE TOPPLED KINGS AND FOUNDED NEW DYNASTIES, BUT NOT IN JAPAN... OVERTHROWING THE EMPEROR WAS OUT OF THE QUESTION! SO WHAT WAS A POWER-HUNGRY JAPANESE CLAN TO DO?

IT'S SO FRUSTRATING!

IN THE MID-500s, A FAMILY CALLED THE **SOGA** FOUND A CLEVER AND **PEACEFUL** ANSWER:

MARRY THE EMPEROR!

WHO, ME?

THE PLAN: IF THE EMPEROR MARRIED A SOGA GIRL, THEIR CHILDREN'S **GENES** WOULD BE HALF SOGA AND HALF IMPERIAL. IF A SON ALSO WED A SOGA, THEIR CHILDREN HAVE **75%** SOGA GENES... IN THE NEXT GENERATION, SOGA GENES RISE TO **87.5%** OF THE TOTAL... ETC!

EMPERORS

SOGA WIVES

▬▬ = IMPERIAL GENE
▭▭ = SOGA GENE

*THE EFFECT IS LESS EXTREME IF IMPERIAL DAUGHTERS MARRY SOGA SONS, MIXING IMPERIAL GENES BACK INTO THE SOGA CLAN.

AFTER MANY GENERATIONS, THE SOGA WOULD EFFECTIVELY HAVE **HIJACKED** THE **IMPERIAL GENOME** UNTIL NOTHING WAS LEFT OF THE FIRST EMPEROR BUT HIS **Y CHROMOSOME!**

Y'CAN'T HAVE EVERY-THING!

AND SO IT HAPPENED... FOR ABOUT A CENTURY, SOGA PRIME MINISTERS MARRIED THEIR DAUGH-TERS TO IMPERIAL SONS AND SURROUNDED THE EMPEROR WITH OFFICERS FROM THE SOGA CLAN.

JAPAN DEVELOPED A UNIQUE TRADITION: INSTEAD OF FIGHTING TO **TOPPLE** THE EMPEROR, POWER-HUNGRY CLANS FOUGHT TO **MARRY** HIM! IN 644, ASSASSINS CUT DOWN THE SOGA, AND A NEW CLAN, THE **FUJIWARA**, BECAME THE IMPERIAL IN-LAWS.

YOUR SERVANT, MAJESTY!

ALL THIS TIME, CHINESE IMMIGRANTS WERE ARRIVING IN JAPAN, BRINGING THEIR OWN IDEAS ABOUT RELIGION, CEREMONY, TECHNOLOGY, CITY PLANNING, DRAINAGE, IRRIGATION, BUREAUCRACY, AND GOOD MANNERS.

PLUS THEY KNOW HOW TO READ AND WRITE!

THEY'RE AWESOME!

THE SOGA AND FUJIWARA AGREED ON ONE THING: JAPAN FACED A **CHOICE**.

SHOULD WE MAKE UP OUR OWN INSTITUTIONS AND CIVILIZATION AS WE GO ALONG, WHICH COULD EASILY TAKE CENTURIES...?

OR SHOULD WE **COPY** THEIR **ENTIRE CIVILIZATION** WHOLESALE?

TO POSE THE QUESTION IS TO KNOW THE ANSWER!

THE FUJIWARA EMBRACED ALL THINGS CHINESE: THEY SEIZED ALL THE LAND AND PARCELED IT OUT, TANG-STYLE, PACIFYING THE NOBLES WITH A STRONG DOSE OF BUDDHISM, FANCY CHINESE TITLES, AND PERFECT MANNERS.

BRONZE BUDDHA AT NARA (C. 740), 56 FT. TALL SITTING DOWN

THEY EVEN ADOPTED CHINESE **WRITING**, WHICH SUITED THE JAPANESE LANGUAGE NOT AT ALL...

SHOULD WE INVENT A NEW SCRIPT...?

OR IMPROVE THIS ONE?

TO HOUSE THIS NEW CIVILIZATION, THE FUJI-WARA LAID PLANS FOR A GRAND NEW CAPITAL CITY BUILT ON A CHINESE DESIGN. SO WHAT IF JAPAN LACKED THE PEOPLE TO FILL IT?

WE'RE OPTIMISTS!

AND SO, IN THE 790s, **KYOTO** AROSE, MOSTLY... THOUGH THE WEST SIDE OF TOWN WAS A SLUM FROM THE START.

OOP!

ON THE EAST SIDE, MEANWHILE, CULTURE BLOSSOMED. A NEW, SIMPLIFIED SCRIPT BOOSTED POETRY AND PROSE... PEOPLE POLISHED THEIR MANNERS INSTEAD OF THEIR WEAPONS (IT WAS ILLEGAL TO OWN THEM)... AT ONE POINT, KYOTO'S CHIEF OF POLICE WAS A 16-YEAR-OLD BOY!

BY THE LATE 900s, PEOPLE SENSED THAT AN ERA WAS PASSING. YOU CAN SEE THE PESSIMISM IN LADY MURASAKI'S GREAT NOVEL OF THE 990s, *THE TALE OF GENJI*, IN WHICH THE AMOROUS, GLAMOROUS PRINCE GENJI BEGETS A DEPRESSED, NEUROTIC SON—LITERATURE'S FIRST **ANTIHERO**.

I HATE MY OWN GRAPHIC STYLE!

BUT WHY DWELL ON IT?! LIFE WAS A PARTY! POETRY! MUSIC! DANCE! COSTUMES WITH SEVEN LAYERS OF COLOR-COORDINATED SLEEVES! CERTAINLY, THE FRONTIER, WITH ITS GROWING POPULATION OF **FREELANCE SWORD SWINGERS**, WAS FAR FROM EVERYONE'S MIND...

HALF THE SUNG BUDGET WENT TO THE **MILITARY,*** FUNDING THE DEVELOPMENT OF **EX-PLOSIVES**... E.G., BOMBS FLUNG FROM CATAPULTS...

OR THE UNIQUELY CHINESE **FIRE OX:** STRAP A TUB OF EXPLOSIVES TO ITS BACK, GIVE IT A WHACK, AND HOPE IT KEEPS GOING FORWARD...

AND THEN THE FIRST **GUNS:** BAMBOO TUBES STUFFED WITH A POWDER CHARGE TOPPED WITH BROKEN CROCKERY THAT SPEWED OUT WHEN FIRED.

RETIRE THE OX...

AND AT LAST, IN THE EARLY 1200s, CHINESE METALLURGISTS MANAGED TO BORE OUT A **TUBE** TO MAKE A **SNUG FIT** WITH A LARGE **BALL**...

?

AND HERE WE MUST LEAVE CHINA FOR A WHILE...

THIS MILITARY ERA WAS ALSO AN AGE OF FEMALE HELPLESSNESS, WHEN CHINESE MOTHERS BEGAN BINDING THEIR DAUGHTERS' FEET. **FOOT-BINDING** FIRST GAINED A TOEHOLD IN TANG TIMES, WHEN A SLAVE-MASTER BOUND SOME DAN-CERS' FEET FOR A MINIATURE, ULTRA-FEMME EFFECT.

KINKEHH...

UNDER THE SUNG, ARISTOCRATS TOOK IT UP: MOTHERS VIED TO MAKE THEIR DAUGHTERS MORE DESIRABLE BY BINDING AND RE-BINDING THEIR FEET, BREAKING AND BENDING THE YOUNG BONES, FOLDING THE FOOT INTO A TINY CARICATURE OF THE REAL THING.

"YOU CAN'T LOVE YOUR DAUGHTER AND HER FEET."
—CHINESE SAYING

POETS RAVED ABOUT SEXY FEET: THE PETITE LOOK, EVEN THE FINE AND FUNKY AROMA OF THE BIND-INGS! SOON COMMON PEOPLE WERE DOING IT TOO, AND SO FOR **NINE CENTURIES** (UNTIL THE PRACTICE ENDED IN THE 1900s) HALF OF CHINA WAS CRIPPLED.

IT'S NORMAL...
IT'S NORMAL...
IT'S NORMAL...

TURKS AND THE WEST

DURING THE EARLY TANG, WHILE THE WESTERN TURKS WERE FRIENDLY TOWARD CHINA, THEY RESISTED CHINESE CIVILIZATION. ONE TURKISH KING HAD THESE WORDS CARVED INTO THE ROCKS:

"GOLD... SILVER... AND SILK ARE SWEET, BUT ENERVATING. BY THESE ENTICEMENTS... THE CHINESE DREW THE TURKIC PEOPLE TO THEM. THROUGH YIELDING TO THE LURE, MANY OF YOUR FOLK DIED, O TURKS! DESERTING THE DARK FOREST, MANY LOOKED TOWARD THE SOUTH, SAYING, 'I WOULD SETTLE ON THE PLAIN'... BUT IF YOU REMAIN IN THE FOREST, WHERE THERE ARE NEITHER RICHES NOR CARES, YOU WILL PRESERVE AN EVERLASTING EMPIRE, O TURKS!"

AND SO, MANY TURKS MAINTAINED THEIR TRADITIONAL WAY OF LIFE, THEIR WANDERING, INDEPENDENCE, TOUGHNESS, AND AMAZING SKILL IN HORSEMANSHIP AND WAR.

IN 751, THEY COMBINED WITH THE MUSLIMS TO DRIVE THE CHINESE OUT OF CENTRAL ASIA.

WITH THE FOUNDATION OF **BAGHDAD** AND ITS ABBASID DYNASTY, THE TURKS BEGAN A LONG RELATIONSHIP WITH THE MUSLIM WORLD.

"RELATIONSHIP"? THOSE IRAQIS KIDNAP OUR DAUGHTERS!

WE SAW ON P. 44 THAT THE CALIPH **HARUN AL RASHID** HAD TURKISH SLAVES IN HIS PALACE AND HAREM...

THAT ONE OF THESE SLAVES' SONS BECAME CALIPH IN 836 AND INVITED **4,000 TURKISH GUARDS** TO BAGHDAD...

AND THAT THE GUARDS ASSASSINATED FIVE CALIPHS IN TEN YEARS (860-869).

THEN, ON PAGE 83, WE SAW HOW BAGHDAD, IN THIS CRAZY STATE, FAILED FOR **14 YEARS** TO STOP THE REVOLT OF THE **ZANJ** (869-883)...

AND HOW, IN ITS WAKE, THE CALIPH LOST EGYPT AND THE REST OF NORTH AFRICA.

TO SOME TURKS, BAGHDAD'S WEAKNESS LOOKED LIKE AN OPPORTUNITY!

TRIBES OF TURCOMANS (NOMADIC TURKS) BEGAN CROSSING THE RIVERS JAXARTES AND OXUS, MOVING THEIR FLOCKS SOUTH INTO IRANIAN MUSLIM COUNTRY.

SOON, MANY IRANIAN WARLORDS HAD TURKISH GUARDS OF THEIR OWN!

ARE YOU SURE THIS IS A GOOD IDEA?

YOU HAVE ANOTHER ONE?

AND MANY TURKS CONVERTED TO ISLAM—THOUGH THEY WERE OFTEN LAX ABOUT DRINK AND THE VEIL.

JUST SO LONG AS THIS DOESN'T MAKE US GO SOFT AND PEACEABLE...

THAT WOULD BE BUDDHISM...

ONE TURKISH TRIBE THAT REJECTED ISLAM WAS THE **KHAZARS**, WHO LIVED ON THE NORTH SHORE OF THE BLACK SEA, CLOSER TO CHRISTIAN ARMENIA AND "ROME."

THIS WAS PRIME TRADING TERRITORY, WHERE AMBER, FURS, AND SLAVES ARRIVED FROM NORTH AND EAST ON THEIR WAY TO CHRISTIAN WEST AND MUSLIM SOUTH. TAKING AN ACTIVE HAND IN THIS TRADE, THE NOMADS SETTLED DOWN NEAR THEIR WAREHOUSES.

ACROSS THE WATER IN CONSTANTINOPLE, THE JEWS TOOK NOTE!

THEY DO GOOD BUSINESS OVER THERE, AND THEY DON'T KNOW A JEW FROM THE BUDDHA!

PERSECUTED FOR CENTURIES BY "ROMAN" LAW, MANY BYZANTINE JEWS SAILED FOR THE SAFE HAVEN OF KHAZAR COUNTRY.

KHAZARS AND JEWS HIT IT OFF... INTERMARRIED... AND THE JEWS ASSIMILATED.

ASSIMILATE? WHAT'S THAT MEAN?

YOU KNOW— "WHEN IN ROME, DO AS THE ROMANS."

WE **TRIED** THAT! THEY WOULDN'T **LET** US!

OH... I THOUGHT IT MEANT GETTING SADDLE SORES...

AROUND 850, IN FACT, WHEN THE KHAZAR NOBLES MET TO CHOOSE A NEW KHAGAN, IT SEEMS THEY ELECTED ONE OF THESE KHAZAR-IFIED JEWS!

UNCLE MOISHE?

Panel 1: JUST ONE COMPLICATION: THE KHAGAN'S WIFE, WHO STILL KEPT KOSHER, URGED HER HUSBAND TO REMEMBER HIS ROOTS!

O.K., **DON'T**... SNIF... IT'S ALL RIGHT...

OH, GOD, NO! **PLEASE** NOT THE COLD SHOULDER!

Panel 2: HE HIRED A RABBI, STUDIED UP, AND FINALLY BROUGHT IT UP WITH THE NOBLES.

MEN, THIS SKY-WORSHIP IS **SO** OUT OF DATE... WE NEED A MORE **INDOOR** TYPE OF RELIGION...

Panel 3: LEGEND HAS IT THAT THE CHIEF SPONSORED A GREAT **DEBATE,** IN WHICH CHRISTIANS, JEWS, AND MUSLIMS ALL PITCHED THEIR PATHS.

JESUS PROMISES **ETERNAL LIFE!**

MUHAMMAD PROMISES ETERNAL LIFE— WITH **CHICKS!**

MOSES FAVORS CHICKS IN **THIS** LIFE!

Panel 4: WHO KNOWS WHAT THEY SAID (OR IF ANYONE REALLY SAID ANYTHING)?

WE HAVE COMMERCIAL CONTACTS IN THE **ENTIRE CHRISTIAN WORLD,** MUCH OF WHICH IS ADMITTEDLY MIRED IN IGNORANCE, POVERTY, AND FILTH AT THE MOMENT...

WE CAN OFFER MARKETS IN THE **ENTIRE MUSLIM WORLD!** REAL MONEY... NICE...

WE CAN DO BOTH!

WHO KNOWS WHAT DECIDES THESE THINGS?

THE DEBATE, IF IT EVER HAPPENED, WAS PROBABLY RIGGED, BUT NEVER MIND! THE KHAZARS CHOSE **JUDAISM**... AND FOR THREE CENTURIES, THIS SETTLED-NOMAD-TURKISH-JEWISH KINGDOM SURVIVED ON THE NORTH SHORE OF THE BLACK SEA... THE KHAZARS' ULTIMATE FATE IS ONE OF **HISTORY'S MYSTERIES**...

MEANWHILE, BACK IN THE CALIPH'S WORLD, AN ASSORTMENT OF IRANIAN NOBLEMEN, WARLORDS, AND BANDITS, EACH WITH HIS OWN MOTLEY BAND OF ARABS, PERSIANS, AND TURKS, CHOPPED UP BAGHDAD'S EASTERN PROVINCES.

WHAT'S THE DIFFERENCE BETWEEN A BANDIT AND A NOBLEMAN?

AS LITTLE AS A MONTH!

IN 945, A PERSIAN PRINCE FINALLY CHASED THE TURKISH GUARD OUT OF BAGHDAD, BUT ONLY AFTER THE GUARD HAD BLINDED THREE CALIPHS, LEAVING THEM TO BEG IN THE STREETS.

I'D BE HAPPY TO SEE THEM GO, IF I COULD SEE...

WAIT! I KNOW THAT VOICE!

NOT TO BE OUTDONE, THE PERSIAN BLINDED A FOURTH, TOSSED HIM OUT WITH THE REST, AND SET UP A NEW CALIPH MORE TO HIS LIKING.

HEY!

WATCH IT!

YET SOMEHOW, IN ALL THIS TURMOIL, HIGH CULTURE THRIVED AND EVEN SPREAD. THE MINI-SHAHS ADORNED THEIR OWN CITIES WITH MOSQUES, PALACES, TOMBS, HOSPITALS, LIBRARIES, AND ASTRO-NOMICAL OBSERVATORIES. **SHIRAZ, BUKHARA,** AND **SAMARKAND** ALL FLOURISHED, AND THE PERSIAN LANGUAGE REVIVED AS A LITERARY VEHICLE.

A LITERARY VEHICLE.

BOOKMOBILE

FAMOUS NAMES OF THE CENTURY 950–1050 INCLUDE AL-BIRUNI (GEOGRAPHER), IBN-SENA OR AVICENNA (PHILOSOPHER), AND FIRDAUSI (POET).

134

AROUND 950, THE IRANIAN LORD OF BUKHARA, A CITY THEN FAMOUS FOR APRICOTS, CARPETS, AND SCHOLARSHIP, HAD A **FALLING-OUT** WITH HIS BEST GENERAL, A TURK NAMED **ALPTIGIN**.

YOU STARTED IT!

NO, **YOU** STARTED IT!

ALPTIGIN AND HIS PEOPLE DEPARTED, EXPOSING THE CITY TO A NEW WAVE OF NORTHERN TURKS. (THE IRANIAN DYNASTY FELL IN 992.)

HE STARTED IT!

HE STARTED IT!

ALPTIGIN AND COMPANY HEADED SOUTH... CROSSED THE OXUS... CLIMBED THE MOUNTAINS...

AND THE NEXT THING YOU KNEW, HIS FAMILY RULED MOST OF **AFGHANISTAN**!

A SIMPLE MATTER OF EXTERMINATING OUR RIVALS...

ALPTIGIN'S MOST AGGRESSIVE AND ZEALOUSLY MUSLIM HEIR WAS **MAHMOUD OF GHAZNI,** WHO SET HIM-SELF UP IN 999. FROM HIS RUG-GED, ROCKY LAIR, HE SOUGHT NEW PLACES TO SPREAD THE FAITH—LUSH, TAXABLE PLACES, PREFERABLY.

ONWARD!

SO MAHMOUD LED HIS ARMIES OVER THE PASSES AND DOWN INTO THE PLAINS OF **INDIA**—AND WHAT HE FOUND THERE AROUSED BOTH HIS GREED AND HIS ZEAL...

SHOCKING!

INDIA 300–1000

WHEN LAST WE LOOKED, INDIA WAS RULED BY FOREIGN BUDDHIST KINGS (SEE P. 109)... WHEN THEY WEAKENED, HINDU KINGS REBELLED... WON TERRITORY... FOUGHT AMONG THEMSELVES... UNTIL ONE, **CHANDRAGUPTA**, CONQUERED THE OTHERS AROUND THE YEAR 300.

THESE SPORT UTILITY VEHICLES REALLY GIVE YOU A FEELING OF POWER...

CHANDRAGUPTA VOWED TO **PURGE INDIA** OF CENTRAL ASIAN "ELEMENTS" LIKE THE YUEH-CHI AND SAKAS AND GREEKS LEFT OVER FROM ALEXANDER THE GREAT.

*NO MORE OF THESE **HYPHENATED INDIANS!** FROM NOW ON, WE'RE **PURE INDO-ARYAN!***

EXCUSE ME?

*I WISH I COULD SAY THIS **ETHNIC CLEANSING** POLICY WAS A **FAILURE**, BUT IN FACT, THE GUPTA DYNASTY BROUGHT INDIA A **CLASSICAL AGE** OF SCIENCE, TECHNOLOGY, ART, PHILOSOPHY, POETRY, AND THEATER...*

DELHI'S IRON PILLAR, OUTDOORS FOR 1,600 YEARS AND STILL NO RUST.

BUDDHIST FRESCOES AT AJANTA

DEVELOPMENT OF WRITTEN ARITHMETIC WITH TEN SYMBOLS INCLUDING ZERO

1 2 3 8 4
6 7 < 9 0

PRODUCTION OF CHEMICALS AND DYESTUFFS SUCH AS INDIGO

JUST LOOK AT THOSE COLORS!

GOSH.

THE PLAYS OF KALIDASA

HERMITS, I'VE BEEN RACKING MY BRAINS, BUT I HAVE NO MEMORY OF MARRYING THIS WOMAN!

IN THE MID-400s, WHILE ATTILA THE HUN TERRORIZED EUROPE, ANOTHER BRANCH OF THE HUNS, THE **YE-TA,** INVADED INDIA WITH MANY MASSACRES.

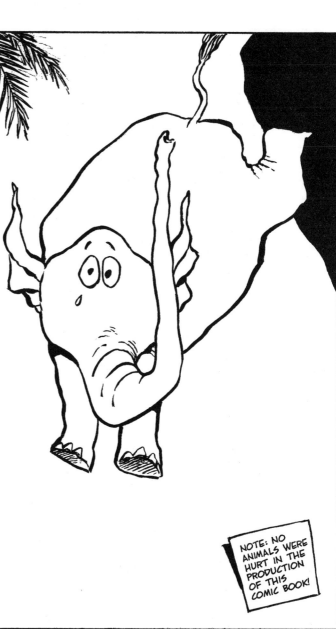

JUST REMEMBER— IT'S NOT CRUELTY, IT'S A LIFESTYLE OPTION!

WELL, ALL RIGHT THEN.

ONE HUN CHIEFTAIN AMUSED HIMSELF BY WATCHING ELEPHANTS BEING DRIVEN OVER CLIFFS.

MY EMOTIONS ARE VALID!

UNDER THE ONSLAUGHT, GUPTA POWER DWINDLED, UNTIL NOTHING WAS LEFT OF IT BY 550...

NOTE: NO ANIMALS WERE HURT IN THE PRODUCTION OF THIS COMIC BOOK!

AT WHICH POINT, THE TURKS CAME TO POWER IN CENTRAL ASIA, ATTACKED THE YE-TA IN THEIR NORTHERN PROVINCES, AND WIPED THEM OUT THERE.

IN THE SOUTH, THE REMAINING YE-TA FELL TO HINDU REBELLIONS, AND SO THE HUNS VANISHED FROM HISTORY.

ELEPHANTS EVERYWHERE CAN RELAX!

THEN, OF COURSE, THE INDIAN ARMIES HAD TO FIGHT AMONG THEMSELVES...

HEY, WAIT A MINUTE!

UNTIL, IN 606, ONE OF THEM CAME OUT ON TOP: KING **HARSHA**, FAMOUS FOR HIS POSH COURT, HIS LAVISH GIFTS, HIS GENEROSITY.

GIFTS ARE **GOOD**! THEY MAKE PEOPLE **HAPPY**!!

BEWARE OF **"GENEROUS"** KINGS! WHATEVER THEY GIVE AWAY, THEY HAVE TO TAKE FROM SOMEONE ELSE!

LOVE YOUR JACKET! GIVE IT TO ME...

DURING THEIR REIGNS, THE PEOPLE FALL INTO POVERTY, AND MANY TURN TO BANDITRY AND REBELLION.*

*&%$ COMMONERS JUST AREN'T AS GENEROUS AS THEY OUGHTA BE...

THIS PRETTY MUCH DESCRIBES WHAT HAPPENED UNDER HARSHA... AND HELPS EXPLAIN WHY HIS KINGDOM FELL APART WHEN HE DIED, LEAVING INDIA DIVIDED ONCE AGAIN.

FOLLOW ME! I'M ONLY **SEMI**-GENEROUS!

I'M A COMPLETE MISER!

INSPIRED NO DOUBT BY THE CLASH OF ARMIES, AN INDIAN **GAME DESIGNER** AROUND THIS TIME CAME UP WITH A NEW ONE FEATURING AN ASSORTMENT OF SPECIALIZED WARRIORS PROTECTED BY A HORDE OF PAWNS WITH LIMITED POWER: **CHESS**.

I JUST ADORE THE CONCEPT!

THANK YOU, HIGHNESS!

SOME OF HISTORY'S GREATEST **TYRANTS** PLAYED CHESS AVIDLY. ONE CHRONICLER WROTE THAT "NO ONE COULD BEAT" THE 14TH-CENTURY ASIAN CONQUEROR **TAMERLANE**... BUT THEN, WHO WOULD DARE TO?

MY KNIGHT CIRCLES AROUND AND GRABS SIX OF YOUR PAWNS!

HEY! WHERE'D THAT MOVE COME FROM?

I JUST MADE IT UP. ANY PROBLEM WITH THAT?

THE GAME SOON GAINED WIDE APPEAL, SINCE IT OFFERS AN OPPORTUNITY TO TEST ONE'S SKILL IN BATTLE STRATEGY WITHOUT ACTUALLY HURTING ANYBODY.

HAH! GOT YOUR CASTLE! POW!

SIGH... THESE ACTION GAMES ARE RUINING TODAY'S YOUTH...

MEANWHILE, **SOUTH** INDIA WAS THRIVING. FROM SEA-PORTS EAST AND WEST, INDIAN SHIPS TRADED WITH THE WORLD.

SHORE TEMPLE, MAHABALIPURAM, LATE 600s.

AS EARLY AS THE FIRST CENTURY, HINDU CULTURE SPREAD EASTWARD... AND THIS WAS ODD, BECAUSE HINDUISM'S PRIESTS, THE BRAHMINS, **FORBID** HINDUS TO CROSS THE SEA OR MARRY OUTSIDE CASTE.

NEVER NEVER NEVER!

ANGKOR

SUMATRA

SINGAPORE

BORNEO

JAVA

BALI

AND YET...

AMBITIOUS PRINCES AND BRAHMINS DID SAIL FROM INDIA'S EAST COAST.

BUT, MY GURU, IS IT NOT FORBIDDEN TO CROSS THE SEA?

YES, MY DISCIPLE, UNLESS UPSIDE POTENTIAL IS VERY VERY HIGH...

THEY CAME TO SUMATRA OR JAVA OR THE MALAY PENINSULA... BEFRIENDED LOCAL FAMILIES...

WE'LL BUY ALL THE **GINGER** AND **PEPPER** YOU CAN GROW!

MARRY MY DAUGHTER!

SET UP TRADING POSTS... MADE FORTUNES IN THE SPICE TRADE... MARRIED LOCAL WOMEN... TAUGHT THEM HINDUISM... HIRED AN ARMY...

BUT MY GURU, IS IT NOT **FORBIDDEN** TO MARRY OUTSIDE CASTE?

YES, MY DISCIPLE, UNLESS GIG IS VERY VERY GOOD...

SUDDENLY, SHIVA TEMPLES WERE ON THE MOUNTAIN-TOPS AND HINDU KINGS WERE LORDING IT OVER THE LOCALS!

YOU'LL **GROW** ALL THE GINGER AND PEPPER WE CAN **BUY!**

!

THE MOST SPLENDID HINDU KINGDOM IN SOUTHEAST ASIA WAS **ANGKOR**, CAMBODIA, IN THE 800s, BUT THERE WERE AT LEAST A DOZEN OTHERS.

A LITTLE WHILE AGO, I NEVER HEARD OF THEIR GODS... NOW I **WORSHIP** THEM!

STRANGE HOW THAT HAPPENS...

EVEN TODAY, MANY INDIAN NAMES REMAIN, LIKE **SINGAPORE** (SINGH-PUR = LIONVILLE) AND **CAMBODIA** (NAMED AFTER THE KAMBUJA VALLEY IN AFGHANISTAN!).

BUT MY GURU—

OH, SHUT UP...

AT THE SAME TIME, BACK IN INDIA, SOMETHING STRANGE WAS GOING ON: **BUDDHISM** WAS DYING OUT.

BORN IN INDIA, OPPOSED TO **CASTE** AND **CUSTOM,** BUDDHISM APPEALED TO MANY INDIANS... YET HINDUISM, BOUND BY CASTE AND CUSTOM, THRIVED, WHILE BUDDHISM WITHERED AWAY. WHY?

PSST! PSST!

WELL, HINDUISM HAS NEVER BEEN SHORT OF **NEW IDEAS**... AND IN THE MIDDLE AGES, IT CAME UP WITH THIS ONE: **SEX** RUNS THE **UNIVERSE!**

COME TO OUR, AHEM, **PRAYER MEETING** TONIGHT! YOU'LL SEE...

CERTAIN CULTS BEGAN TO MEET SECRETLY, AT NIGHT, BY INVITATION ONLY...

IN THE DARK, THEY VIOLATED CASTE AND CUSTOM... ALL CASTES SAT SIDE-BY-SIDE AND INDULGED IN THE FIVE "FORBIDDEN Ms": MEAT, MEAD, *MACHLI* (FISH), MAGIC...

AND MM-**MMM!**

THE NEXT MORNING, THEY WENT BACK TO AVOIDING EACH OTHER'S SHADOWS.

AT NIGHT, THERE **IS** NO SHADOW!

WELL, A GOOD SECRET IS HARD TO KEEP... IN THE 900s, TEMPLES WENT UP IN INDIA THAT LOOKED LIKE **THIS!** HOW COULD BUDDHISM **COMPETE?**

IT'S JUST SO **UNFAIR!**

AND SO, BUDDHISM SLOWLY RECEDED IN INDIA, WHILE HINDUISM FLOURISHED IN A RIOT OF SCULPTURE...

THAT OLD-TIME RELIGION STILL HAS SOME LIFE IN IT!

SO NOW YOU KNOW WHAT **MAHMOUD OF GHAZNI** SAW WHEN HE CAME KNOCKING AT THE DOOR!

BLOODY &%$#! PERVY HORSE!

IN A PIOUS SNIT, MAHMOUD TOLD HIS MEN TO SMASH EVERY IDOL IN SIGHT.

IMAGES ARE BAD ENOUGH— BUT **THESE** IMAGES!

SEVENTEEN TIMES HE INVADED INDIA, ALWAYS SMASHING... THE FIRST MUSLIM TO DO REAL DAMAGE TO HINDU CULTURE...

THERE GO THE MODELING JOBS!

MEANWHILE, IN AFGHANISTAN, MAHMOUD TRIED TO ADORN GHAZNI WITH WHATEVER SMALL CHANGE WAS LEFT AFTER HIS MILITARY SPENDING.

HERE'S THE MINIATURE MOSQUE AND THE 5-BED HOSPITAL AND THE THRONE ENCRUSTED WITH A SINGLE PRECIOUS GEM...

HE DIED IN 1033.

ONCE THEY GOT SETTLED, THE TURKS CULTIVATED PERSIAN LEARNING. MAHMOUD HIRED **FIRDAUSI**, THE GREAT PERSIAN POET, TO WRITE A HISTORY OF THE PERSIAN KINGS, AND PROMISED TO REWARD HIM WITH **1000 GOLD COINS**.

PAYABLE ON DELIVERY!

FIRDAUSI TOILED FOR YEARS TO CREATE THE **SHAH-NAMEH**, NOW THE PERSIAN NATIONAL EPIC, BUT MAHMOUD PAID HIM ONLY **1000 COPPERS** INSTEAD!

YOUR POEM IS WONDERFULLY... AH... **LONG**... BUT UNFORTUNATELY, I'M A LITTLE BIT **SHORT**...

FIRDAUSI THEN ATTACKED MAHMOUD'S STINGINESS WITH THESE PECULIAR LINES:

THE HAND OF KING MAHMOUD, OF NOBLE DESCENT, IS **NINE TIMES NINE** AND **THREE TIMES FOUR**.

(=93)

FOOTNOTE TO THE FOOTNOTE: MUSLIM TRADERS BARGAINED USING NUMERICAL HAND-SIGNALS—SO EVERYONE WOULD KNOW THAT 93 MEANT A **TIGHT FIST!**

MANZIKERT

NOW WE COME TO A **HISTORIC TURNING POINT,** AS THE TURKS TURN TO THE **WEST...**

IT BEGAN AMONG THOSE TURKS PASSING BUKHARA AFTER 950 (SEE P. 135)... A CHIEFTAIN CALLED **SELJUK,** OF THE TRIBE OF GHUZZ OR OGHUZ, HAD SONS NAMED **DAVID, ISRAEL,** AND **MOSES.** (THEIR MOM MAY HAVE BEEN A KHAZAR.) LITTLE MORE IS KNOWN.

BY THE YEAR 1000, WE FIND SELJUK'S SONS AS FERVENT MUSLIMS IN THE SERVICE OF **MAHMOUD OF GHAZNI...**

AFTER MAHMOUD'S DEATH IN 1033, WE NOTICE THE SELJUKS ATTACKING THEIR NEIGHBORS...

BY 1037, WE SEE THEIR FLAG AT THE HEAD OF QUITE AN ARMY...

HEY... YOU LOOKING OVER MY SHOULDER?

THIS HORDE, COMMANDED BY SELJUK'S GRANDSON **TUGHRIL BEY,** IN 1055 BORE DOWN ON **BAGHDAD** ITSELF. THE CITY'S EYE-GOUGING PERSIAN OVERLORDS (SEE P. 134) FLED AT THE SIGHT!

TSK! HORSES! ALWAYS **RUNNING...**

ONCE IN THE CAPITAL, THE SELJUK HAD SOME WORDS WITH THE CALIPH... LUCKILY THEY BOTH HAD INTERPRETERS, SINCE TUGHRIL TALKED TURKISH... HE ORDERED TWO HIGH PLATFORMS TO GO UP... ATOP ONE, THE CALIPH, WEARING THE PROPHET'S OWN ROBE, BLESSED TUGHRIL, ON THE OTHER, WITH A BRAND NEW TITLE: **SULTAN,** WHICH MEANS GRAND HIGH POOH-BAH IN ANY LANGUAGE.

HEY! NO TIPTOES!

I CAN'T UNDERSTAND YOU!

IT'S GOOD THEY'RE PUTTING THINGS ON A FIRM FOUNDATION.

UNLIKE THE PERSIAN "PROTEC-TORS," WHO WERE SHIITES, THE SELJUK SULTAN SHOWED THE CALIPH SOME RESPECT.

LIKE HOW?

WELL, I CAN STILL SEE, FOR ONE THING...

ALAS FOR HIM, THE SELJUKS HAD TO DUCK OUT BRIEFLY TO SUPPRESS A REVOLT... THE SHIITES RETURNED, FORCED THE CALIPH TO ABDICATE, AND SENT HIS HAT AND CALIPHAL GEAR TO EGYPT, THRILLING THE **OTHER** CALIPH, ALSO A SHIITE, IN CAIRO (SEE P. 98).

THIS MARKS THE HIGH POINT OF SHIITE POWER...

BUT TUGHRIL AND ALL CAME STRAIGHT BACK TO BAGHDAD, KILLED THE SHIITE GENERAL, AND RESTORED THE OFFICIAL CALIPH. THE TURKISH SULTAN NOW CONTROLLED THE HEART OF THE MUSLIM WORLD.

RATS!

SOON TUGHRIL DIED, AND THE SECOND SELJUK SULTAN **ALP ARSLAN** ("LION HERO") KEPT UP THE WESTWARD PUSH. IN 1064 HE INVADED CHRISTIAN **ARMENIA**, WHERE HIS TROOPS MASSACRED ENTIRE CITIES.

WHOA!

MANZIKERT
LAKE VAN
TIGRIS R

FROM ARMENIA THE TURKS BEGAN RAIDING THE BYZANTINE HEARTLAND, WHILE THE "ROMAN" EMPEROR DID NOTHING.

WHADDAYAMEAN, "NOTHING"? I'M ACTIVELY WRINGING MY HANDS HERE!

IN 1067, THE EMPEROR DIED... HIS WIDOW DECIDED TO MARRY A **GENERAL**, SOMEONE WITH **FIGHT**, AND MAKE **HIM** THE NEW EMPEROR.

EXCELLENT! I'M A GENERAL!
SO AM I!
SO AM I!

NATURALLY, WHEN SHE CHOSE ONE, **ROMANOS DIOGENES**, THE OTHERS FELT SORRY FOR THEMSELVES.

NOW GIT THEM TURKS!
RRI-I-IGHT...

AND ROMANOS DIOGENES HAD TO BUILD UP HIS MILITARY AMID BACKBITING AND BYZANTINE INTRIGUE.

MY MEN AND I ARE DEEPLY ATTACHED TO YOUR CAUSE, MAJESTY!

IN THE SPRING OF 1071, THE NEW EMPEROR LED OUT HIS FORCES, WHICH INCLUDED PROFESSIONAL SOLDIERS, RAW RECRUITS, SOME PRIVATE ARMIES LED BY PEOPLE WHO HATED HIM, AND EVEN A FEW TURKISH CAVALRY UNITS.

WAIT. WHOSE SIDE ARE WE ON?
BOTH OF THEM, FOR NOW...

ALP ARSLAN WAS WAITING FOR THEM IN ARMENIA WITH HIS OWN ARMY AT A PLACE CALLED **MANZIKERT**.

ON FRIDAY, AUGUST 19, OR POSSIBLY AUGUST 26, THE "ROMANS" MARCHED OUT IN BATTLE ARRAY, KEEPING THE QUESTIONABLE PRIVATE ARMIES IN THE REAR AS RESERVES. AS THE "ROMAN" LINE ADVANCED, THE TURKS FELL BACK... AND BACK... AND BACK... UNTIL, AT LAST, LATE IN THE DAY, ROMANOS DIOGENES SIGNALED FOR A RETURN TO CAMP. THEN, JUST AS THE "ROMANS" WERE ROTATING, THE TURKS MADE THEIR CHARGE. THE "ROMAN" REINFORCEMENTS FAILED TO REINFORCE... SOME "ROMAN" TURKS DESERTED... AND AFTER A BLOODY STRUGGLE, THE BYZANTINE ARMY WAS ROUTED AND THE EMPEROR HIMSELF TAKEN PRISONER.

WHAT A LOSER!

IN THE SELJUK CAMP, ALP ARSLAN PUT HIS FOOT ON THE EMPEROR'S NECK AND MADE HIM SAY SOMETHING SUBMISSIVE.

FLOG ME! BEAT ME! TIE ME UP, GAG ME, AND PLAY WITH MY—

DON'T OVERDO IT, EH?

THEY STRUCK A DEAL: "ROME" CEDED THE TURKS SEVERAL EASTERN CITIES AND PROMISED A MOUNTAIN OF MONEY. THE TURKS SWORE TO LEAVE THE BYZANTINES IN PEACE.

NOW HE'LL **HAVE** TO FREE ME, SO I CAN GO HOME AND SUPERVISE THIS DEBACLE. EXCELLENT!

WHILE THESE BOZOS **PAY** ME, I CAN FIGHT MY **REAL** ENEMIES, THE SHIITES... SECURE JERUSALEM... CONQUER EGYPT... YESS!!

THE SULTAN THEN SENT THE EMPEROR STUMBLING HOMEWARD WITH THE REMAINS OF HIS ARMY.

BEFORE HE COULD ARRIVE, ROMANOS'S ENEMIES HAD SEIZED THE THRONE. THEY ATTACKED HIS ARMY WITH ONE OF THEIR OWN...

WEE'RE BACK!

CAPTURED HIM, AND PUT OUT HIS EYES. HE DIED OF INFECTION WITHIN DAYS.

SIGH... THE THINGS YOU GOTTA DO IN THE SOLDIER BIZNESS...

DON'T WORRY! I'M A MEDIEVAL DOCTOR!

SOON AFTER, ALP ARSLAN WAS ASSASSINATED IN CAMP BY ONE OF HIS OWN MEN.

WITH BOTH LEADERS GONE, THEIR AGREEMENT COLLAPSED.

NOW HORDES OF TURCOMAN NOMADS ROLLED AND RUMBLED AND TROTTED AND GALLOPED INTO ASIA MINOR... BY 1080, THEY CONTROLLED SOME 30,000 SQUARE MILES—LAND THAT HAD BEEN GREEK FOR 1,400 YEARS, SINCE ALEXANDER THE GREAT. CONSTANTINOPLE YELLED FOR HELP.

HURRY UP, OR THEY'LL BE CALLING IT **TURKEY!**

A FEW YEARS LATER, EUROPE ANSWERED THE CALL... AND SO THE BATTLE OF MANZIKERT SET IN MOTION THIS TRAIN OF EVENTS:

THE CRUSADES,
THE REVIVAL OF EUROPE,
THE RUIN OF "ROME,"
THE RENAISSANCE,
THE DISCOVERY OF AMERICA,
 AND
THE FORMATION OF THE MODERN WORLD!

READ ON...

NEXT: DARKNESS AT NOON AND ONE AND TWO AND...

IN THE LAST VOLUME, WE FOLLOWED THE FORTUNES OF THE TURKS... IN THIS ONE, WE TURN BACK TO EUROPE!

CLIK

AND I DO MEAN **BACK!** THESE ARE THE **DARK AGES**, WHEN EUROPEANS WERE BADLY FED, BADLY LED, AND BADLY EDUCATED!

BUT THAT'S ONLY **HALF** THE STORY... BECAUSE ALL ALONG THERE WAS "ROME": THE **BYZANTINE EMPIRE**, A REAL **CIVILIZATION** WITH LAWS, LIBRARIES, AND LEARNING!

ALTHOUGH EUROPEAN HISTORY MAKES **NO SENSE** WITHOUT THE BYZANTINES, WE IN THE WEST TEND TO **IGNORE** THEM—MAINLY BECAUSE THEY BELONGED TO THE "WRONG" CHURCH!

TWISTED $#%& REASON...

WE EVEN USE THE WORD "BYZANTINE" AS A KIND OF **INSULT**—AND, TO BE **FRANK**, IT WASN'T THE MOST **ENLIGHTENED** OR **PLEASANT** CIVILIZATION AROUND!

AK! I CAN'T SEE!

SO... AS WE SET THE **TIME MACHINE** TO THE YEAR 600, WE'LL BE VISITING **TWO DIFFERENT** EUROPES—AT LEAST! I CALL THEM...

ICONS WITHOUT COMPUTERS

THE CARTOON HISTORY OF THE UNIVERSE

Volume 17

DIM AND DIMMER

IT WAS FOUNDED IN 322 BY THE EMPEROR **CONSTANTINE**... EIGHTY YEARS LATER, ITS MASSIVE WALLS WENT UP IN THE REIGN OF **THEODOSIUS**... AND THEN, THROUGH ALL THE PILLAGING COMMITTED BY THE GERMANS, **CONSTANTINOPLE** HELD FAST.

TRULY, WE ARE THE BASTION OF WESTERN CIVILIZATION!

UH... FRIEND, AT THE MOMENT, WE **ARE** WESTERN CIVILIZATION...

THOSE WALLS ENCLOSED A CITY STILL RULED BY ROMAN TRADITIONS: AN ALL-POWERFUL EMPEROR, A WEAK (BUT POMPOUS!) SENATE, A CHRISTIAN ESTABLISHMENT, A COMPLEX ("BYZANTINE") BODY OF LAW, CHARIOT RACES, PUBLIC BATHS, LIBRARIES, AND A ROMAN FLAIR FOR BIG BUILDINGS. STILL, THERE WERE DIFFERENCES BETWEEN THIS "ROME" AND THE ORIGINAL: HERE EVERYONE SPOKE GREEK... AND HERE THE PRIESTS GREW BEARDS, MARRIED, AND OTHERWISE SCANDALIZED THE CLEAN-SHAVEN CELIBATES OF ROME.

ST. SOPHIA, BUILT IN THE 500s, WORLD'S LARGEST CHURCH FOR MANY CENTURIES

YOU DISOBEY OUR POPE... YOUR EMPEROR APPOINTS THE HEAD OF YOUR CHURCH... YOU STAND WHEN WE SIT... YOU DO EVERYTHING **BACKWARD**... IS THERE **ANY** WAY WE'RE ALIKE?

UM... WE BOTH OPPOSE FREEDOM OF THOUGHT?

O.K.... YOU'RE NOT ALL BAD...

CONSTANTINOPLE'S STRATEGIC POSITION—AT A DOUBLE BOTTLENECK BETWEEN ASIA AND EUROPE—PRODUCED ITS WEALTH. IT COULD TAX OR GET HOLD OF ANYTHING IMPORTED FROM ANYWHERE.

EUROPE SEA ROUTE LAND ROUTE ASIA

JUSTINIAN I (REIGNED 525–565), FOR EXAMPLE, ORDERED HIS AGENTS TO SMUGGLE SILK-MAKING TECHNOLOGY OUT OF CHINA—AND THEY DID!

FUNNY... I COULD SWEAR THEY LOOK LIKE **WORMS**...

THE BYZANTINES BUILT UP THEIR INDUSTRY AND BECAME THE SILK MERCHANTS OF THE WESTERN WORLD.

SO THE SECRET IS LOCATION, LOCATION, AND LOCATION?

THAT, AND WALLS.

RUSTLE CRINKLE

153

YES, THE BYZANTINES WERE CIVILIZED, AND THEY KNEW IT! SO THEY TRIED HARD TO SET A **HUMANE EXAMPLE.** FOR INSTANCE...

LIKE MANY OTHERS, THE "ROMANS" BELIEVED THAT THEIR EMPEROR'S FACE MUST BE **BLEMISH-FREE.** DISFIGUREMENT MEANT DISQUALIFICATION.

THIS ONE?

SQUINTY.

THIS ONE?

BOTH EYES ON THE SAME SIDE OF HIS NOSE.

THIS ONE?

HAS A WART ON THE FOOT GROWING OUT OF HIS FOREHEAD.

SO, WHEN THEY **OVERTHREW AN EMPEROR,** HIS ENEMIES WOULD **DEFACE** HIM IN SOME WAY, MAKING HIM UNFIT TO RULE AGAIN—SO MUCH KINDER THAN KILLING!

THAT IS, UNTIL EMPEROR **JUSTINIAN II** AND HIS NOSE...

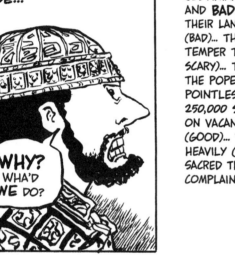

WHY? WHA'D WE DO?

TO THE NOBILITY, THIS JUSTINIAN WAS **SCARY** AND **BAD:** HE TOOK AWAY THEIR LAND AND POWER (BAD)... THREW VIOLENT TEMPER TANTRUMS (BAD, SCARY)... TRIED TO KIDNAP THE POPE (BAD, SCARY, POINTLESS)... SETTLED 250,000 SLAVIC PEASANTS ON VACANT ASIAN LAND* (GOOD)... TAXED THEM TOO HEAVILY (BAD)... AND MASSACRED THEM WHEN THEY COMPLAINED (BAD, SCARY).

IN 695, A GROUP OF NOBLES ARRESTED JUSTINIAN II AND **SLIT HIS NOSE.**

AARGH!

OO! YOU SHOULDA HELD STILL!

LOOKS NASTY...

*THE LAND HAD BEEN VACATED BY PEOPLE FLEEING ALL THE ARAB ATTACKS OF THE LATE 600s. TO STOP THESE ATTACKS, BYZANTINE SCIENTISTS BEGAN TRYING TO IMPROVE THEIR **MILITARY TECHNOLOGY.**

DURING THE INVASION OF 674, THE GREEKS SQUIRTED OUT A NEW **SECRET WEAPON: GREEK FIRE,** A SORT OF **FLAMING GEL** SHOT FROM NOZZLES. IT BURNED ON WATER!

THE BYZANTINE MILITARY GUARDED THE GREEK FIRE RECIPE CLOSELY FOR CENTURIES, AND NOW IT'S COMPLETELY FORGOTTEN.

WHAT A TERRIBLE LOSS TO HUMANITY!

JUSTINIAN WAS BANISHED TO THE FAR SIDE OF THE BLACK SEA, IN KHAZAR COUNTRY (NOT YET JEWISH—SEE P. 133).

THUMBING HIS RUNNY NOSE AT FATE, JUSTINIAN MADE FRIENDS WITH THE KHAZAR KHAGAN, MARRIED A KHAZAR PRINCESS, AND PLOTTED A RETURN TO POWER.

FFFFF
FFFFFF

☆✳⚡✺!

IN 700, HE MARCHED ON CONSTANTINOPLE WITH AN ARMY OF KHAZARS AND BULGARS AND REGAINED THE BYZANTINE THRONE.

SO IT TURNED OUT A BYZANTINE EMPEROR **COULD** HAVE A BLEMISH! JUSTINIAN RULED FOR SIX MORE YEARS BEFORE BEING MURDERED.

ARF FFYOU FMAKING **FFFFUN** OF ME?

NO, YOUR MAJESTY!

NOW THE "ROMANS" REALIZED THEIR ERROR... SO WHEN THE NEXT EMPEROR WAS OVERTHROWN IN 710, THEY PUT HIS EYES OUT.

AFTER THIS, I SHOULD WARN YOU, BYZANTINE HISTORY CONTAINS AN **AMAZING** AMOUNT OF EYE-GOUGING... BE WARNED...

HUMANE, THOUGH!

THE WEST, BY CONTRAST, LACKED THIS PARTICULAR KIND OF CIVILIZATION...

FRANKS, GOTHS, LATINS, JEWS, ARABS, BERBERS, ALL IN ONE CHAPTER!

OF ALL THE GERMANS WHO WRECKED ROME'S WESTERN EMPIRE, THREE TRIBES WON OUT IN THE END: FRANKS, VANDALS, AND GOTHS. AFTER LENDING THEIR NAME TO **ANDAL**UCIA, THE VANDALS PASSED ON TO AFRICA, LEAVING GOTHS AND FRANKS TO HACK UP EUROPE.

THESE NEW OVERLORDS OF THE WEST SPOKE **GERMAN**, WHILE EVERYONE ELSE SPOKE **LATIN**... BELONGED TO A **SPLINTER CHURCH**, WHILE EVERYONE ELSE FOLLOWED **ROME**... AND THEY LIVED BY THEIR OWN **LAWS*** AND **CUSTOMS.**

GAUL

FRANKS

DID YOU SPEAK OR CLEAR YOUR THROAT?

GOTHS

GOTHS

MACHT MACHT RECHT!

(MIGHT MAKES RIGHT.)

SPAIN

ANDALUCIA

VANDALS

I'VE NEVER BATHED!

WAS IST LOS DAMIT?*

THEY COMPLETELY FAILED TO STOP EUROPE'S DECAY... WEEDS SPROUTED IN THE ROADS... PEOPLE STOLE PAVEMENT... AQUEDUCTS BROKE... SCHOOLS CLOSED... MEDICAL CARE DWINDLED... PUBLIC BUILDINGS, MARKETS, AND BATHS FELL INTO RUIN... FIELDS WENT UNTENDED... FORESTS SPREAD... LIFE GREW SIMPLER, SHORTER, AND LESS SECURE.

*WHAT'S WRONG WITH THAT?

GERMAN LAW USED A ROUGH-AND-READY METHOD CALLED THE **ORDEAL** TO DECIDE TOUGH CASES.

"ORDEAL"? QUOD EST?

YOU WOULDN'T UNDERSTAND! IT'S A GERMAN THING!

SAY, FOR EXAMPLE, ONE PERSON SUES ANOTHER, BUT BOTH SIDES SEEM EQUALLY RIGHT (OR WRONG, OR RICH, OR POWERFUL). THEN CAME **ORDEAL BY COMBAT**, AND TO THE VICTOR WOULD GO THE VERDICT!

SO MUCH EASIER THAN LISTENING TO TESTIMONY!

OR: SOMEONE ACCUSED OF WITCHCRAFT MIGHT UNDERGO **ORDEAL BY WATER**, I.E., BE THROWN IN THE RIVER. FLOTATION EQUALED GUILT.

AND IF SHE SINKS?

TRIAL OVER, PROBLEM GONE!

THE CHURCH EM-BRACED THESE CUS-TOMS, SINCE GOD SUPPOSEDLY DECIDED THE OUTCOME, AND TRIAL BY ORDEAL REMAINED A PART OF EUROPEAN "JUSTICE" ALMOST UNTIL MODERN TIMES.

WHY NOT JUST FLIP A COIN? DOESN'T GOD DECIDE **THAT**, TOO?

DUNK THE WITCH!

AFTER THE FRANKS BECAME CATHOLIC, THE SPANISH GOTHS FELT PRESSURE TO DO THE SAME.

OTHERWISE, THOSE DANG FRANKS WILL BE ON US IN A MINUTE, AND THEN WON'T OUR OWN PEOPLE STAB US IN THE BACK?

EH?

AT LAST, IN 586, THE GOTHIC KING RECARED (RICHARD, RICARDO) CONVERTED, AND SOON ALL SPAIN BELONGED TO THE ROMAN CHURCH— OR ALMOST ALL...

I FEEL SO MUCH MORE SECURE NOW...

THE MAIN EXCEPTION BEING SPAIN'S LARGE POPULATION OF JEWS.

ULP... THEY'RE TALKING ABOUT US IN THERE...

FOR WHATEVER REASON, THE SPANISH CHURCH SPEWED UNUSUALLY VENOMOUS VENOM AGAINST THE JEWS.

ALL JEWS ARE GUILTY FOREVER FOR SOMETHING A FEW OF THEIR ANCESTORS MAY HAVE DONE!

SHOULDN'T THEY SUFFER HORRIBLY?

THE VATICAN'S POSITION UNTIL 1973

BEFORE CONVERSION, THE GOTHS HAD NO PROBLEM WITH THE JEWS, BUT AFTERWARD, THERE WAS THE ROMAN CHURCH, EGGING THEM ON.

ALL RIGHT! ALL RIGHT!!

A NERVE-WRACKING CENTURY FOLLOWED... ONE CHURCH COUNCIL AFTER ANOTHER URGED THE GOVERNMENT TO ANNOY, DISPOSSESS, ENSLAVE, FLOG, OR DEPORT THE JEWS, WHILE KINGS PING-PONGED BACK AND FORTH BETWEEN DEFYING THE CHURCH AND OBEYING IT.

TALK ABOUT A CROSS TO BEAR!

IN 694, THE CHURCH RECOMMENDED **EN-SLAVING ALL ADULT JEWS** AND RAISING THEIR CHILDREN AS CHRISTIANS; THE GOTHIC KING, **WITIZA,** REFUSED TO LISTEN.

YOUR MAJESTY CONDEMNS THESE INNOCENTS TO **ETERNAL DAMNATION!**

YOU CONDEMN THEM TO LIFELONG MISERY, AND WHO KNOWS FOR CERTAIN WHAT HAPPENS AFTER DEATH?

WHEN WITIZA DIED IN 709, THE CHURCH OPPOSED HIS SON **WOMBA** AND BACKED A MORE OBEDIENT ANTI-SEMITE, LORD **RODERICK.**

RODERICK'S ARMY DEFEATED WOMBA, CREATING KING ROD.

HA!

WOMBA'S FRIENDS LOOKED DESPERATELY FOR **SOMEONE** TO HELP THEM.

AS LUCK WOULD HAVE IT, THE **MUSLIMS** WERE JUST THEN WRAPPING UP THEIR CONQUEST OF **NORTH AFRICA,** ONLY A FEW MILES AWAY.

A FEW GOTHS SLIPPED ACROSS THE STRAITS AND (WITH JEWS AS TRANSLATORS) INVITED THE ARABS TO SPAIN—EVEN ARRANGING THE SHIPS TO FERRY THEM OVER.

WELL? CAN YOU **HELP** US?

AND SO...

WHOTTA A BUNCH OF **IDIOTS...**

159

IN 711, AN ARAB AND BERBER FORCE, LED IN PERSON BY THE GOVERNOR OF MOROCCO, **TARIQ IBN ZIYAD,** CROSSED FROM AFRICA TO SPAIN'S GREAT ROCK THAT NOW BEARS HIS NAME, **GIBRALTAR** (= JEBEL AL TARIQ, ROCK OF TARIQ).

SAY, DO WE HAVE ANY INSURANCE?

AS THEY PILLAGED THE SOUTH, KING ROD SUMMONED TROOPS FROM ALL HIS BARONS.

COME ON!!

YES, KING SCUMBAG!

BUT OF COURSE, MORE THAN A FEW OF THE GOTHS WERE ROD'S ENEMIES.

ARE YOU BEHIND ME, MEN?

SOON AS YOU TURN AROUND!

AT THE ALL-OR-NOTHING BATTLE OF LAGUNAS DE JANDA, HALF THE GOTHS DESERTED THE OTHER HALF... KING ROD VANISHED FOREVER... AND THE **MOORS,** OR MOROCCANS, PREVAILED.

ALL RIGHT! EVERYTHING'S GOING ACCORDING TO PLAN... ISN'T IT?

AH... BUT THEN TARIQ'S MOORS WENT AFTER THE **FRIENDLY** GOTHS TOO! SUDDENLY, NO ONE COULD STOP THE INVADERS. ALL THEY LACKED WAS ENOUGH MEN TO GUARD ALL THEY'D WON.

I SAY!

THE MOORS CALLED FOR SPANISH VOLUNTEERS, AND WHO CAME FORWARD? MILITANT YOUNG **JEWS,** READY TO TRADE IN 125 YEARS OF CATHOLIC PERSECUTION FOR SOMETHING NEW.

WHAT? AFTER ALL WE'VE DONE TO—I MEAN, **FOR** YOU?

TAKE A SWORD, ANY SWORD...

SO THE MOORS ARMED THE JEWS AND LEFT THEM TO POLICE THE CONQUERED TOWNS.

SOME FOLKS HAVE **NO** SENSE OF GRATITUDE...

HOW WOULD THE MOORS REWARD THEIR FRIENDS AND ALLIES? NOT WELL, IT TURNED OUT... JUST AS IN AFRICA (SEE PP. 72-73), THE ARABS TOOK THE BEST LAND AND TREASURE, SLIGHTED THE BERBERS, AND DUMPED THE GOTHS.

HOW COME YOU GET THAT COOL CASTLE, AND I ONLY GET A PEASANT'S HOVEL?

WELL, THERE AREN'T REALLY ENOUGH CASTLES TO GO AROUND, ARE THERE?

THE CONQUERORS BEGAN TO FIGHT AMONG THEMSELVES.

AARGH!

OPEN THE GATE! OPEN THE GATE!

BY THE LATE 720s, THE MOORISH COMMANDERS REACHED A KIND OF AGREEMENT: THEY WOULD SEND ALL THIS PENT-UP RESENTMENT OUT OF THE COUNTRY...

IT IS KIND OF HOW WE GOT TO SPAIN IN THE FIRST PLACE...

AND SO IN 729, A MUSLIM ARMY INVADED FRANCE.

LET'S HOPE THEY HAVE SOME CASTLES OVER THERE...

AFTER TARIQ'S FIRST TRIUMPHS, THE GOVERNOR OF NORTH AFRICA HIMSELF CAME TO SPAIN TO FINISH THE CONQUEST—AND TAKE THE CREDIT! IN FACT, HE HAD TARIQ WHIPPED.

MOAN... WHA'D I DO?

YOU DIDN'T WAIT FOR ME!

THEN (714) THE TWO OF THEM TOOK A HUGE TRAIN OF TREASURE AND GOTHS OFF TO DAMASCUS.

STILL SQUABBLING, THEY SHOWED THE TROVE TO THE AGING CALIPH AL-WALID.

LO, A GEM-ENCRUSTED TABLE, UM, MINUS A LEG!

HERE'S THE LEG! YOU STOLE THAT TABLE FROM ME!

THE NEXT CALIPH CASHIERED THE GOVERNOR, WHO DIED A BEGGAR IN ARABIA. WHAT BECAME OF TARIQ I DON'T KNOW.

I HAD AN UNDERLING ONCE! I'D STILL LIKE TO KILL HIM...

161

MEANWHILE, IN FRANCE, LOTHAR AND PIPPIN HAD BOTH SPAWNED A LONG LINE OF WEAK KINGS WITH STRONG MAJORDOMOS ALL NAMED PIPPIN, EXCEPT FOR AN OCCASIONAL KARL FOR VARIETY'S SAKE.

MAJORDOMO, MAY I PEE NOW?

O.K., I'LL LIFT YOUR LEG.

WHEN THE MUSLIMS ARRIVED, THE MAJORDOMO KARL "THE HAMMER"—CHARLES MARTEL IN BAD LATIN—LED OUT THE FRANKS.

THEY STOPPED THE MOORS AT THE BATTLE OF TOURS IN 732—THE MUSLIMS' FARTHEST ADVANCE INTO WESTERN EUROPE.

TOURS

SPAIN

ALL FRANCE CHEERED THE NAMES OF CHARLES AND PIPPIN...

PIP PIP HURRAY

THE BATTERED MUSLIMS STAGGERED BACK TO SPAIN, WHERE THEY FOUND THE SAME SORRY STATE THEY HAD LEFT BEHIND.

THEN CAME **750,** THE REVOLTS IN THE EAST, THE UMAYYAD COLLAPSE, THE ABBASID DYNASTY, BAGHDAD...

AND, YOU MAY RECALL, A LONE UMAYYAD PRINCE WHO SWAM THE EUPHRATES RIVER WHILE HIS BROTHER WAS MURDERED ON THE SHORE.

MAN, AM I GLAD MY FAMILY BUILT SWIMMING POOLS...

THIS 19-YEAR-OLD, **ABDAR RAHMAN,** SPENT FIVE YEARS IN HIDING, INCHING WESTWARD WITH A FEW TRUSTED SERVANTS.

HE REACHED MOROCCO... SENT WORD TO HIS KINFOLK IN SPAIN... AND SOON HE HAD AN INVITATION TO COME AND TAKE CHARGE OF THE MESS OVER THERE.

TAKE IT SON! TAKE IT!

IN 756, HE ARRIVED... THE LEADERS—MOSTLY—PLEDGED ALLEGIANCE... AND AFTER QUICKLY DISPOSING OF A FEW NAYSAYERS, ABDAR RAHMAN BECAME EMIR (COMMANDER, GOVERNOR) OF ALL SPAIN.

STILL ALIVE! CAN YOU BELIEVE IT?

SO ABU SUFYAN'S FAMILY, THE UMAYYADS, SURVIVED, AFTER ALL... AND (ONCE THEY DEVISED A FAIR TAX SYSTEM!), THEY MADE SPAIN A RICH AND HAPPY COUNTRY FULL OF POETRY, ART, AND RELIGIOUS TOLERATION...

I JUST CAN'T GET USED TO IT!

NEITHER CAN I!

DOWN WITH PICTURES!

ISLAM'S SUDDEN SUCCESS—FROM ZERO TO HUGE IN 70 YEARS—SHOOK THE CHRISTIAN WORLD. HOW COULD ONE FAITH REPLACE ANOTHER SO FAST?

CHRISTIANS SEARCHED THEIR SOULS, WONDERING IF THEIR RELIGION HAD **GONE OFF** SOMEHOW. IN THE BIBLE, SINNERS ARE PUNISHED... MAYBE **THEY** WERE SINNERS... BUT WHAT, EXACTLY, WAS THEIR **SIN?**

HMM... NOTHING WRONG WITH MY SOUL... MIND IF I SEARCH YOURS?

TO SOME PEOPLE, THE ANSWER WAS OBVIOUS.

JUST LOOK AROUND!

CHRISTIANS, THEY SAID, **WORSHIPPED IDOLS.** PRAYING TO STATUES OF SAINTS, MAKING OFFERINGS TO PAINTINGS—HOW DID THIS DIFFER FROM SACRIFICING TO BAAL?

UM... LESS BLOOD?

MUSLIMS, ON THE OTHER HAND, STRICTLY OBEYED THE SECOND COMMANDMENT AGAINST MAKING "GRAVEN IMAGES." THEY DREW LEAVES, STEMS, AND GEOMETRY, BUT NO PEOPLE! WAS NOT THEIR FAITH MORE **PURE?**

SO BASICALLY YOU'RE SAYING THEY'RE SUCCESSFUL BECAUSE THEY HAVE BETTER **ART?**

IN 711, THE SAME YEAR SPAIN WAS INVADED, A NEW EMPEROR TOOK THE BYZANTINE THRONE. **LEO "THE ISAURIAN"** HAD LIVED AT THE EASTERN EDGE OF THE EMPIRE... SPOKE ARABIC... AND SYMPATHIZED WITH THE MUSLIM POINT OF VIEW.

IT'S ALL OUR FAULT!

A FEW YEARS LATER IN DAMASCUS, THE CALIPH **YAZID** ORDERED THE DESTRUCTION OF EVERY CHRISTIAN IMAGE IN THE MUSLIM WORLD—EVERY PAINTING, MOSAIC, AND STATUE OF JESUS, MARY, AND THE SAINTS.

THEY CAN STILL BE CHRISTIANS WITHOUT THEM, RIGHT?

AS THE WRECKAGE BEGAN, PEOPLE LOOKED TO THE CHRISTIAN EMPEROR FOR HELP—A **PROTEST** AT LEAST!

LEEEEO!

LEO'S REACTION SURPRISED THEM ALL!

GOOD IDEA!

HE VOWED TO DO THE **SAME THING** IN HIS OWN EMPIRE! HE SENT A WRECKING CREW UP TO A HUGE IMAGE OF JESUS ABOVE THE DOOR OF ONE OF CONSTANTINOPLE'S BIGGEST CHURCHES. THEY CHIPPED IT OFF AND SENT IT HURTLING TO EARTH.

CLAST!

AFTERWARD, A CROWD OF WOMEN BEAT THE CREW'S FOREMAN TO DEATH.

!

BUT LEO PRESSED ON... AND SO BEGAN FIFTY YEARS OF IMAGE-SMASHING, OR **ICONOCLASM**, AS THE GREEKS WOULD SAY. THE ICON POLICE INVADED CHURCHES ACROSS THE EMPIRE, ROOTING OUT IMAGES!

THERE WAS A LOT OF **GOLD** AND **SILVER** ON THOSE IMAGES, PURELY BY COINCIDENCE, NO DOUBT! THE EMPEROR TOOK IT ALL.

ANOTHER ARAB ADVANTAGE: THEY DON'T WASTE A LOT OF **PRECIOUS METAL** ON THEIR MOSQUES!

SO WHEN THE ARABS AGAIN ATTACKED CONSTANTINOPLE IN 744, THE IMPERIAL ARMY COULD AFFORD MEN AND EQUIPMENT ENOUGH TO THRASH THEM SO BADLY THEY NEVER CAME BACK!

ICONOCLASM WORKS!

SHALL WE CELEBRATE BY PARADING SOME ICONS AROUND THE WALLS?

YOU MOCK YOUR EMPEROR?

AFTER LEO'S DEATH, HIS SON, EMPEROR CONSTANTINE V "COPRONYMUS" SMASHED ICONS AS AVIDLY AS HIS DAD!

THIS IS **SO** MUCH BETTER!

IN ENGLISH, "COPRONYMUS" MEANS "POOP-NAME." SUPPOSED-LY, THE NICKNAME CAME FROM AN "ACCIDENT" THE INFANT PRINCE HAD AT HIS BAPTISM.

BY A STRANGE COINCIDENCE, LATER IN LIFE, HIS FAVORITE PRIEST, THE ICONOCLAST PATRIARCH ANASTA-SIUS, DIED OF **CONSTIPATION**.

WHOA!

IT IS ENTIRELY POSSIBLE THAT BOTH THESE STORIES WERE INVENTED BY PEOPLE OPPOSED TO ICONOCLASM.

AND DON'T FORGET GEORGE STINKY-FINGERS!

ALEXIUS CACA-CAP!

DIOGENES PEEPEE PANTS!

PLENTY OF PEOPLE LOVED ICONS AND HATED ICONO-CLASTS... AND THESE PEOPLE HAD A FRIEND AT COURT IN POOP-NAME'S DAUGHTER-IN-LAW **IRENE.** WHEN THE THRONE CAME VACANT, HER SON BECAME EMPEROR, BUT SINCE HE WAS A SMALL BOY, IRENE REALLY RULED.

TIME TO CUT THE CRAP.

BUT **MOM!**

IN 786, SHE CALLED AN ALL-EMPIRE CHURCH COUNCIL AND PACKED IT WITH **ICONO-DULES** (THE OPPOSITE OF THE OTHER THING). AFTER A VERY INTERESTING DISCUS-SION (TO A CARTOONIST), THEY VOTED ICONS BACK IN!

"THE MORE CONTINUOUSLY THESE (JESUS, MARY, AND THE SAINTS) ARE SEEN BY MEANS OF **PICTORIAL REPRESENTATIONS,** THE MORE BEHOLDERS ARE LED TO **REMEMBER** AND **LOVE** THE ORIGINALS..."

YOU GET THAT, COMICS FANS? IMAGES CAN PACK AN EMOTIONAL **WALLOP!**

GOT THAT RIGHT!

IRENE'S FAITH WAS STRONG... SO WHEN HER SON THE BOY EMPEROR CAME OF AGE AND ANNOUNCED HIS SUPPORT OF ICONOCLASM, SHE HAD HIS EYES PUT OUT.

HE **SAID** HE DIDN'T WANT TO SEE ICONS...

BUT NEVER MIND! THE WESTERN CHURCH CHEERED HER ON! **ROME** HAD ALWAYS LIKED IMAGES, AND NOW THE POPE HAD HOPES OF AN **EAST-WEST MERGER.**

WRITE A LETTER, YOUR MAJESTY!

I CAN'T WRITE...

IN 801, IRENE RECEIVED A PRO-POSAL OF MARRIAGE FROM A **FRANKISH** KING—AND WEIRD-LY, HE CALLED HIMSELF THE "**ROMAN EMPEROR.**"

BUT— THAT'S **ME!**

WHAT WAS THIS ALL ABOUT?

THE GREAT

WHEN WE LAST VISITED THE FRANKS, A FEW PAGES AND 70 YEARS AGO, MAJORDOMOS CALLED KARL AND PIPPIN WERE PULLING THE STRINGS OF THEIR KINGS, AND KARL THE HAMMER HAD JUST BEATEN THE MOORS.

NOW—AROUND 750—KARL'S SON **PIPPIN "THE SHORT"** DECIDED TO CUT THE STRINGS, DUMP THE KING, AND TAKE THE THRONE FOR HIMSELF.

HOW DID YOU DUMP A KING IN THOSE DAYS—DUMP HIM WELL, SO HE STAYED DUMPED?

A KING NEEDS **LEGITIMACY!**

YOU NEEDED LEGITIMACY.

YES.

MEANING: PEOPLE HAD TO THINK YOU WERE DOING THE **RIGHT THING**... SOMETHING LIKE GETTING MARRIED BEFORE HAVING SEX... ALTHOUGH MAYBE NOT IN THIS CASE...

GET SERIOUS! THIS IS FRANCE...

IN SHORT, YOU NEEDED THE POPE'S BLESSING.

OTHERWISE, THE PREACHERS WILL BE ALL OVER ME EVERY SUNDAY...

SO PIPPIN SENT PEOPLE TO APPEAL TO THE POPE!

PLEASE, PAPA! PLEASE, PAPA! PAPA, PAPA, **PLEASE!**

THE POPE'S REPLY: IF PIPPIN COULD SAVE HIM FROM THE **LONGBEARDS**, THEN PIPPIN WOULD HAVE HIS BLESSING.

GHASP! N-N-NOT THE **L-L-LONG-B-B-BEARDS!**

WHO ARE THE LONG-BEARDS?

THE LONG-BEARDS, OR **LOMBARDS,** ANOTHER GERMAN TRIBE, HAD INVADED ITALY AND MENACED THE POPE.

PIPPIN, A MILITARY MAN LIKE HIS FATHER, MOUNTED HIS HORSE AND MARCHED A FRANKISH ARMY TO ITALY.

HIS LONG **BREADS** MET THE LONG **BEARDS** AND SMASHED THEM—BLESSING GIVEN!

GOOD JOB, MY SON!

IN 751, PIPPIN WENT HOME, ASSEMBLED THE FRANKS, ASKED THEIR SUPPORT, AND SHOWED THEM THE POPE'S LETTER—INSTANT LEGITIMACY!

THE POPE SAYS... SAYS... UM... CAN ANY OF YOU READ?

NO!

GOOD, IT'S UNANIMOUS! I'M KING!

PIPPIN PACKED OFF THE LAST OF CLOVIS'S LINE TO BECOME A MONK—WITH HIS EYES INTACT, BY THE WAY.

WE ARE GETTING MORE CIVILIZED, AREN'T WE?

JUST MIND THE RAZOR!

TO THANK THE POPE, PIPPIN IN 756 GAVE HIM A HUGE PRESENT: A STRIP OF LAND STRETCHING RIGHT ACROSS ITALY. THIS **PAPAL STATE,** OR **DONATION OF PIPPIN,** BLOCKED ITALY'S UNIFICATION UNTIL THE LATE **19TH CENTURY!**

THERE ARE **TWO KINDS** OF KINGS, VARLET! ONE KIND, LIKE THE ICONOCLASTS, TAKES FROM THE CHURCH... THE OTHER, LIKE PIPPIN, GIVES US PRESENTS! WHAT USE DO I HAVE FOR THE FIRST KIND OF KING?

I DON'T KNOW! WHAT?

AHEM... VARLET, HAVE YOU EVER HEARD OF A **RHETORICAL QUESTION?**

I DON'T THINK SO... GIVE ME AN EXAMPLE!

ARE YOU AN IDIOT?

THANK YOU, SIRE!

WHY ALL THOSE PAGES ON PIPPIN? WHAT MAKES HIM DESERVE OUR ATTENTION? TWO THINGS: HIS GIFT TO THE POPE WITH ITS LASTING EFFECT, AND HIS SON **KARL** (OF COURSE!), WHO BECAME THE GREATEST KING OF THE DARK AGES: CHARLES THE GREAT, KARL DER GROSSE, OR **CHARLEMAGNE.** WHAT MADE HIM SO GREAT? GREAT BLOODSHED, TO BEGIN WITH. SOON AFTER TAKING THE THRONE IN 768, KARL LAUNCHED HIS FIRST INVASION... AND FOR THE NEXT **FOUR DECADES** HE WENT TO WAR ALMOST EVERY YEAR.

HE FIRST ATTACKED HIS EASTERN NEIGHBORS THE **SAXONS**, WHO STILL WORSHIPPED THE OLD GODS. CHARLEMAGNE OFFERED THEM A CHOICE: SUBMIT AND BE CHRISTIAN, OR DIE.

THEY RESISTED... HE BEAT THEM... EXECUTED 4,500 PRISONERS AND DROVE 10,000 WOMEN AND CHILDREN OFF THEIR LAND... STILL THEY REBELLED... AGAIN AND AGAIN HE HAMMERED THEM UNTIL ALL RESISTANCE ENDED.

THEN THE **AVARS**, INDEPENDENT NOMADS IN CENTRAL EUROPE. WE KNOW LITTLE ABOUT THE AVARS, BECAUSE BY THE TIME CHARLEMAGNE FINISHED WITH THEM, THERE WERE NO MORE AVARS.

CHARLEMAGNE ALSO CROSSED THE PYRENEES INTO SPAIN, BUT THE MOORS PUSHED HIM BACK.

EVEN A SUPERPOWER HAS LIMITS, I GUESS...

ON THE WAY HOME, THE FRANKISH REAR GUARD FELL INTO AN AMBUSH SET BY A MOUNTAIN PEOPLE, THE **BASQUES**, WHO KILLED ONE OF CHARLEMAGNE'S FRIENDS, COUNT **ROLAND.**

(FOUR CENTURIES LATER, A POET SANG OF THE MASSACRE IN THE **SONG OF ROLAND**— BUT CHANGED THE BASQUES TO **MOORS** FOR DRAMATIC EFFECT!)

DETAILS AREN'T FOR POETS!

THOUGH HARSH IN WAR, CHARLEMAGNE WAS A LOVING, MAYBE **TOO** LOVING, PARENT. HE CARED ABOUT HIS CHILDREN **SO MUCH** THAT HE NEVER DINED WITHOUT THEM.

IS IT LOVE OR CONTROL MANIA?

BLAH BLAH BLAH BLAH BLAH

EXCEPT FOR ONE, HE NEVER LET ANY OF HIS DAUGHTERS MARRY. NO ONE WAS GOOD ENOUGH TO BE HIS SON-IN-LAW, APPARENTLY.

IF YOU MARRY, HOW WILL I EAT?

BUT HE ALSO LOVED THEM WELL ENOUGH TO **LOOK THE OTHER WAY** WHILE HIS DAUGHTERS HAD **BABIES** BY VARIOUS PALACE "FRIENDS"!

CUTE LI'L BASTARD! PASS THE ROAST!

WHILE NOT FIGHTING OR PREPARING TO FIGHT, CHARLEMAGNE RAN EVERY ASPECT OF THE EMPIRE: TAXES, LAWS, MINES, PORTS, AND SCHOOLS—**FREE SCHOOLS** OPEN TO ALL, RUN BY THE WEST'S BEST SCHOLARS (MEDIOCRE, BUT THE BEST!)...

HE ALSO ORDERED **FORTS** AND **CASTLES** DEMOLISHED TO KEEP HIS NOBLES FROM HIDING BEHIND THEM.

THERE'S SO MUCH TO BE DONE!

AACHEN

PARIS

TOLEDO

BARCELONA

CORDOBA

ROME

THIS IS GOING TO BACKFIRE, I WARN YOU!

TO PROMOTE COMMERCE, HE INVITED JEWS INTO HIS EMPIRE, SINCE THEY COULD TRADE WITH THE MUSLIM WORLD.

I WANT GEMS! PEARLS! METALWORK, SILKS, THE ACCOUNTING SYSTEMS OF THE MYSTIC EAST!

WHAT CAN YOU OFFER IN EXCHANGE?

PRISONERS OF WAR! LOADS OF 'EM! DOESN'T ANYBODY HERE SELL **SLAVES??**

WELL, WE **WERE** THINKING MORE ALONG THE LINES OF **USED CLOTHES**...

FRANK-LAND'S JEWS DID MORE THAN TRADE; THEY ALSO DISCUSSED RELIGION. A PROMINENT GERMAN PRIEST NAMED **BODO** LIKED WHAT THEY SAID... IN 837, HE WENT TO SPAIN, CONVERTED TO JUDAISM, AND BEGAN WRITING LETTERS BLASTING CHRISTIANITY.

CENSORED
CENSORED
CENSORED
CENSORED
(SEE LAST PANEL)

PABLO ALVARO, A SPANISH CHRISTIAN OF JEWISH DESCENT (!), WROTE A BUNCH OF REBUTTALS, AND FOR OVER A DECADE, EUROPE RANG WITH THIS LETTER-WAR BETWEEN THE JEWISH CHRISTIAN AND THE CHRISTIAN JEW!

"THERE YOU SIT, BEARDED AND MARRIED..."

UNFORTUNATELY, ONLY ALVARO'S SIDE OF THE ARGUMENT HAS SURVIVED, SINCE ZEALOUS CHRISTIANS DESTROYED BODO'S LETTERS.

THIS IS THE ONLY HEAT THESE PAPERS SHOULD GENERATE!

EXCEPT FOR THE BUSINESS WITH THE JEWS, THE POPE LOVED EVERYTHING ABOUT CHARLEMAGNE! ON CHRISTMAS DAY, 800, POPE LEO III PUT A CROWN ON KARL'S HEAD AND CALLED HIM **EMPEROR** OF **ROME.**

NOTE THE SYMBOLISM HERE: I AM CROWNING *YOU.*

BUT YOU SNUCK UP BEHIND ME!

AT THE TIME, NO OTHER "ROMAN" EMPEROR EXISTED— CONSTANTINOPLE HAD AN EMPRESS, IRENE, AND CHARLEMAGNE PROPOSED TO **MARRY** HER!

THE BYZANTINE COURT GASPED IN HORROR... WHISKED IRENE OFF TO A NUNNERY... AND INSTALLED A PROPER "ROMAN" EMPEROR IN HER PLACE.

AND SO IT SEEMED THERE MUST BE TWO "ROMAN" EMPERORS, ONE GERMAN AND ONE GREEK.

DUMBEST THING I EVER HEARD.

IRKED BY REJECTION, CHARLEMAGNE TRIED TO MAKE A PACT WITH **BAGHDAD** AGAINST BYZANTIUM... THE CALIPH SENT BACK AN ELEPHANT, BUT NO GUAR-ANTEES. (CONSTANTINOPLE, MEANWHILE, TRIED TO ALLY WITH SPAIN AGAINST THE FRANKS.)

CHARLEMAGNE DIED, AGE 72, IN 814. HIS SON, A KINDLY SORT, LET THE SQUABBLING GRANDSONS GRAB AS MUCH AS THEY COULD, UNTIL IN 843 THEY AGREED TO SPLIT THE REALM THREE WAYS.

GERMANY (MORE OR LESS)

FRANCE (MORE OR LESS)

LORRAINE (AND THEN SOME)

THESE KINGDOMS MIGHT WELL HAVE DEVELOPED VERY NICELY, WERE IT NOT FOR A FEW LITTLE THINGS...

THINGS?

THINGS LIKE THE **VIKING RAIDS** ON FRANCE...

HUNDREDS OF SHIPS AT A TIME, THE VIKINGS ROWED UP FRANCE'S RIVERS BENT ON PILLAGE, MURDER, AND ENSLAVEMENT. THEY CAME IN 840, 842, 843, 845, 846, 853, 862, 872...

THE WORST PART WAS THAT THE FRENCH HAD NO PLACE TO HIDE, BECAUSE CHARLEMAGNE HAD BANNED FORTS!

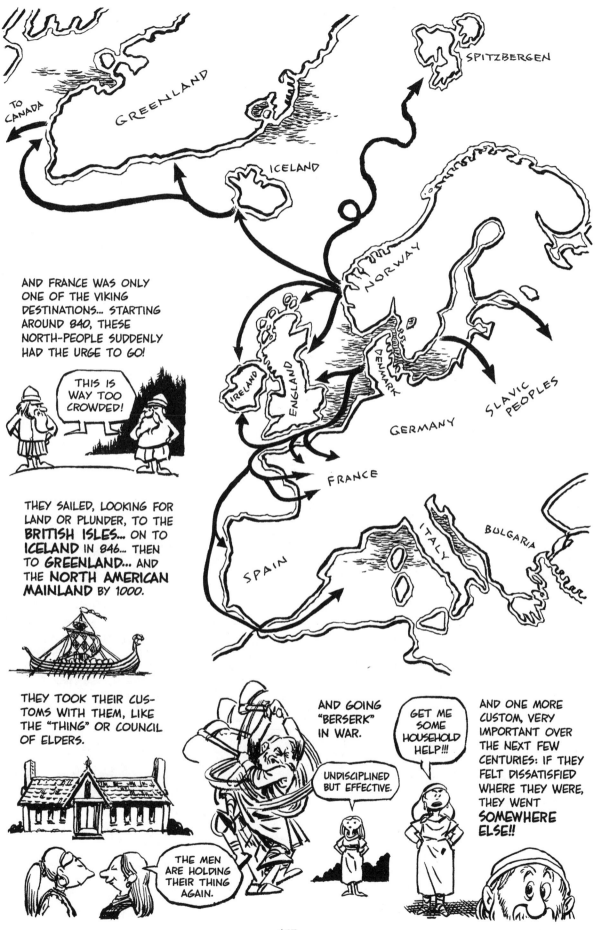

AND FRANCE WAS ONLY ONE OF THE VIKING DESTINATIONS... STARTING AROUND 840, THESE NORTH-PEOPLE SUDDENLY HAD THE URGE TO GO!

THIS IS WAY TOO CROWDED!

THEY SAILED, LOOKING FOR LAND OR PLUNDER, TO THE **BRITISH ISLES**... ON TO **ICELAND** IN 846... THEN TO **GREENLAND**... AND THE **NORTH AMERICAN MAINLAND** BY 1000.

THEY TOOK THEIR CUSTOMS WITH THEM, LIKE THE "THING" OR COUNCIL OF ELDERS.

THE MEN ARE HOLDING THEIR THING AGAIN.

AND GOING "BERSERK" IN WAR.

UNDISCIPLINED BUT EFFECTIVE.

GET ME SOME HOUSEHOLD HELP!!!

AND ONE MORE CUSTOM, VERY IMPORTANT OVER THE NEXT FEW CENTURIES: IF THEY FELT DISSATISFIED WHERE THEY WERE, THEY WENT **SOMEWHERE ELSE!!**

SPITZBERGEN

TO CANADA

GREENLAND

ICELAND

NORWAY

IRELAND

ENGLAND

DENMARK

SLAVIC PEOPLES

GERMANY

FRANCE

SPAIN

ITALY

BULGARIA

IN FRANCE, THE COUNTS* WROTE THE KING, BEGGING PERMISSION TO BUILD DEFENSES AGAINST THE NORSE. RELUCTANTLY, THE KING SAID YES.

BUILD FIRST! ASK LATER!

SIGH... BEHIND WALLS, COUNTS STOP BEING ACCOUNTABLE... AND IF I CAN'T COUNT ON MY COUNTS, WHAT AM I? A NO-ACCOUNT... OH, WELL... IT WAS NICE OF THEM TO ASK...

*A COUNT, FRENCH COMTE, FROM LATIN COMES = FRIEND (OF THE KING), WAS THE ADMINISTRATOR OF A COUNTY.

UP WENT THE WALLS... FIRST EARTHWORKS WITH WOODEN PALISADES...

?

THEN STONE ENCLOSURES...

HEY! THIS IS STARTING TO FEEL LIKE WORK!

AND FINALLY...

I'M GOING HOME...

THESE FRENCH ARE CRAZY!

SOME DAYS, BERSERK IS NOT ENOUGH...

A PROPER CASTLE MADE A COUNT FEEL SO MUCH MORE SECURE, POWERFUL, AND INDEPENDENT! NOW HE COULD COMMAND THE PEOPLE TO SWEAR FEALTY TO HIM, NOT THE KING... AFTER ALL, HE, NOT THE KING, WAS PROTECTING THEM.

OH, AND PROMISE ME 3 DAYS' LABOR A WEEK AND HALF YOUR CROPS WHILE YOU'RE AT IT...

AS EXPECTED, THE KING LOST POWER... LOCAL LORDS GAINED IT... THE PEASANTS LOOKED NO FARTHER THAN THE NEAREST CASTLE... AND FEUDALISM WAS BORN IN FRANCE.

AT LEAST THE VIKINGS HAVE BACKED OFF...

YES... NOW WHO PROTECTS US FROM THE COUNT?

THOUGH MOST VIKINGS CAME TO PILLAGE AND GO, THERE WAS ONE ESPECIALLY TOUGH BUNCH WHO **STAYED**... IN NORTHWEST FRANCE THEY MARRIED THE LOCALS, LEARNED FRENCH, AND CAME TO BE KNOWN AS THE **NORMANS**.

SAY "FROMAGE," MON CHER!

IN 911, THEIR LEADER, DUKE **ROLLO**, CAME TO TERMS WITH THE FRENCH KING, CHARLES "THE SIMPLE." CHARLES "GAVE" THE NORMANS THEIR LAND... WHILE ROLLO AGREED TO PROTECT PARIS FROM THE OTHER VIKINGS—AND ALSO TO BECOME A CATHOLIC.

O.K.! NOW WHAT?

UM... NOW YOU **KNEEL**... THAT IS, IF YOU DON'T MIND...

IN A GRAND CEREMONY DURING WHICH THE NORMANS LAUGHED IN THE KING'S FACE, ROLLO SWORE TO BE CHARLES'S VASSAL.

CHUCK, YOU'VE GOT HANDS AS SOFT AS **PICKLED HERRING!**

HEH HEH...

WHEN ROLLO DIED, THEY SACRIFICED **100 VIRGINS** AND SENT THEM OFF WITH HIS BODY IN A BURNING SHIP, VIKING-STYLE.

THESE NORMANS WILL PLAY A BIG ROLE AS OUR STORY UNFOLDS...

ONCE IN THEIR CASTLES, THE FRENCH COUNTS AND DUKES AND ALL BEGAN TO FIGHT AMONGST THEMSELVES. ONCE AGAIN, FARMERS COULD EXPECT ARMED MEN TO TRAMPLE THEIR CROPS AT ANY TIME.

OH, FOR—

IN THE EARLY 1000s, THE CHURCH MERCIFULLY STEPPED IN AND CALLED ON THE NOBLES TO OBSERVE A **"TRUCE OF GOD."** NO MORE FIGHTING!

NO FIGHTING ON **FRIDAY** THROUGH **MONDAY**, THAT IS... TUESDAY, WEDNESDAY, AND THURSDAY WERE O.K.!

AHEM! SOMETIMES EVEN **RELIGION** IS THE ART OF THE POSSIBLE!

VOLGA BOATMEN

ANOTHER VIKING EXPLOIT TOOK PLACE IN THE EAST. FROM THE INLAND WATERS OF THE BALTIC SEA, NORSE SHIPS PLIED SOUTHWARD, UPRIVER INTO THE CONTINENT'S HEART, HOME OF THE **SLAVS.**

NORWAY

GOTLAND

DENMARK

SLAVIC PEOPLES

THIS HISTORY IS AS OBSCURE AS THE NORTHERN WOODS. IT PROBABLY RESEMBLED THE HINDU COLONIZATION OF SOUTHEAST ASIA THAT WE SAW LAST VOLUME: FIRST, A WANDERING PRINCE AND HIS RETINUE FIND A LIKELY PLACE...

THEY BEFRIEND SOME LOCALS... TERRORIZE OTHERS... MARRY THEIR FRIENDS' DAUGHTERS AND KIDNAP THEIR ENEMIES'... AND SOON THERE'S A **NEW BOSS** IN THE NEIGHBORHOOD.

HOW "LIKELY" WAS THIS PLACE? A NORTHERN TRAVELER COULD FOLLOW THESE RIVERS DOWN TO THE BLACK SEA... CARRY AMBER, FUR, AND SLAVES TO BYZANTINES, KHAZARS, AND ARABS...

PLUS, THERE ARE ALWAYS PEASANTS TO TAX!

BY 850, A NEW NATION HAD SUDDENLY EMERGED: **RUSSIA.**

THIS NEW RUSSIA POSED A **CHALLENGE** TO CONSTANTINOPLE. THE BYZANTINES REFUSED TO SHARE THE BLACK SEA WITH **ANYONE!**

EXCUSE ME!

THE GREEK NAVY MUST HAVE ANNOYED THE RUSSIAN TRADERS SOMEHOW, SUNK THEIR SHIPS, OR TAXED THEIR CARGO, OR SQUIRTED THEM WITH FIRE.

AS EARLY AS 866, THE RUSSIANS LAUNCHED A **NAVAL ASSAULT** ON CONSTANTINOPLE—AT A TIME, CONVENIENTLY, WHEN THE EMPEROR AND HIS ARMY WERE AWAY IN THE EAST.

THE GREEKS, SHORT OF MEN, COULD DO NO MORE THAN LIGHT INCENSE, CHANT, AND PARADE AN ICON OF THE VIRGIN MARY AROUND THE WALLS. (ICONS WERE BACK!)

THE RUSSIANS TURNED AROUND AND WENT HOME WITHOUT A FIGHT, AND THE BYZANTINES CALLED IT A MIRACLE!

MAN, WOULD YOU LOOK AT THOSE WALLS??!!

YES... BY THE WAY, COULD YOU MAKE OUT SOMETHING TINY MOVING ALONG THE PARAPET?

THE CITY WAS SAVED AGAIN... AND THE RUSSIANS COVET ISTANBUL TO THIS DAY!

YET CONSTANTINOPLE ALSO VIEWED RUSSIA AS A POTENTIAL ALLY IN THE STRUGGLE AGAINST THE **BULGARS.**

RUSSIA

BULGARS

BYZANTIUM

BYZANTINES HAD BATTLED BULGARS FOR CENTURIES, BUT LATELY THINGS HAD TURNED ESPECIALLY NASTY.

SMALL-MINDED BASTARD!

HAHAHA

AFTER ONE ESPECIALLY TOTAL BULGAR VICTORY, IN 811, THE KHAN **KRUM** MADE A WINE CUP FROM THE BYZANTINE EMPEROR'S SKULL.

THEY'RE UNCIVILIZED, I TELL YOU!

EXCUSE ME? MY ATTENTION WANDERED WHILE I WAS PUTTING OUT THIS PRINCE'S EYES...

BYZANTIUM'S STRATEGY TOWARD THE BULGARS: FIRST CONVERT THEM TO CHRISTIANITY, THEN HOPE THEY GROW SUBMISSIVE AND FRIENDLY.

THEN GET 'EM!

BUT AS CHRISTIANS, THE BULGARS ACTED JUST AS ORNERY AS BEFORE, SO SOMETHING ELSE WOULD HAVE TO BE DONE.

CONVERT THE RUSSIANS!

YES, CONVERT THE RUSSIANS, AND THEN URGE THEM TO ATTACK THE BULGARS FROM THE REAR!

AGREED! JUST AS SOON AS WE FINISH ONE MORE FUTILE ATTACK ON CONSTANTINOPLE...

TAKE YOUR TIME.

(IN 941.)

THE RUSSIANS SUCCEEDED **TOO WELL**... IN 970, CZAR SVIATA-SLAV INVADED BULGARIA AND NOW MENACED CONSTANTI-NOPLE ITSELF.

ARGH!

☆@✱

DON'T WORRY... THIS GUY IS NO MATCH FOR US... JUST WATCH...

THE GREEKS PULLED A RUSE: THEY OFFERED TO **BUY OFF** THE CZAR AND HIS ARMY. HOW MUCH MONEY DID HE NEED? I HAVE **20,000** SOLDIERS, HE REPLIED... HEARING WHICH, THE GREEKS SENT **100,000** TROOPS AND CRUSHED THE RUSSIANS.

HOW BYZANTINE!

SVIATASLAV ESCAPED BUT FELL INTO A PECHENEG AMBUSH, AND SOON HIS SKULL WAS A WINE CUP TOO!

HOW'S HE TASTE?

JUST LIKE CAVIAR!

(THE PECHENEGS WERE ANOTHER TURKISH-DESCENDED PEOPLE.)

THE BULGARS REVIVED... ATTACKED BYZANTIUM AGAIN... THE WAR DRAGGED ON... UNTIL AT LAST, IN 1014, THE BYZANTINE EMPEROR **BASIL "BULGAR-SLAYER"** COMMITTED HISTORY'S ULTIMATE EYEBALL ATROCITY: HE DIVIDED 15,000 BULGAR PRISONERS INTO GROUPS OF 100... IN EACH HUNDRED, 99 WERE BLINDED, AND ONE WAS LEFT WITH A **SINGLE EYE** TO GUIDE THE OTHERS HOME. WHEN THE BULGAR CZAR SAMUEL SAW THIS PARADE, HE FELL INTO A COMA AND DIED.

THE BULGAR EMPIRE WAS FINISHED, AND "ROME" RULED.

DO YOU **LIKE** BEING REMEMBERED AS "BULGAR-SLAYER"?

THE FUNNY THING IS, IT WAS MEANT AS A COMPLIMENT!

SLAV TRAD

THESE BALKAN WARS AND OTHERS HARVESTED A GREAT CROP OF **CAPTIVES** IN THE 800s AND 900s, MAINLY FROM AMONG THE **SLAVIC** PEOPLES.

THE GERMANS ATTACKED THE SLAVS... SO DID THE BYZANTINES... THE KHAZARS MAY HAVE TOO... EVEN A LITTLE ITALIAN CITY DID IT!

IT MAY NOT BE FAIR TO INTRODUCE A PLACE AS PRETTY AS **VENICE** IN A SECTION ON THE SLAVE TRADE... BUT THERE IT IS... A SWAMPY ITALIAN PORT, SURROUNDED BY WATER, PROTECTED BY SANDBARS AS EFFECTIVELY AS CONSTANTINOPLE WAS BY ITS WALLS: NO ENEMY TOUCHED VENICE FOR A THOUSAND YEARS!

BONK BONK BONK

THE VENETIANS BASED THEIR WEALTH ON "RESOURCES" TAKEN FROM THE DALMATIAN COAST OPPOSITE— THE CHIEF RESOURCES BEING TIMBER AND HUMANS.

VENICE

DALMATIA

ROME

SOME OF VENICE'S PRISONERS MUST HAVE WORKED AS **PILE DRIVERS**, SINKING TIMBERS INTO THE SWAMP TO SUPPORT THEIR MASTERS' CITY. TODAY VENICE SITS ON MORE THAN A MILLION ANCIENT PILINGS SET VERY CLOSE TOGETHER.

PULL!

BONK

PULL!

SLAVS

VENICE

CONSTANTINOPLE

BARI

TO SPAIN

TO EGYPT

BUT VENICE, LIKE OTHERS, ALSO ENRICHED ITSELF BY **SELLING** PEOPLE, MOSTLY AT THE GREAT CLEARINGHOUSE AT **BARI**, CONSTANTINOPLE'S LAST TOEHOLD ON THE ITALIAN BOOT.

AT BARI, JEWS DOMINATED THE BUSINESS, FOR A FAMILIAR REASON: THEY COULD SELL TO THE MUSLIM WORLD.

EXCUSE ME... DO YOU ALSO, UM... "DO" EUNUCHS?

SURE! IT'S JUST LIKE A **BRIS**, ONLY MORE SO!

AND THE MUSLIM WORLD BOUGHT IN VOLUME... THE "SAKALABA" CAPTIVES WENT TO SPAIN, MOROCCO, AND FATIMID EGYPT WITH ITS EUROPEAN LEGION.

SO WIDESPREAD WAS THIS TRADE, AND SO HEAVILY SLAVIC, THAT MANY EUROPEAN LANGUAGES—AND ARABIC—HAVE A WORD FOR **SLAVE** THAT COMES FROM **SLAV.**

PEOPLE WERE SO **INSENSITIVE** BACK THEN!

YES, COULDN'T THEY HAVE CALLED THEM "UNFREE PERSONS OF SLAVIC DESCENT"?

FOURTEEN DAYS

THOUGH MOSTLY SPARED BY THE VIKINGS, MUSLIM SPAIN IN THE 800s SUFFERED FROM REBELLIOUS GOVERNORS, DISGRUNTLED BERBERS, AND ORDINARY BANDITS.* BY 900, THE CHRISTIAN KINGDOMS OF THE NORTH HAD EXPANDED AT THE MUSLIMS' EXPENSE.

○ LEON

○ TOLEDO   ○ VALENCIA

SEVILLE ○ ○ CORDOBA

○ GRANADA

CADIZ ○

GIBRALTAR

THEN, IN 912, A YOUNG WORKAHOLIC INHERITED THE EMIRATE OF CORDOBA: **ABDAR RAHMAN III.**

WORRY WORRY WORRY

ABDAR RAHMAN III PLAYED POLITICS BY WEIGHING ALL OPTIONS, USING TALENTED PEOPLE (NOT JUST HIS RELATIVES), AND INVENTING CREATIVE SOLUTIONS. TAKE THE CASE OF **SANCHO THE FAT.**

YES, TAKE IT, PLEASE!

SANCHO, A CHRISTIAN PRINCE, WAS THE WOULD-BE KING OF LEON—WOULD BE, THAT IS, IF HE **WEIGHED** ANY LESS. AS IT WAS, LEON WOULDN'T HAVE HIM.

HE BREAKS HORSES IN HALF!

SANCHO'S GRANDMOTHER WROTE TO THE MUSLIM EMIR, ASKING IF HE COULD HELP OUT HER GRANDSON.

DEAR EMIR...

AFTER THE **BODO-ALVARO** LETTERS (SEE NOTE, P. 172), THE GOVERNMENT **CRACKED DOWN** ON CHRISTIANS WHO ILLEGALLY TRIED TO WIN CONVERTS. SOME CHRISTIANS PROTESTED BY REVILING MUHAMMAD IN PUBLIC—A CAPITAL CRIME!

IGNORANT CAMEL DRIVER! TOOL OF SATAN!

THAT'S ENOUGH.

AFTER MANY EXECUTIONS, THE MILITANTS FLED TO THE **BOBASTRO GORGE,** JOINING THE BANDIT **UMAR IBN HAFSUN**—THE SPANISH ROBIN HOOD—WHO EVENTUALLY BECAME A CHRISTIAN HIMSELF IN 892.

THE BANDIT FELL... THE PROTESTS ENDED... BUT THE SPANISH CHURCH'S **FERVENT RESENTMENT** SMOLDERED FOR MANY CENTURIES...

WHAT ABOUT FORGIVENESS? LOVING THINE ENEMY?

I DON'T THINK SO.

ABDAR RAHMAN CALLED ON ONE OF HIS AIDES, **HASDAI IBN SHAPIRUT,** A JEW TRAINED IN MEDICINE, FLUENT IN MANY LANGUAGES, AND A VERY PERSUASIVE PERSON.

SHAPIRUT, I NEED YOUR TONGUE AND YOUR MEDICAL BAG...

IBN SHAPIRUT BRAVELY AGREED TO TRAVEL INTO ENEMY TERRITORY AND TALK TO THE GRANDMA.

MAKE **THEM** COME TO ME— AND **NO** COMPROMISES!

HE USED EVERY TRICK IN THE DIPLOMAT'S HANDBOOK TO PERSUADE HER TO BRING SANCHO TO CORDOBA FOR TREATMENT.

YES NO YES YES NO
NO YES NO
NO YES NO NO YES

(THIS TRICK IS CALLED "HAVING A LEADEN BUTT.")

AT LAST SHE AGREED... AND THE EMIR MADE A SPECTACLE OF THE CHRISTIAN PRINCE WHO CAME TO ASK FOR AID.

CREAK GROAN

THEN DR. SHAPIRUT PUT SANCHO THROUGH MONTHS OF WEIGHT-LOSS THERAPY.

NO! NO! NO MORE GEFILTE FISH!!

OO! HARSH!

THE PRINCE EMERGED FAIRLY SVELTE AND RETURNED TO THE NORTH.

CLAP CLAP CLAP

TO SHOW HIS THANKS, SANCHO JOINED HIS ARMY TO ABDAR RAHMAN'S FOR AN ATTACK ON **LEON.**

RESULT: SANCHO THE FAT GOT HIS THRONE—BUT HE OWED EVERYTHING TO THE EMIR IN CORDOBA!

AND THAT, MY FRIEND, IS HOW TO PLAY POLITICS!

ABDAR RAHMAN III RECONQUERED MOST OF SPAIN... HASDAI IBN SHAPIRUT, WHO BECAME HIS PRIME MINISTER IN ALL BUT NAME, PROMOTED HEBREW SCHOLARSHIP AND POETRY, CORRESPONDED WITH THE RABBIS IN BAGHDAD, AND INVESTIGATED, WITHOUT MUCH SUCCESS, THE MYSTERIOUS FATE OF THE KHAZARS.

UNDER ABDAR RAHMAN III SPAIN FLOURISHED... CORDOBA, WITH NEARLY A MILLION PEOPLE, WAS ONE OF THE WORLD'S LARGEST CITIES... BY MID-CENTURY, THE EMIR WAS CALLING HIMSELF CALIPH. (SEE P. 86.)

GOTTA STAY AHEAD OF THOSE SHIITES!

HE ENLARGED CORDOBA'S MAIN MOSQUE TO THE HUGE BUILDING YOU CAN VISIT TO-DAY: A FOREST OF COLUMNS, NO TWO ALIKE, SALVAGED FROM ROMAN AND GOTHIC RUINS, SOME LAVENDER, SOME PALE GREEN, SOME WHITE, SUPPORT THE FAMOUS DOUBLE ARCHES STRIPED WITH RED AND WHITE.

ABDAR RAHMAN'S FIFTY-YEAR REIGN ENDED IN 962... "AND IN ALL THAT TIME," WROTE THE OLD WORRIER, "I HAVE NUMBERED THE DAYS OF PURE AND GENUINE HAPPINESS THAT HAVE FALLEN MY LOT... THEY AMOUNT TO FOURTEEN... PUT NOT THEREFORE YOUR HOPES IN THE THINGS OF THIS WORLD."

CORDOBA'S HAPPINESS LASTED A CENTURY, BUT ALL THINGS MUST PASS.

IN 1002, FIGHTING BROKE OUT AMONG ARABS, BERBERS, AND SLAVS. MASSES OF PEOPLE FLED THE CITY.

BRIDGE BUILT BY ROMANS, RESTORED BY ARABS, STILL THERE!

IN 1023, A REVOLT CREATED A WORKER-RUN GOVERNMENT...

...WHICH WAS PUT DOWN AND REPLACED BY A COUNCIL OF PROPERTY OWNERS.

THIS CITY COUNCIL, WHICH RULED CORDOBA FOR ALMOST **FIVE CENTURIES,** GETS THE CREDIT FOR SAVING CORDOBA'S GREAT MOSQUE LATER, WHEN CATHOLIC ZEALOTS TRIED TO TEAR DOWN MOST OF SPAIN'S MUSLIM MONUMENTS.

SORRY, IT'S AN ARCHITECTURAL MASTERPIECE!

WE SEE THAT AS A PROBLEM...

THE REST OF MUSLIM SPAIN BROKE INTO PETTY EMIRATES. ONE, GRANADA, HAD A **JEWISH GENERALISSIMO** FOR A WHILE.

OY! IT'S SATURDAY!

(HIS SON'S CORRUPTION LED TO A MASSACRE OF GRANADA'S JEWS.)

EXPLOITING THE SPLIT, THE NORTHERN CHRISTIANS CONQUERED TOLEDO, AND BY SOME MIRACLE SPARED ITS LIBRARIES.

?

IN THE 1090s, THE **ALMORAVIDS** (SEE P. 92) CROSSED FROM AFRICA AND PULLED MOST OF MUSLIM SPAIN BACK TOGETHER AGAIN...

FOR GOD AND ONE-STORY HOUSES!

BUT SOME CITIES RESISTED, LIKE VALENCIA UNDER THE CHRISTIAN SOLDIER OF FORTUNE RUY DIAZ, CALLED **EL CID** (AL SAYEED=THE KNIGHT).

SANTIAGO!

AS ALL THIS WENT ON, THE CHRISTIAN WEST BEGAN TO GET THE IDEA THAT ISLAM MIGHT BE PUSHED BACK EVEN FARTHER...

AFTER DUKE ROLLO'S FLAMING FUNERAL, THE NORMANS BEGAN TO TAKE THEIR CATHOLICISM SOMEWHAT MORE SERIOUSLY.

IN THE EARLY 1000s, SOME NORMAN KNIGHTS WENT ON PILGRIMAGE TO JERUSALEM,* TAKING A ROUTE THAT PASSED THROUGH ITALY.

*THEN POSSIBLE UNDER THE FATIMIDS (SEE P. 87).

THEY LIKED ITALY WELL ENOUGH TO STAY!

WHAT DO YOU **LIKE** ABOUT IT?

THE GIRLS, THE FOOD, THE WEATHER, THE OPPORTUNITY TO **PILLAGE!**

THEY FOUND WORK AS SOLDIERS, SERVING ITALIAN LORDS IMPRESSED BY THE NORMAN LANCERS' THUNDEROUS **CAVALRY CHARGES** (WHICH DEPENDED ON STIRRUPS, A RECENT ARRIVAL FROM THE EAST).

MAMA MIA! YOU'RE HIRED!

THUDDA RUMP THUDDA RUMP

THE SONS OF THESE KNIGHTS—THEY HAD A LOT OF SONS—FORMED A SMALL ARMY WHICH GREW BIGGER WITH NEW ARRIVALS FROM NORMANDY. THESE BOYS FOUGHT FOR THEMSELVES!

STAND ASIDE!

IN 1053, ONE OF THEM, **ROBERT GUISCARD,** OR THE **WEASEL,** LED AN INVASION OF SOUTHERN ITALY, FIGHTING AGAINST THE **POPE'S OWN ARMY.**

SMASH

GUISCARD ("WEE-SCAR") = WILY, WISEACRE, OR WEASEL.

THE NORMANS CAPTURED THE POPE AND HELD HIM PRISONER, WHILE TREATING HIM WITH THE UTMOST RESPECT, OF COURSE!

WE'RE BELIEVERS, HOLY FATHER, **BELIEVE** ME!

YOU REALLY ARE WEASELLY, AREN'T YOU?

THE POPE WAS FORCED TO GIVE HIS BLESSING TO THE WEASEL AS **KING OF CALABRIA** (THE "TOE" OF THE ITALIAN BOOT).

WOW! A **KING!** YOU CAN GO NOW, POPEY!

THE BYZANTINES BERATED THE POPE! HE HAD BLESSED A RECKLESS, RUTHLESS MAN WITH OBVIOUS DESIGNS ON **BARI,** THE GREEKS' PROFITABLE, STRATEGIC SLAVE MARKET AND NAVY BASE.

WHAT WERE YOU **THINKING?**

THIS STARTED A SHOUTING MATCH BETWEEN ROME AND CONSTANTINOPLE.

WELL, **YOU** DIDN'T LIFT A FINGER TO **HELP,** DID YOU?

IT ENDED IN 1054 WHEN THE POPE EXCOMMUNICATED THE **ENTIRE EASTERN CHURCH.** THIS SPLIT, OR **SCHISM,** BETWEEN ROMAN CATHOLICS AND GREEK ORTHODOX HAS NEVER HEALED TO THIS DAY.

YOU'RE OUT!

WHO CARES?

NONE OF WHICH TROUBLED THE WEASEL IN THE LEAST! IN 1060, HE SENT HIS LITTLE BROTHER ROGER WITH AN ARMY TO **SICILY** TO TRY THEIR ARMS AGAINST THE FATIMIDS.

NOT MUCH FAMILY RESEMBLANCE, IS THERE?

QUITE A LOT OF TROUBLE THE WEASEL HAD STIRRED UP IN VERY LITTLE TIME... AND THERE WAS MORE TO COME...

O.K... NEXT WE GET **BARI**... THEN **GREECE**... THEN **ROME** AND **CON-STANTINOPLE** BOTH...

MEANWHILE, BACK IN NORMANDY...

AS 1065 TURNED TO 1066, NORMANDY'S DUKE **WILLIAM** "THE BASTARD" AWAITED NEWS FROM **ENGLAND** AND CONSIDERED AN ADVENTURE OF HIS OWN: TO INVADE, OR NOT TO INVADE? LET'S LOOK AT THE BACKGROUND TO THIS DECISION... THE VERY DEEP BACKGROUND...

DRUM DRUM

DRUM DRUM

THERE HASN'T ALWAYS BEEN AN ENGLAND!

IN ANCIENT TIMES, THE ROMAN LEGIONS THAT CONQUERED BRITAIN LATER WENT TO **JUDAEA** TO QUELL THE REVOLT OF 69.

SEE BOOK II, VOL. 12, P. 242!

AND SO, PLAUSIBLY, SOME REFUGEES FROM THAT REVOLT MAY HAVE GONE THE OTHER WAY.

TRADITION SAYS THAT EARLY CHRISTIANS CAME TO BRITAIN CARRYING JESUS' OWN DRINKING CUP, OR **HOLY GRAIL**.

WHATEVER THE TRUTH, BY 350, SOUTHERN BRITAIN WAS FULLY ROMAN, AND CHURCHES DOTTED ITS DAMP, GREEN LANDSCAPE.

AND NORTHERN BRITAIN?

HOSTILE! PAGAN! WALLED OFF!

AS THE EMPIRE COLLAPSED, BRITAIN FELL PREY TO PIRATES LIKE THE ONES WHO KIDNAPPED A BOY NAMED **PATRICIUS** (VERY ROMAN NAME!) AROUND 385.

SOLD AS A SLAVE IN PAGAN IRELAND, PATRICIUS FOUND HIMSELF HERDING SHEEP AMONG PEOPLE WITH STRANGE GODS AND ASSERTIVE WOMEN. HE PRAYED.

YAK YAK YAK YAK YAK YAK YAK

SOME YEARS LATER, HE HEARD A VOICE SAYING "GO."

GO!

WHY DIDN'T I THINK OF THAT?

PATRICIUS FLED... HE FOUND A SHIP HOME TO BRITAIN... THERE HE STUDIED FOR THE PRIESTHOOD... BECAME A BISHOP... AND IN 431 SAILED BACK TO IRELAND ON A MISSION FROM THE POPE!

IRELAND

BRITAIN

385

c. 395

431

WELL, I DO SPEAK THE LANGUAGE!

AND HE TOOK ALONG A TEAM... A TEAM OF **EXORCISTS**. (THE EARLY CHRISTIANS BELIEVED THAT STRANGE GODS WERE REAL—REAL DEMONS, THAT IS!)

MAGIC SPELLS

FOR MANY YEARS, BISHOP PATRICIUS, OR **SAINT PATRICK** AS WE KNOW HIM, ROAMED IRELAND, PREACHING, TEACHING, BLESSING, CURSING, AND CHALLENGING DRUIDS TO DUELS OF MAGIC...

IN THE END, THE IRISH CONVERTED, THOUGH THEY NEVER DID GIVE UP THE OLD GODS COMPLETELY— THEY JUST MADE THEM SMALL— AND THE WOMEN WERE ALWAYS TOO ASSERTIVE FOR ROME'S TASTE.

I RUN THIS MONASTERY, AND YOU'LL DO AS I SAY!

YES, MIZ BRIGID!

THE LAST ROMAN SOLDIER LEFT BRITAIN AROUND 407... THE RAIDS CONTINUED... AROUND 420, A LOCAL MAGISTRATE THOUGHT OF A WAY TO RESTORE ORDER.

I KNOW! LET'S HIRE SOME GERMANS! THEY'RE ORDERLY!

THE WORD GOT AROUND NORTHERN GERMANY... ONE THING LED TO ANOTHER...

NORTH SEA

BRITONS

ANGLES
VOT?

SAXONS
VOT?

AND AT MID-CENTURY, THE GERMAN INVASIONS BEGAN.

THESE WERE THE **ANGLES** AND **SAXONS**, PAGANS WHO ENJOYED PILLAGING A GOOD CHURCH... THE GRAIL DISAPPEARED, AND THE ANGLO-SAXONS TRAMPED OVER THE EAST COUNTRY.

A GREAT, DRIZZLING DUMPPE OF A LANDE!

BUT SOMETHING HELD THEM BACK... HISTORY RECORDS NO FACTS... BUT FROM POETRY WE HEAR OF **KING ARTHUR** AND HIS CHRISTIAN KNIGHTS, WHO BATTLED SAXONS AND VAINLY SOUGHT THE GRAIL, UNTIL ARTHUR FELL IN BATTLE AROUND 525...

AS THE BATTLEAXE-WIELDING, BEOWULF-BELLOWING PAGANS CARVED OUT AN ANGLE-LAND, OR ENGLAND, THE BRITISH CHURCH FLED WEST.

SAVE THE BOOKS!

MANY SETTLED IN IRELAND AND SPENT CENTURIES COPYING THE MANUSCRIPTS THEY HAD SAVED.

IF ONLY I KNEW WHAT THEY MEANT...

IN THE 600s, THE ANGLO-SAXONS CONVERTED... BY THE 700s THEY PRODUCED SOME REAL SCHOLARS: **BEDE**, WHO PERFECTED THE CALCULATION OF EASTER DAY, AND **ALCUIN**, WHO HEADED CHARLEMAGNE'S EDUCATION DEPARTMENT.

WELCOME! I'M BARELY CIVILIZED MYSELF!

THANK YOU VERY MUCH.

NOW FAST-FORWARD THROUGH MORE INVASIONS, BY NORSEMEN AND DANES THROUGH THE 800s, 900s, AND EARLY 1000s. BY 1013, ENGLAND HAD A DANISH KING, AND SOME ANGLO-SAXONS TURNED TO THE **NORMANS** AS ALLIES, CEMENTING THE FRIENDSHIP WITH MARRIAGE.

IT'S EITHER NORSEMEN FROM FRANCE OR NORSEMEN FROM DENMARK!

IN 1042, ONE OF THESE ANGLO-NORMANS TOOK THE THRONE. EDWARD "THE CONFESSOR"—FATHER ENGLISH, MOTHER NORMAN—SURROUNDED HIMSELF WITH FRENCH-SPEAKERS, TO THE ANGLOS' DISGUST.

BAISER BAISER, MON ROI!

PFECH!

PFACH!

PFLUGH!

AND NOW, IN NORMANDY, DUKE WILLIAM "THE BASTARD" LOOKS ON WITH INTEREST, BECAUSE EDWARD IS **DEATHLY ILL.**

DRUM DRUM DRUM DRUM DRUM

THE NORMANS HAD PROTECTED EDWARD FOR YEARS... AND AFTERWARD, HE HAD PROMISED TO MAKE WILLIAM THE NEXT **KING** OF **ENGLAND.**

WILL HE KEEP HIS PROMISE? **THAT'S** THE QUESTION!

CALM YOURSELF WILLIE... YOU'RE IN THE SOUP!

IN EARLY 1066, EDWARD DIES... BUT THE ENGLISH NOBLES REBUFF WILLIAM AND GIVE THE CROWN TO A "PURE" ANGLO-SAXON, **HAROLD**, EARL OF WESSEX.

ARGH! THE INVASION IS **ON!**

SOON AS I GET THE POPE'S PERMISSION!*

*QUICKLY GRANTED!

IN ENGLAND, THE NEW KING EXPECTED WILLIAM AND PREPARED TO FIGHT HIM OFF, POSTING LOOKOUTS ALONG THE COAST...

SIRE! URGENT BUSINESS!

BUT FIRST ANOTHER PROBLEM: HAROLD'S BROTHER **TOSTIG** WAS INVADING FROM THE NORTH, IN LEAGUE WITH **HARALD HARDRADA** ("TOUGH ADVICE"), KING OF NORWAY, VETERAN OF THE BYZANTINE WARS, A FEROCIOUS GIANT OF 50-SOMETHING.

IN EARLY SEPTEMBER, THE ENGLISH AXEMEN HAD TO TROT NORTH TO FACE TOSTIG AND HARDRADA.

THE ENGLISH WON THAT BAT-TLE—JUST AS DUKE WILLIAM'S NORMANS ARRIVED IN THE SOUTH.

URGENT!

THE AXEMEN TROTTED BACK AND, BARELY RESTED, FACED THE NORMANS.

OCTOBER 14, 1066: THE BATTLE OF HASTINGS... THE NORMANS DEFEATED THE ENGLISH... KING HAROLD TOOK AN ARROW IN THE EYE BEFORE THE NORMANS CHOPPED HIM TO PIECES... THEY HAD TO ASK HIS MISTRESS, EDITH SWANSNECK, TO IDENTIFY THE BITS... AND A NUMBER OF ANGLO-SAXONS ESCAPED TO FIGHT ANOTHER DAY IN ANOTHER PLACE...

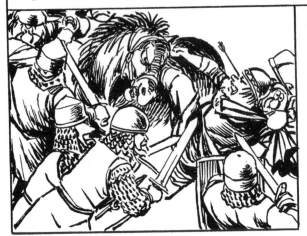

DOES THIS LOOK LIKE HIS LARGE INTESTINE?

AFTER A CHRISTMAS-DAY CORONATION, WILLIAM BEGAN SEIZING SAXON LAND FOR HIMSELF AND HIS BARONS. IN THE FUTURE, HE ANNOUNCED, ENGLAND WOULD RUN ON THE FEUDAL, FRENCH PLAN: BARONS MIGHT BUILD CASTLES AND FORTS, BUT EVERY LORD, GREAT AND SMALL, MUST **SWEAR ALLEGIANCE** TO THE KING. WILLIAM SUMMONED EVERY LANDOWNER IN ENGLAND TO GATHER FOR THE OATH-TAKING CEREMONY, AND THEY CAME, SOME 60,000 LANDLORDS, PLUS FAMILIES, SERVANTS, AND REFRESHMENT VENDORS...

FROM THIS MOMENT ON, NO NATION HAS SUCCESSFULLY INVADED BRITAIN... ON THE CONTRARY, BRITAIN BEGAN TO INVADE OTHER NATIONS FOR THE FIRST TIME... AND WILLIAM THE BASTARD IS KNOWN TO THIS DAY AS **WILLIAM THE CONQUEROR!**

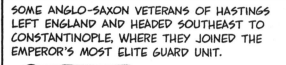

SOME ANGLO-SAXON VETERANS OF HASTINGS LEFT ENGLAND AND HEADED SOUTHEAST TO CONSTANTINOPLE, WHERE THEY JOINED THE EMPEROR'S MOST ELITE GUARD UNIT.

PRESENT **ARMS!**
OO! SCARY!

HE NEEDED THE HELP! ALP ARSLAN'S TURKS HAD JUST OVERRUN ARMENIA (SEE P. 145), AND THE WEASEL'S NORMANS WERE HACKING AROUND ITALY, WITH THE POPE'S BLESSING.

WEASEL... TURKS...

BETTER DO TURKS FIRST...

IN 1071 CAME THE DISASTER AT **MANZIKERT,** ARMENIA, WHERE THE TURKS CAPTURED THE BYZANTINE EMPEROR AND SLAUGHTERED HIS ARMY (SEE THE END OF THE LAST VOLUME).

TIME FOR A NEW EMPEROR!

IN THE SAME YEAR, ROBERT THE WEASEL OVERRAN **BARI,** TAKING AWAY BYZANTIUM'S MOST IMPORTANT WESTERN NAVY BASE.

IT'S THAT TIME AGAIN...

AT SOME POINT DURING THESE PROCEEDINGS, ROBERT THE WEASEL **FELL IN LOVE.** HE DIVORCED HIS FIRST WIFE AND MARRIED THE AWE-INSPIRING **SICHELGAITA,** A SIX-FOOTER WHO STRODE INTO BATTLE AT HIS SIDE.

WOW!

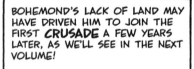

ENTHRALLED BY SICHELGAITA, THE WEASEL DISINHERITED HIS OLDEST SON **BOHEMOND** (BY WIFE #1), BUT KEPT HIM AT HIS SIDE, WHERE BOHEMOND LEARNED WARFARE AND GUILE.

YOU'LL JUST HAVE TO WIN YOUR OWN KINGDOM, LIKE YOUR DAD!

YES, FATHER...

BOHEMOND'S LACK OF LAND MAY HAVE DRIVEN HIM TO JOIN THE FIRST **CRUSADE** A FEW YEARS LATER, AS WE'LL SEE IN THE NEXT VOLUME!

WHILE THE BYZANTINES TRIED OUT NEW LEADERS ONE BY ONE, THE WEASEL RESOLVED TO TAKE THE WAR TO **CONSTANTINOPLE**.

IN 1081, THE NORMANS INVADED GREECE... THE EMPEROR THREW HIS CRACK TROOPS AGAINST THEM... ONCE AGAIN, **ANGLO-SAXONS** BATTLED **NORMANS**... AND THE NORMAN LINE BUCKLED!

REVENGE!

INSPIRED BY SICHELGAITA'S BELLOWING, THE NORMANS REGROUPED, CHARGED, AND KILLED THE ANGLO-SAXONS TO A MAN.

STILL, THE WEASEL'S LOSSES WERE HEAVY... HE HAD TO GO HOME FOR MORE MEN AND SUPPLIES—NOT SO EASY, BECAUSE HIS SHIPS HAD BEEN DESTROYED BY THE VENETIANS!

THE NORMAN LEADER FOUND SOMETHING TO CARRY HIM BACK TO ITALY.

HE RAISED THE MEN—BUT WHERE WERE THE SUPPLIES? THE ARMY ENTERED **ROME** AND PLUNDERED IT AS IT HADN'T BEEN PLUNDERED FOR CENTURIES.

SUDDENLY, IN 1085, ROBERT THE WEASEL FELL ILL AND DIED IN SICHELGAITA'S ARMS.

GAITA... THAT SOUND... WHAT IS IT...?

THE ENTIRE MEDITERRANEAN BASIN SIGHING WITH RELIEF.

EVEN SO, GREECE AND ITALY STILL HARBORED HORDES OF NORMANS DROOLING OVER CONSTANTINOPLE'S WEALTH.

TO THEM ADD **SICILY**... IN 1090, THE WEASEL'S BROTHER **ROGER** FINALLY GAINED CONTROL OF THE WHOLE, HUGE ISLAND AFTER THIRTY YEARS OF WAR.

THIS IS GETTING TOTALLY OUT OF HAND...

WOULD CONSTANTINOPLE FALL? NOT YET... THE POPE AND EMPEROR HAD BEGUN SPEAKING AGAIN... THE SACK OF ROME HAD COOLED THE POPE ON THE NORMANS, TO SAY THE LEAST... SO THE LATINS WERE READY TO LISTEN WHEN THE GREEK EMPEROR EXPLAINED THE **BIG PICTURE** AS HE SAW IT: IN ATTACKING THE BYZANTINE EMPIRE, HE SAID, THE WEST WAS ONLY BUYING ITSELF A MUCH MORE **SERIOUS PROBLEM:**

IT'S THE **TURKS,** STUPID!!

NEXT! ISLAM SQUEEZED!

THE CARTOON HISTORY OF THE UNIVERSE

Volume 18

CROSS PEOPLE

During the 1070s, the Byzantine empire fell apart east and west.

In Asia, the **SELJUK TURKS** had come nearly to Constantinople's door. In Europe, the **NORMANS** grabbed Byzantine holdings in **ITALY** and **GREECE**... **SERBS, BULGARS, HUNGARIANS,** and **PECHENEGS** fought to take over the **BALKANS**...

And in Constantinople, the throne passed from one useless emperor to another with the usual loss of eyeballs.

WHOA!

THE FIRST CRUSADE

ENTER **ALEXIUS COMNENUS**, CONSTANTINOPLE'S TOP GENERAL, A SHORT MAN, BUT A COMMANDING FIGURE, AT LEAST WHEN HE WAS SITTING UP HIGH, ON A THRONE OR A HORSE. HE SEIZED POWER IN 1081.

I'VE HEARD OF WALLS HAVING EARS, BUT...

SQUEEZING THE PEOPLE AS HARD AS HE COULD, BEGGING THE CHURCH FOR ITS GOLD, ALEXIUS MANAGED TO HIRE ENOUGH TROOPS TO HOLD OFF THE NORMANS, PUT DOWN THE SERBS, AND KILL **STUNNING** NUMBERS OF PECHENEGS...

GOOD, GOOD...

BUT STILL HIS COUNTRY WAS FULL OF TURKS.

SIGH...

AND THEN, A BREAK: IN 1092 THE SELJUK SULTAN DIED... HIS SONS BEGAN FIGHTING AMONG THEMSELVES... ANOTHER TURKISH CLAN ENTERED THE FRAY... AND SUDDENLY, PRESSURE ON CONSTANTINOPLE EASED.

NOW IT'S **OUR** TURN TO GET **THEM!**

YES, SIRE... AND SHALL WE TAKE UP YOUR HEM, SIRE?

DURING THIS LULL, SOME VISITORS ARRIVED, SENT BY THE POPE IN ROME TO SEE THE EMPEROR.

THE EMPEROR RECEIVED THEM WITH COMPLAINTS: HIS FELLOW CHRISTIANS, HE SAID, SEEMED AWFULLY KEEN TO ATTACK HIM... THIS WAS **INSANE**... BYZANTIUM WAS HOLDING BACK THE MUSLIM TURKS... THE WEST SHOULD WORK WITH HIM, NOT AGAINST HIM... THERE MUST BE SOMETHING THE POPE COULD **DO**...

UNITED WE STAND, DIVIDED YADDA YADDA!

YADDA YADDA?

AN AMBIGUOUS PHRASE USED IN DIPLOMACY TO KEEP THINGS VAGUE AND AVOID HARD FEELINGS.

AROUND THE SAME TIME, IN ROME, POPE **URBAN II** HAD A VISITOR TOO: A TRAVELING PREACHER NAMED **PETER** THE **HERMIT**.

THE HERMIT HAD JUST COME FROM **JERUSALEM**, AND HE WAS FULL OF COMPLAINTS!

HOLY FATHER, THEY **ROB** US, THEY **CHEAT** US, THEY DON'T ALLOW **PIGS** IN OUR ROOMS!

THE TURKS, WHO NOW RULED JERUSALEM, MADE CHRISTIAN PILGRIMS FEEL UNWELCOME, HE SAID.

THEY'RE A BUNCH OF FANATICS!

LOVE HIS HAIR SHIRT!

PETER URGED URBAN TO GIVE HIS BLESSING TO A **HOLY WAR** TO WIN BACK THE **HOLY LAND** FROM THE UNBELIEVERS.

AND I HUMBLY VOLUNTEER TO **TAKE COMMAND!**

THE POPE **LIKED** THIS IDEA! AS A SLOGAN, "TAKE THE CROSS TO JERUSALEM" SOUNDED **SO** MUCH BETTER THAN "HELP OUT THE GREEK EMPIRE," AND IT MIGHT EVEN **WORK**—IF HE COULD JUST FIND GOOD **LEADERS**...

WHERE IS THE WEASEL, NOW THAT YOU NEED HIM?

SO THE WORD WENT OUT... THE POPE WOULD BE MAKING AN **IMPORTANT STATEMENT**... THOUSANDS OF NOBLES, KNIGHTS, AND PRIESTS GATHERED TO HEAR HIM AT CLERMONT, FRANCE, IN THE FALL OF 1095...

WE ALL KNOW HOW THESE GLITTERING PAGEANTS LOOK FROM THE MOVIES... THE BLAZES OF COLOR, THE FLAPPING BANNERS... BUT WHAT ABOUT THE **SMELL?** IT MUST HAVE BEEN SOMETHING, SINCE THE FRANKS RARELY BATHED IN THOSE DAYS! THE POPE CALLED ON THE REEKING CROWD TO CARRY THE WAR TO JERUSALEM... THIRTY THOUSAND MOUTHS FULL OF DECAYING TEETH BELLOWED BACK... AND TWO BYZANTINE BYSTANDERS NEARLY FAINTED, POSSIBLY OVERWHELMED BY THE AROMA...

DEUS LE VOLT!

(GOD WILLS IT!)

IN A FRENZY OF PEER PRESSURE, THE CROWD BEGAN RIPPING CLOTH INTO STRIPS AND SEWING CROSSES ON THEIR SLEEVES.

RIP
RIP
RIP

BARONS AND KNIGHTS AND COUNTS AND DUKES THEN WENT HOME TO COLLECT MEN, WEAPONS, WAGONS, FOOD, AND THE MONEY TO PAY FOR THEM ALL.

NOW WHERE CAN I REFINANCE THE ENTIRE DUCHY OF NORMANDY?

THE HERMIT, WHO KNEW HOW LONG IT CAN TAKE TO PROCESS A LOAN APPLICATION, IMPATIENTLY TRAMPED ACROSS FRANCE, URGING CHURCHGOERS TO JOIN UP RIGHT NOW!

BUT WHAT ABOUT FOOD?

GOD WILL PROVIDE!!

AN AMAZING NUMBER DROPPED WHATEVER THEY WERE DOING (OFTEN NOT MUCH) AND FOLLOWED PETER AND HIS STRATEGIST WALTER SANS-AVOIR (HAVE-NOTHING) TO JOIN THE FIGHT.

HEY, THE POPE SEZ CRUSADERS GO STRAIGHT TO HEAVEN, GUARANTEED... GOOD DEAL... 'SPECIALLY FOR A SINNER LIKE ME... I KILLED SIX GUYS... HOW MANY GUYS DID YOU KILL?

UM...

SPRING 1096: IN THE QUAINT TOWNS OF GERMANY'S RHINE VALLEY, THEY FOUND THEIR FIRST INFIDELS: THE JEWS, WHOM THE CHURCH STILL BLAMED FOR KILLING CHRIST.

AHEM. OUR OFFICIAL POSITION IS TO LET THE JEWS LIVE, BUT WRETCHEDLY, TO "REMIND" THEM WHAT "THEY" DID!

TOO COMPLICATED FOR ME!

AND SO THE MURDERS BEGAN... EACH NEW WAVE OF CRUSADERS WENT AFTER THE JEWS... BY THE END OF THE FIRST YEAR, THOUSANDS HAD DIED...

PETER'S MOB TURNED SOUTH, PLUNDERING HUNGARY AND THE BALKANS FOR FOOD, AND CAME AT LAST TO CONSTANTINOPLE. THE EMPEROR WAS UNNERVED!

IF YOU'LL PARDON THE EXPRESSION— JESUS CHRIST!

ALEXIUS URGED THEM TO TURN BACK AND SAVE THEIR SKINS... THEY SCOFFED... SO HE FERRIED THEM OVER TO ASIA.

HOW CAN WE LOSE? THE TURKS DON'T BELIEVE IN JESUS!!

WHO TOLD YOU THAT?

THEN HE SHOWED THEM THE ROAD, AND OFF THEY WENT...

THIS WAY, WATER! THAT WAY, NO WATER!

HA HA! GOD WILL PROVIDE!

AS EXPECTED, THE TURKS MADE SHORT WORK OF THIS LOT, KILLING NEARLY ALL OF THEM...

WHAT A WASTE...

EXCEPT, THAT IS, FOR PETER THE HERMIT, WHO SOMEHOW ESCAPED TO BRING BACK THE BAD NEWS.

IT'S A MIRACLE!

MEANWHILE, AFTER MORE MASSACRES OF JEWS, "REAL" CRUSADERS ARRIVED IN CONSTANTINOPLE: BIG ARMIES BEHIND GREAT LORDS, LIKE **BOHEMOND**, SON OF ROBERT THE WEASEL.

HOW COULD THE EMPEROR **CONTROL** THESE PROUD COUNTS? THEY HAD LOYALTIES BACK HOME... BOHEMOND WAS AN OLD ENEMY... YET THEY WERE SUPPOSED TO HELP HIM WIN BACK HIS EMPIRE... WEREN'T THEY?

OTHERWISE, WHY AM I FEEDING THEM?

ALEXIUS ASKED THEM TO SWEAR AN OATH TO BE "HIS MAN" AND RETURN TO THE EMPIRE EVERY EASTERN CITY WON BACK FROM THE TURKS.

WELL?

UPON MY HONOR, WE FEUDAL LORDS TAKE THESE OATHS SERIOUSLY... HOW CAN I HONORABLY WRIGGLE OUT OF THIS ONE?

BOHEMOND AND MOST OF THE OTHERS GLIBLY SWORE..

I KNOW! I'LL CROSS MY FINGERS BEHIND MY BACK!

I SWEAR!

THE FEW WHO REFUSED WERE ATTACKED BY THE **IMPERIAL ARMY**—SO THE CRUSADES' FIRST BATTLES SET **FRANKS** AGAINST **GREEKS!**

OO! BAD START!

AT LAST, IN JUNE 1099, AFTER TWO YEARS OF MARCHING, ARGUMENTS, BATTLE, DISEASE, AND DESERTION, THE CRUSADERS REACHED THEIR GOAL: **JERUSALEM.** IT SEEMED LIKE A MIRACLE.

AFTER A 4-MONTH SIEGE, THESE KNIGHTS, THE MOST FAITHFUL OF ALL—AND HALF-CRAZED WITH THIRST, AS THE MUSLIMS HAD PLUGGED EVERY WELL FOR MILES AROUND—FOUGHT THEIR WAY OVER THE WALLS...

AND KILLED EVERY NON-CHRISTIAN IN JERUSALEM—MEN, WOMEN, AND CHILDREN—AT LEAST 40,000 IN ALL.

DO I REALLY NEED TO ADD THAT THIS MASSACRE SEEMED ESPECIALLY HEINOUS BECAUSE IT WAS COMMITTED IN THE NAME OF A RELIGION THAT PREACHES LOVE, MILDNESS, AND FORGIVENESS?

NAAAAH...

THE NEWS OF JERUSALEM SHOCKED THE MUSLIM WORLD. DEMONSTRATORS FILLED THE STREETS, CALLING FOR ACTION.

WE DIDN'T DO THIS WHEN **WE** TOOK JERUSALEM!!

BUT THE CALIPH WAS POOR... THE ARABS RESENTED THE TURKS... THE TURKS RESENTED EACH OTHER... THE **OTHER** CALIPH (IN EGYPT) WAS A SHIITE, AND **NO ONE** WANTED TO DEAL WITH HIM...

I'D **LIKE** TO HELP, BUT FIRST LET ME PLUNGE THIS DAGGER INTO YOU!

AND SO THE CRUSADERS MANAGED TO STAY... THEY MADE THEMSELVES LORDS OF THE LAND... REPLACED GREEK ORTHODOX PRIESTS WITH ROMAN CATHOLICS... BUILT MASSIVE CASTLES... FEUDALIZED SYRIA AND PALESTINE... AND EVEN LEARNED TO LIVE WITH THEIR MUSLIM NEIGHBORS... AND GRADUALLY, PEACE BROKE OUT, SOMETIMES.

IN FACT, VISITORS FROM FRANCE THOUGHT THESE GUYS HAD "GONE NATIVE"!

QUEL HORREUR! NOW YOU **BATHE?**

THE BYZANTINES, MEANWHILE, HAD MIXED FEELINGS... THEY HAD REGAINED SOME LAND, BUT THE TURKS STILL THREATENED, AND NOW THERE WERE THESE FRANKISH ARMIES TOO... BEST TO KEEP UP A FROSTY FRIENDSHIP WITH EVERYONE, IF POSSIBLE.

TRULY, WE ARE MASTERS OF DIPLO-MACY!

WHO WOULDN'T BE, SURROUNDED BY SERBS, NORMANS, HUNGARIANS, TURKS, RUSSIANS, FRANKS, AND ARMENIANS?

THE HOME FRONT

CATHOLIC EUROPE CHEERED ON THE CRUSADERS, AND EVERY YEAR MORE PEOPLE HEADED FOR THE WARS IN THE EAST.

PEOPLE HAD MORE REASONS TO CHEER THAN YOU MIGHT THINK. FOR ONE THING, THE STAY-AT-HOMES GOT SOME GREAT **BARGAINS** WHEN CRUSADERS SOLD OFF THEIR STUFF TO PAY FOR THE TRIP!

ITALIAN SHIPPERS CHEERED TOO: TICKET SALES SOARED AS MEN AND MATERIEL PASSED THROUGH PISA, GENOA, AND VENICE. (ONE EXAMPLE: TIMBER FOR THE SIEGE EQUIPMENT AT JERUSALEM ARRIVED ON GENOESE SHIPS AT THE LAST MINUTE.)

AND EVERY WAR-BATTERED FIEF IN EUROPE SIGHED WITH RELIEF TO SEE ALL THAT HEAVY ARMOR LEAVING THE CONTINENT.

AS ALL THIS TESTOSTERONE DRAINED AWAY, EUROPE CALMED DOWN!

ABOVE ALL, THE CRUSADES SHOWED THE PRESTIGE OF THE **ROMAN CATHOLIC CHURCH.** THINK OF IT: THE POPE CALLED FOR WAR, AND AN ARMY RESPONDED!

BY 1096, THE CHURCH HAD COME A LONG WAY FROM THE "PORNOCRACY" OF THE 900s, WHEN THE POPES' HENCHMEN AND MISTRESSES RULED ROME BY FAIR MEANS AND FOUL.*

WHOA! KINKY!

SHE'S POISONED FOUR LIKE THAT...

THERE'S ONLY ONE POSSIBLE EXPLANA-TION!

OVERPOPULATION?

ALL ACROSS EUROPE, IN FACT, FUN-LOVING FRIARS RUBBED ELBOWS WITH POSH NOBLES... RUBBED FACES IN WILD BOAR HAUNCHES... RUBBED OTHER PORTIONS OF THEIR ANATOMY AGAINST VARIOUS OTHER HAUNCHES...

WHY, FATHER, I DIDN'T KNOW YOU WERE A **LAYMAN!**

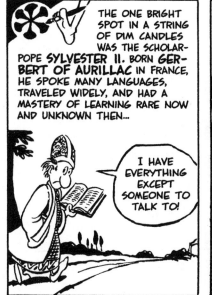

THE ONE BRIGHT SPOT IN A STRING OF DIM CANDLES WAS THE SCHOLAR-POPE **SYLVESTER II.** BORN **GER-BERT OF AURILLAC** IN FRANCE, HE SPOKE MANY LANGUAGES, TRAVELED WIDELY, AND HAD A MASTERY OF LEARNING RARE NOW AND UNKNOWN THEN...

I HAVE EVERYTHING EXCEPT SOMEONE TO TALK TO!

LONG BEFORE HE WAS POPE, IN 976, GERBERT WAS THE FIRST TO BRING **ARABIC NUMERALS** (THE KIND WE USE NOW!) FROM MUS-LIM SPAIN TO CHRISTENDOM.

COOL, EH?

WE DON'T DO "COOL"!

THE ROMANS DISLIKED SYLVESTER... THEY CALLED HIM A MAGICIAN... BESIDES, HIS FAMILY WAS JEWISH! HE WAS POISONED IN 1002 AFTER ONLY FOUR YEARS AS POPE, AND ARABIC NUMERALS HAD TO WAIT **200 YEARS** BEFORE CHRISTEN-DOM FINALLY TRIED THEM OUT...

CCXXVI YEARS, TO BE EXACT!

THEN, IN THE 1000s... INVASIONS FROM ASIA EASED (THE TURKS MOVED INTO SOUTH ASIA RATHER THAN EUROPE), AND THE CHURCH STRUGGLED TO KEEP EUROPEANS FROM FIGHTING EACH OTHER.

ON TUESDAY, WEDNESDAY, AND THURSDAY ONLY, PLEASE!

CATHOLIC MISSIONARIES CONVERTED THE PAGAN NORWEGIANS, HUNGARIANS, AND DANES—WHILE CATHOLIC ARMIES CARRIED THE CROSS TO MUSLIM SPAIN AND SICILY.

CALL IT THE PRE-CRUSADES!

IN ROME, REFORMERS WORKED HARD TO CLEAN UP THE CHURCH,* AND BY CENTURY'S END, THE POPE WAS RUNNING AN EFFECTIVE INTERNATIONAL ORGANIZATION. THE RESULT?

SIMPLE!

MORAL AUTHORITY
+
STANDING ARMIES
=
CRUSADES

IN 1070, POPE GREGORY VI SENT OUT AN ORDER THAT ALL PRIESTS MUST BE **CELIBATE.** WIVES, GIRL-FRIENDS, SIGNIFICANT OTHERS— ALL MUST GO IMMEDIATELY!

WHAT IS THE **PROBLEM?**

WHY? AT THE TIME, PRIESTS OFTEN MARRIED, ALTHOUGH THE CHURCH ROUTINELY DENOUNCED SEX AS FILTHY AND LOW (IF SOME-TIMES NECESSARY!). PRIESTS WERE SUPPOSED TO SET A "HIGHER" EXAMPLE OF SELF-CONTROL, SELF-DENIAL, EVEN SELF-MOR-TIFICATION.

WHAT ABOUT SELF-ABUSE?

JUST CONFESS IN THE MORNING...

BUT THE POPE HAD SOMETHING ELSE IN MIND AS WELL: A MARRIED PRIEST OFTEN WANTED TO LEAVE HIS PARISH TO A **SON,** WHEREAS THE CHURCH WANTED **COMPLETE CONTROL** OVER ALL **PERSONNEL DECISIONS...** SO A CELIBATE PRIEST AVOIDED **CONFLICT OF INTEREST.**

IS IT **MY** FAULT THE POPE'S A **CONTROL FREAK?**

THE CRUSADES, ONCE THEY BEGAN, CREATED A NEW CHALLENGE TO THE CHURCH: CHRISTIANS IN MUSLIM LANDS SAW A MORE **ADVANCED CIVILIZATION!**

WELL, THEY'RE **ONLY** AHEAD OF US IN MATH, SCIENCE, AGRICULTURE, ARCHITECTURE, ENGINEERING, SHIPBUILDING, GEOGRAPHY, MEDICINE*...

AND BATHING...

SO—OUT WITH THE OLD AND IN WITH THE NEW! CHURCH ARCHITECTS WENT FOR A LIGHTER LOOK... INSTEAD OF MASSIVE WALLS, THEY PUT UP JUST ENOUGH STONEWORK TO SUPPORT ENORMOUS WINDOWS... DECORATION SPROUTED... HORRIFIED CLASSICISTS BLASTED THE NEW STYLE, NAMING IT AFTER THE BARBARIANS WHO RUINED THE ROMAN WORLD...

IT'S SO... UGH... **GOTHIC**...

 A MUSLIM DOCTOR OF THOSE DAYS LEFT THIS MEMOIR: TREATING A FRANKISH PATIENT WITH A WOUNDED LEG, THE MUSLIM CAREFULLY CLEANED AND BANDAGED THE WOUNDS, WHEN A **FRANKISH PHYSICIAN** ARRIVED.

STAND BACK! STAND BACK!

"DOCTOR FRANK" OPINED THAT ONLY **AMPUTATION** WOULD DO AND IMMEDIATELY HOISTED HIS AXE.

WHOCK

CRUNCH

ONE SWIFT BLOW, AND—NO, MAKE THAT **TWO** SWIFT BLOWS... WELL, THREE... AT WHICH POINT THE LEG CAME OFF, AND THE PATIENT DIED ON THE SPOT.

DON'T LOOK AT ME LIKE THAT! I WAS TRAINED BY THE GREATEST LUMBERJACK IN ALL FRANCE!

MEANWHILE, THE "LIBERATED" ARAB LIBRARIES OF SPAIN SAW **TAG-TEAM TRANSLATION:** JEWS TRANSLATED FROM ARABIC TO SPANISH, THEN CHRISTIANS WENT FROM SPANISH TO LATIN.

SERVANTS AND MULES CARTED THE NEW STUFF OFF TO FRANCE, WHERE SCHOLARS AND COPYISTS SNAPPED IT UP!

IDEAS ARE HEAVY...

THAT'S WHY I TRY NEVER TO HAVE ONE...

NOW THAT THERE WAS SOME-THING TO TEACH, NEW **SCHOOLS** SPRANG UP—LIKE THE MEDICAL SCHOOL IN SALERNO, SICILY, WHERE STUDENTS LEARNED ANATOMY BY DISSECTING PIGS.

WHY PIGS?

KEEPS THE JEWS AND MUSLIMS AWAY!

FOR PHILOSOPHY, ONE WENT TO **PARIS**, TEEMING WITH PROFESSORS AND STUDENTS EXPLORING THE LIFE OF THE MIND, MOSTLY...

THOUGH AT LEAST ONE FAMOUS TEACHER, THE PRIEST **PETER ABELARD**, WENT INTO A FEW **OTHER** THINGS WITH HIS GIFTED TEENAGE TUTEE, **HELOISE**...

WHAT HAVE YOU LEARNED UNDER ME?

SOME BOOKS ARE HARDER THAN OTHERS...

HELOISE BORE HIM A SON, AS-TROLABE*(!), AND THEY WED—BUT SECRETLY, TO PROTECT ABELARD'S PRIESTLY CAREER.

CUTE LI'L ASTROLABE...

TSK! ACADEMICS!

*AN ARAB ASTRONOMICAL GIZMO

HER UNCLE—ALSO A PRIEST—TOLD THE WORLD... HELOISE DENIED EVERYTHING... THE UNCLE BEAT HER... ABELARD PACKED HER OFF TO A NUN-NERY... SO THE UNCLE AND HIS BOYS AMBUSHED THE TEACHER AND **CASTRATED** HIM.

I HATE IT WHEN THAT HAPPENS...

HELOISE GAVE UP THE BABY AND BECAME A NUN... YEARS LATER, SHE WROTE ABELARD TO SAY SHE REGRETTED NOTHING... THOUGH HIS ARDOR, BY THAT TIME, HAD COOLED QUITE A BIT.

WE'LL ALWAYS HAVE PARIS!

OUCH! YES, WE WILL...

HERE WAS ONE MORE 12TH-CENTURY NOVELTY: AN **EDUCATED WOMAN**...

ANOTHER ABBESS, **HILDEGARD VON BINGEN,** WROTE MUSIC, HAD VISIONS, PREACHED TO PRINCES—AND ALSO COMPILED AN ENCYCLO-PEDIA OF MEDICINAL HERBS.

I GET SOME OF MY BEST VISIONS FROM MEDICINAL HERBS...

A PROUDER EXAMPLE, **ELEANOR OF AQUI-TAINE,** MARRIED KING LOUIS OF FRANCE AND WENT CRUSADING, TRAILING TROUBADOURS WHEREVER SHE WENT.

THESE POETS, BY THE WAY, WROTE LAYS OF LOVE— ANOTHER NOVELTY AFTER THE HEAD-BASHING, BEOWULF-ISH EPICS OF THE DARK AGES.

O, GUINEVER LOVED LAUNCELOT, AND LAUNCELOT LOVED HERRRR. BUT SHE, BY GOTH, HAD PLEDGED HER TROTH, TO THE SILLY TWIT ARTHURRRR...

AND HOW DID THE CHURCH HANDLE ALL THIS FEMININITY? SUR-PRISINGLY WELL... HELOISE BECAME AN ABBESS... THE POPE LET ELEANOR **DIVORCE** LOUIS... AND NOBODY COMPLAINED ABOUT THE **BIRTH-CONTROL POTIONS** IN HILDEGARD'S HERB KIT...

HEY, THIS CENTURY WE'RE FLEXIBLE!

THE
CRUSADES
BROUGHT
LESS HAPPY
CHANGES TO
EUROPE'S
JEWS...

BEFORE 1096, MANY JEWS WORKED IN LONG-DISTANCE TRADE, BUT AFTER 1096, RAMPAGING CRUSADERS CHASED THEM OFF EUROPE'S LUMPY, RUTTED ROADS.

SEEKING PROTECTION, JEWISH LEADERS APPROACHED THEIR VARIOUS COUNTRIES' KINGS—WITH "PRESENTS" IN HAND.

WE'LL BE DELIGHTED TO HELP.

DRAINED THE ENTIRE COMMUNITY TO RAISE THIS

EVERY KING OFFERED MORE OR LESS THE SAME DEAL: THE JEWS WOULD BECOME HIS OFFICIAL **MONEY MEN:** TAX COLLECTORS, LENDERS, FINANCIERS. HE, IN TURN, WOULD HAPPILY PROTECT THEM AS HE WOULD HIS OWN PROPERTY!

IN FACT, THEY **ARE** MY PROPERTY!

SEZ RIGHT HERE.

THE KING ALSO BARRED THE JEWS FROM OWNING LAND OR HOLDING MOST OTHER JOBS—AND SO THE STEREOTYPE APPEARED OF THE JEW WHO LENDS MONEY AT INTEREST.

THE DEVIL'S BUSINESS! CAN YOU SPARE ME FIFTY?

FUNNY HAT MANDATED BY LAW

IN TIME, A FEW JEWS CAME TO CONTROL HEAPS OF MONEY—¾ OF ALL THE COIN IN ENGLAND, BY ONE EDUCATED ESTIMATE—A FACT WHICH ENDEARED THEM TO NO ONE.

WHUZZAT NOISE? WHUZZAT?

NEVER MIND, YOUR MAJESTY...

POGROM IN LONDON DURING KING RICHARD I'S CORONATION IN 1187.

WERE THEY RICH? IT LOOKED THAT WAY... BUT BY LAW **ALL** THE MONEY REALLY BELONGED TO THE **KING,** WHO TOOK AS MUCH OF IT AS HE LIKED AT ANY TIME!

OY! WHO PROTECTS US FROM **YOU?**

THAT'S THE BEAUTY OF THE ARRANGEMENT...

216

ASIDE FROM THE JEWS, THOUGH, EVERYONE SUPPORTED THE CRUSADES, RIGHT?

WRONG...

A POWERFUL SECT OF DISSIDENT CHRISTIANS, THE **CATHARS** OR PURE ONES, REJECTED THE CATHOLIC CHURCH, ITS CROSS, AND ITS WAR.

NOTHING BUT A WAY TO HELP THE RICH AND VIOLENT!

THE CATHARS BELIEVED:

THE **MATERIAL WORLD** WAS CREATED BY THE DEVIL AND IS **THOROUGHLY EVIL.** GOD IS **PURELY SPIRITUAL.**

JESUS, AS AN EMANATION OF GOD, WAS **NOT MATERIAL,** SO NOT HUMAN... SO **NEVER DIED** ON THE CROSS.

IN THAT CASE, ADORING THE CROSS MADE NO MORE SENSE THAN WORSHIPPING A **HANGMAN'S NOOSE.**

I MEAN, REALLY!

DURING THE 11TH AND 12TH CENTURIES, THIS SECT OF CROSSLESS CHRISTIANS GAINED A BIG FOLLOWING IN FRANCE... CLEARLY, THE CHURCH HAD TO DO **SOMETHING** ABOUT THEM... BUT **WHAT?**

WE **CAN'T** JUST **KILL** THEM, CAN WE...? WE'RE **PRIESTS!**

TO THE CATHARS— ALSO CALLED **BOUGRES** OR BULGARS BECAUSE THE SECT ORIGINATED IN THE BALKANS—HUMANITY'S ULTIMATE GOAL WAS TO SHED OUR MATERIAL BODIES AND BECOME PURELY SPIRITUAL.

BAD BODY!

PINCH

OW!

FOR THIS REASON, THE "BULGARS" BELIEVED IN **BIRTH CONTROL,** INCLUDING ANY SEX ACT THAT REDUCED THE RISK OF PREGNANCY. THE FEWER CHILDREN THE BETTER, THEY THOUGHT!

SO WE CAN **GIVE IN** TO OUR **CARNAL LUST?**

JUST SO LONG AS WE USE THE MOST SPIRITUAL ORIFICES...

THIS IS HOW THE WORD BOUGRE— ENGLISH BUGGER—CAME TO MEAN SOMEONE WHOSE, ER, PRACTICES WERE, UM, BACKWARDS...

DAG, ALPHONSE, ALL THIS SPIRITUALITY IS REAL PAIN IN THE—

BUT WE'RE GOING TO HEAVEN, JULIETTE!

SECOND CRUSADE

As mid-century approaches, we see some new faces.

In Constantinople, a new emperor, **MANUEL**, charming, clever, overconfident.

In Iraq, **ZENGI**, atabeg* of **MOSUL**, pious, militant, determined to attack the crusader states and anyone else in his way.

PSST!

SELJUKS
KONYA
ANTIOCH
MOSUL
JERUSALEM

*A TURKISH TITLE MEANING BARON OR SOME SUCH EQUIVALENT

To Manuel, the atabeg was not all bad, since he bordered the Seljuk Turks. The emperor saw an opportunity to play the Muslim powers one against the other.

EXCELLENT! THE ENEMY OF MY ENEMY IS MY FRIEND!

But to the Latins, Zengi was a pure enemy. In 1142, he attacked Armenia and captured the Frankish cities there—the crusaders' first big loss.

NONE OF YOUR FANCY-NANCY LOGIC! THE MAN IS **EVIL**!

In response, an outspoken French abbot, **BERNARD** of **CLAIRVAUX**, persuaded two **KINGS** to take the cross: **CHARLES** of France and **CONRAD** of Germany.

NO KING AS POWERFUL, WONDERFUL, BEAUTIFUL, AND GOD-FEARING AS YOURSELVES WOULD LET THE WHOLE PROJECT SLIDE DOWN THE TUBES, NOW WOULD HE?

NO. NO.

COULD TALK THE SKIN OFF A TURNIP

Traveling in style, trailing wagonloads of princesses,* silk, troubadours, etc., they reached Constantinople just as Manuel was signing a **PEACE TREATY** with the **SELJUKS**.

THIS IS **GOOD**... IF, I MEAN, WHEN YOU REACH THE HOLY LAND, **ZENGI** WILL BE BUSY FIGHTING THE SEJUKS! YOU SEE? TRY TO TAKE THE LONG VIEW... **MY** VIEW...

*INCLUDING THE YOUNG QUEEN OF FRANCE, ELEANOR OF AQUITAINE.

IN OTHER WORDS, THE CRUSADERS HAD TO PASS THROUGH SELJUK TERRITORY WITH NO HELP FROM THE EMPIRE.

I SAY!

THIS HARDLY SEEMS FAIR...

THE TURKS DESTROYED 90% OF THE GERMANS AND MOST OF FRENCH, THOUGH THE KINGS AND QUEEN ESCAPED, OF COURSE.

I SAY!

THIS HARDLY SEEMS FAIR...

CHARLES LED HIS REMNANT TO PALESTINE AND STUPIDLY ATTACKED DAMASCUS, ONE OF THE CRUSADERS' FEW ARAB ALLIES.

BUT BUT BUT

NONSENSE! THESE ARE INFIDELS! VICTORY MUST BE MINE!

THE ATTACK FAILED... DAMASCUS WENT OVER TO ZENGI... AND CHARLES, AFTER MORE USELESS ADVENTURES, WENT HOME. THE TWO KINGS HAD FAILED COMPLETELY.

AS I WAS SAYING, YOU LIVE HERE... YOU KNOW THE SITUATION... YOU HANDLE IT!

THIS SECOND CRUSADE FAILED TO PUSH BACK ZENGI AN INCH... IN FACT, IT ONLY STRENGTHENED HIM... IT KILLED THOUSANDS... AND IT COST A FORTUNE...

'BYE!

EVEN SAINT BERNARD, WHO STARTED IT, HAD PANGS OF DOUBT.

WEIRD SENSATION! I'VE NEVER FELT IT BEFORE...

IN FRANCE, MORE PEOPLE LEFT THE CHURCH AND JOINED THE CATHARS...

219

VENICE THE MENACE

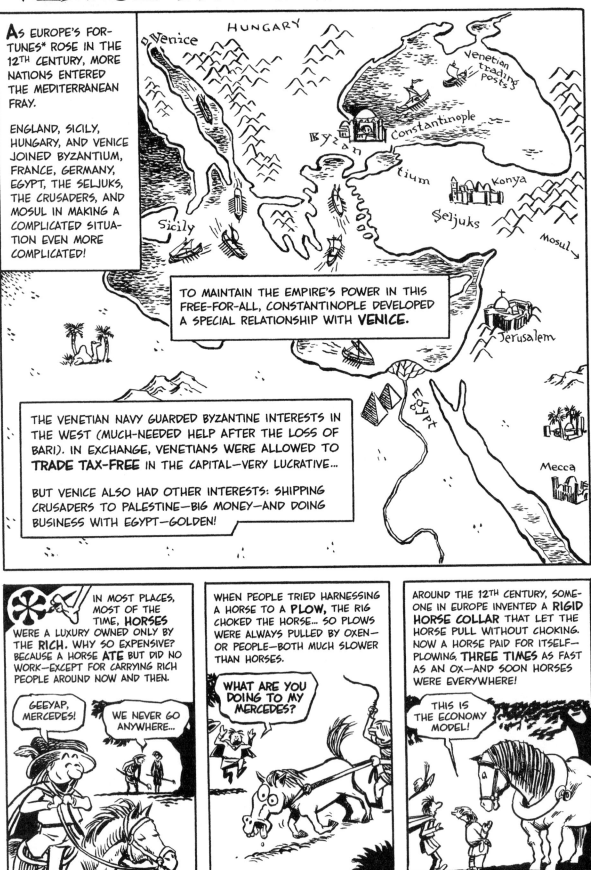

As Europe's For-tunes* rose in the 12th century, more nations entered the Mediterranean fray.

England, Sicily, Hungary, and Venice joined Byzantium, France, Germany, Egypt, the Seljuks, the Crusaders, and Mosul in making a complicated situa-tion even more complicated!

HUNGARY

Venice

Venetian trading posts

Byzantium **Constantinople**

Konya

Seljuks

Sicily

Mosul →

To maintain the empire's power in this free-for-all, Constantinople developed a special relationship with **VENICE.**

Jerusalem

Egypt

The Venetian navy guarded Byzantine interests in the west (much-needed help after the loss of Bari). In exchange, Venetians were allowed to **TRADE TAX-FREE** in the capital—very lucrative...

But Venice also had other interests: shipping crusaders to Palestine—big money—and doing business with Egypt—golden!

Mecca

In most places, most of the time, **HORSES** were a luxury owned only by the **RICH.** Why so expensive? Because a horse **ATE** but did no work—except for carrying rich people around now and then.

GEEYAP, MERCEDES!

WE NEVER GO ANYWHERE...

When people tried harnessing a horse to a **PLOW,** the rig choked the horse... so plows were always pulled by oxen—or people—both much slower than horses.

WHAT ARE YOU DOING TO MY MERCEDES?

Around the 12th century, some-one in Europe invented a **RIGID HORSE COLLAR** that let the horse pull without choking. Now a horse paid for itself—plowing **THREE TIMES** as fast as an ox—and soon horses were everywhere!

THIS IS THE ECONOMY MODEL!

MY BRILLIANT CAREER:

EMPEROR MANUEL HANDLED COMPLEXITY WELL, AT FIRST...

HE BEFRIENDED THE WEST BY MARRYING A CATHOLIC PRINCESS* AND ENCOURAGING WESTERNERS TO LIVE IN CONSTANTINOPLE.

MAYBE THEY'LL LEARN HOW TO BATHE!

STRANGE... YOU GREEKS DON'T SMELL LIKE ANYTHING...

*TWO, ACTUALLY, ONE AFTER THE OTHER.

HE MARCHED A BIG, WELL-TRAINED ARMY TO THE EAST AFTER THE SECOND CRUSADE, LORDED IT OVER THE FRANKS, AND MADE AN ALLIANCE WITH THE ATABEG OF MOSUL IN 1159.

WHO'S BETTER FOR YOU THAN FRANCE?

ARGH... GNASH... YOU ARE...

WITH THAT REGION STABILIZED, HE BROKE HIS TRUCE WITH THE SELJUKS* AND HIT THEM HARD...

GOD, I'M AWESOME!

BY THE 1160s, THE EMPIRE'S MIGHT HAD REACHED A HEIGHT—NOT AN ALL-TIME HEIGHT, MIND YOU... BUT A HEIGHT...

IT'S AMAZING! I CAN DO NO WRONG!

AND THEN CAME AN ASTONISHING FALL...

IN 1162, THE SELJUK SULTAN KILIJ ARSLAN CAME TO CONSTANTINOPLE TO PAY PERSONAL HOMAGE TO MANUEL. THE EMPEROR WOWED HIM WITH SOLID-GOLD PLACE SETTINGS, BUT THE SULTAN SAID HE HAD SOMETHING TO SHOW OFF TOO: A MAN WHO COULD FLY.

PARDON ME? SHALL I KILL MY TRANSLATOR?

YOU HEARD ME.

A HUGE CROWD GATHERED AT THE RACETRACK... THEY SAW A MAN WEARING A COAT WITH **MANY POCKETS** CLIMB A HIGH TOWER.

HE LEAPED—AND MADE A BIG IMPACT ON THE CITY, SAY THE HISTORIANS.

HA HA HA HA HA HA

THESE GREEKS HAVE A STRANGE SENSE OF HUMOR...

AND YOU THOUGHT NOTHING HAPPENED IN THE 1100s?

1174: THE ATABEG OF MOSUL DIES. THE SELJUKS, FREED OF AN EASTERN THREAT, ATTACK THE EMPIRE.

1176: THE TURKS WIPE OUT A BYZANTINE ARMY AT MYRENCEPHALON.

REVENGE!

1171: FEELING STRONG, MANUEL PROVOKES A WAR WITH VENICE (ITS TRADE PRIVILEGES RANKLE!)... PLAGUE RAVAGES THE VENETIAN NAVY, WHICH HAS TO WITHDRAW IN A RAGE.

NO MORE TAX BREAKS? REVENGE!

1180: MANUEL DIES... OUT COME THE EYEBALL KNIVES...

1182: A GREEK ORTHODOX PARTY CHALLENGES MANUEL'S HEIR AND HIS FRANKISH MOTHER. ANTI-WESTERN RIOTERS KILL SOME **10,000 FRANKS** IN CONSTANTINOPLE.

1183: HUNGARY INVADES THE BALKANS.

1185: SICILY INVADES GREECE.

1187: THE EMPRESS PAWNS THE CROWN JEWELS IN VENICE... CONSTANTINOPLE GIVES UP ITS NAVY COMPLETELY. NOW EVERYONE IS ANGRY AT THE EMPIRE, AND THE EMPIRE IS BROKE.

OH, THE PROBLEMS OF A MULTI-POLAR WORLD!

NOW THE SAME YEARS IN THE EAST:

1146: ZENGI DIES, IS SUCCEEDED BY HIS SON **NUR AD-DIN** (JEWEL OF THE FAITH), WHO SPENDS HIS 25 YEARS AS ATABEG WRITING TO MOSQUES, INCITING MUSLIMS AGAINST THE CRUSADERS.

1159: NUR AD-DIN MAKES A PEACE TREATY WITH MANUEL (ALLOWING MANUEL TO ATTACK THE SELJUKS). BUT NUR AD-DIN STILL DREAMS OF OUSTING THE CRUSADERS. HIS STRATEGY: FIRST CONQUER THOSE FATIMID **SHIITES** IN **EGYPT.***

ENTER THE GREATEST HERO OF THE MIDDLE AGES: ME!

1170: THE ATABEG SENDS AN ARMY TO EGYPT BEHIND A TRUSTED LIEUTENANT, YUSUF IBN AYYUB... AFTER AN APPALLING SLAUGHTER OF EGYPT'S BLACK REGIMENTS, YUSUF CONTROLS THE COUNTRY.

1174: NUR AD-DIN DIES. HIS FORMERLY TRUSTWORTHY LIEUTENANT IBN AYYUB DECIDES TO SEIZE THE LEADERSHIP... HE MARCHES OUT OF EGYPT... BEGINS TAKING THE ATABEG'S LANDS... AND GIVES HIMSELF A NEW NAME: **SALADIN,** DEFENDER OF THE FAITH.

1187: WITH EGYPT, IRAQ, SYRIA, AND KURDISTAN BEHIND HIM (SALADIN WAS A KURD), SALADIN MOUNTS AN ALL-OUT OFFENSIVE ON **JERUSALEM.**

THEY'LL NEVER COOPERATE!

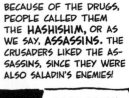

THE FATIMIDS HAD SOME FRIGHTENING FRIENDS: A SMALL SECT OPERATING FROM A CASTLE, THE "EAGLE'S NEST," IN THE MOUNTAINS OF NORTHERN IRAQ.

ITS LEADER, "THE OLD MAN OF THE MOUNTAIN," RECRUITED FOLLOWERS BY DRUGGING YOUNG MEN AND LETTING THEM WAKE IN A BEAUTIFUL GARDEN WITH WOMEN, MUSIC, AND SWEETS. THIS, HE SAID, IS WHAT PARADISE IS LIKE.

WANT MORE?

THEN HE'D SEND THE YOUNG MAN ON A MISSION: SMOKE HASHISH, FIND AN ENEMY IN A CROWD, THEN SIDLE UP AND **STAB** HIM.

BECAUSE OF THE DRUGS, PEOPLE CALLED THEM THE **HASHISHIM,** OR AS WE SAY, **ASSASSINS.** THE CRUSADERS LIKED THE ASSASSINS, SINCE THEY WERE ALSO SALADIN'S ENEMIES!

GOOD STUFF! LET'S GO GET SOME FALAFEL!

THIRD CRUSADE

AS SALADIN'S ARMY APPROACHED, THE KING OF JERUSALEM CALLED FOR ALL THE KNIGHTS IN ALL THE CRUSADER STATES TO TAKE THE FIELD—ABOUT 2,000 IN ALL, PLUS MORE ON FOOT.

IF THE FRANKS HAD ONE MILITARY WEAKNESS (AND THEY DID!), IT WAS THIS: THEY RATED **INDIVIDUAL VALOR** ABOVE **STRATEGY.**

WE'RE OUTNUMBERED LIKE A BILLION TO ONE... SHOULDN'T WE DO SOMETHING CLEVER?

OH, PUH-LEEZE!

CLEVERNESS JUST LOOKS SO **BAD**...

EVEN THE SUGGESTION LOOKS BAD...

SORRY.

DEFYING COMMON SENSE, THEY DASHED AHEAD ONTO SALADIN'S BATTLEFIELD... HIS TROOPS HAD WATER—FROM THE SEA OF GALILEE BEHIND THEM—AND THE FRANKS HAD NONE. ON A BLAZING HOT JULY 4, 1187, BELOW A HILL CALLED THE HORNS OF HATTIN, SALADIN DESTROYED THE CRUSADER ARMY.

ON OCTOBER 2, THE MUSLIMS STORMED JERUSALEM AND MASSACRED NOBODY.

DON'T YOU GET IT? MY RELIGION IS BETTER THAN YOURS!

WHEN THE NEWS REACHED ROME, THE POPE DROPPED DEAD ON THE SPOT.

OH, DEAR... I DIDN'T MEAN TO MAKE HIM DO **THAT**...

FOURTH CRUSADE

WITH JERUSALEM LOST, THE CALL AGAIN WENT OUT... IN 1202, SOME CRUSADING KNIGHTS WENT AHEAD TO **VENICE** TO BUY SHIPS FOR THE ARMY. THEY OPTIMISTICALLY ORDERED ENOUGH TO CARRY 35,000 MEN AND 5,000 HORSES, AT A PRICE OF **84,000** SILVER MARKS TO BE PAID IN ONE YEAR'S TIME.

> WE HAVE FAITH!

THE KNIGHTS THEN LEFT TO RAISE MEN AND MONEY—ONLY TO FIND THAT CRUSADING FEVER HAD FADED BADLY.

> **DEUS LE VOLT,** MEN! MEN?

THEY RETURNED TO VENICE IN 1203, SHORT OF EVERYTHING—BUT THERE WERE THE SHIPS, SHINY NEW!

> OOPS.

> DO YOU KNOW THE OLD VENETIAN SAYING, "A DEAL IS A DEAL"?

WHERE, OH, WHERE, COULD THEY GET THE 84,000? THE DOGE, OR DUKE, OF VENICE HAD AN IDEA: LET HIM, **ENRICO DANDOLO,** TAKE COMMAND, AND **HE** WOULD LEAD THEM TO IT!

> YES, I TOO WILL TAKE THE CROSS...

> AS LONG AS YOU DO WHATEVER I SAY...

AN AMAZING OFFER, CONSIDERING THAT ENRICO DANDOLO WAS STONE BLIND AND AT LEAST 85 YEARS OLD.

> WELL?

> OH, ALL RIGHT...

1202 SAW A MOMENTOUS EVENT OF ANOTHER KIND: THE APPEARANCE OF A NEW **MATH BOOK.** ITS AUTHOR, **LEONARDO OF PISA, "FIBONACCI"** (SON OF BONACCIO), LEARNED MATH IN NORTH AFRICA WHERE HIS FATHER RAN A TRADING HOUSE.

THE BOOK'S TITLE, **LIBER ABACI,** MEANS "BOOK OF THE ABACUS" (THE WAY MOST EUROPEANS CALCULATED THEN), BUT IN FACT IT WAS THE FIRST POPULAR LATIN EXPLANATION OF **ALGORISM** OR CALCULATION WITH ARABIC NUMERALS.

> AMAZING! YOU CAN DO ARITHMETIC WITH A GOOSE QUILL!

EUROPE, NOW EAGER TO ADVANCE, EMBRACED ALGORISM, BUT THE ABACUS STILL HAD ITS DEFENDERS! THE DEBATE BETWEEN **ALGORISTS** AND **ABACISTS** RAGED ON FOR **TWO MORE CENTURIES.**

> ALGORISM IS FOR **CHEATERS!** I CAN TURN A 6 TO A 0 WITH A LITTLE WHITEOUT!

> WHERE WILL THE TEACHERS COME FROM?

> BUT

> BUT

> BUT

> IT'S BAD FOR GEESE!

FIRST DANDOLO LED THEM ACROSS THE ADRIATIC TO ZARA, A TOWN THAT VENICE HAD LATELY LOST.

ANY INFIDELS THERE?

JUST AS BAD: CATHARS!

THE FRANKS STORMED THE WALLS, KILLED A FEW ZARIANS, BUT FAILED TO FIND ENOUGH MONEY TO PAY THE DOGE.

DOESN'T THE TOWN ITSELF COUNT FOR SOMETHING?

NO. READ YOUR CONTRACT...

ONLY **ONE PLACE** HAD THAT KIND OF MONEY, HE SAID, AND THAT PLACE WAS—

VENICE?

BITE YOUR TONGUE!

EGYPT?

WE DON'T DO EGYPT!*

WELL, THEN?

*TRUE. THE TRADE WAS TOO RICH.

SO, IN NOVEMBER, 1203, THE, UM, BLIND VENETIAN BROUGHT THE CRUSADERS UNDER THE FAMOUS WALLS THAT HAD HELD OFF EVERY ASSAULT FOR THE PAST 800 YEARS.

OH, NO-O-O-O...

TO ENCOURAGE THE NERVOUS FRANKS, THE DOGE'S OWN GALLEY RAN AGROUND UNDER THE SEA WALL.

SCRAPE

SCRAPE SCRAPE SCRAPE

HE KNEW THE BYZANTINES HAD LOST THE WILL TO RESIST. WITHIN HOURS, FRANKS AND VENETIANS WERE **INSIDE CONSTANTINOPLE!!**

AT FIRST, THE FRANKS BEHAVED THEMSELVES... THEY "ONLY" DEMANDED THE 84,000 MARKS... BUT AFTER SOME TIME, WHEN NO ONE GAVE IT TO THEM, THEY WENT WILD, BURNING, KILLING, AND RAPING LIKE—WELL, LIKE SOLDIERS SACKING AN ENEMY CITY. THE VENETIANS, WHO KNEW CONSTANTINOPLE BETTER, PILLAGED MORE SELECTIVELY, CAREFULLY PICKING AND PACKING THE BEST TREASURES FOR SHIPMENT HOME TO VENICE, WHERE YOU CAN STILL SEE THEM TODAY.

A FRANK BECAME KING OF CONSTANTINOPLE... VENICE TOOK 3/8 OF THE EMPIRE... AND THE OTHER BARONS DIVIDED UP THE SCRAPS.

SMILE! YOU GOT MORE THAN YOU WANTED!

I AM SMILING.

THE DOGE THANKED THE CRUSADERS FOR A DEBT REPAID, AND THE FOURTH CRUSADE ENDED THEN AND THERE.

SHOULDN'T WE GO ON TO THE HOLY LAND?

ON WHAT?

EVENTUALLY, IN 1260, ONE OF THE OLD GREEK NOBILITY REGAINED CONSTANTINOPLE, BUT THE EMPIRE'S POWER WAS GONE FOREVER.

OH, WELL, IT'S A GRAND TITLE, ANYWAY...

SO THE CRUSADES FAILED TO GAIN THE HOLY LAND, BUT DID SUCCEED IN RUINING THE BYZANTINE EMPIRE.

WELL, AT LEAST WE ACCOMPLISHED **SOMETHING!**

STILL, THE CRUSADING SPIRIT LIVED ON. IN 1210, THE POPE LAUNCHED A NEW ONE— AGAINST THE **CATHARS** OF SOUTHERN FRANCE.

I'LL BE DAMNED IF I LOSE THIS ONE!

THIS CIVIL WAR LASTED TWEN-TY YEARS, UNTIL NO CATHARS REMAINED.

FORTRESS CATHEDRAL

OR DID THEY? THE **LIVING** MIGHT BE THINKING **SECRET THOUGHTS**... HOW CAN YOU **TELL?**

TORTURE... TORTURE IS ALWAYS GOOD...

I MEAN, BAD! IT'S BAD!

IN 1227, THE POPE SET UP THE **INQUISITION,** A PANEL OF JUDGES WHO SNIFFED OUT CRYPTO-CATHARS AND OTHER HERETICS TO BE BURNED AT THE STAKE.

WE DON'T BURN... WE'RE PRIESTS... WE TURN OVER TO THE SECULAR AUTHORITIES, AND THEY BURN.

GOOD TO KNOW.

AS WE MOVE FROM THE 12TH CENTURY TO THE 13TH, WE SEE ANOTHER LEGACY OF THE CRU-SADES: THE CHURCH MEETING **ERROR** WITH **TERROR.**

AFTER THE FOURTH CRUSADE, PEOPLE DISGUS-TEDLY WONDERED IF **GROWN-UPS,** WITH ALL THEIR FLAWS AND NEEDS, COULD EVER BE **GOOD ENOUGH** FOR HOLY WAR. IN 1212, AS IF ON CUE, THE CHILDREN RESPONDED WITH A **CHILDREN'S CRUSADE.**

ONE GROUP OF YOUNGSTERS HIKED FROM GERMANY TO GENOA, WHERE ITALIAN SHIPPERS RE-FUSED TO TAKE THEM ANY FUR-THER. POPE INNOCENT TOLD THE KIDS TO GO HOME.

RATS! DON'T THEY **GET** THAT IT KEEPS US OFF THE STREET?

THE FRENCH GROUP WENT TO MARSEILLE... TWO SHIPOWNERS PACKED THEM INTO SEVEN SHIPS, SENT THEM TO NORTH AFRICA, AND SOLD THEM INTO **SLAVERY.** MOST NEVER RETURNED.

UM... DO YOU THINK WE COULD HAVE BEEN MORE INVOLVED AS PARENTS?

A SABLE COAT

MANY YEARS EARLIER, FAR AWAY IN MON-GOLIA, A PRINCE **YESUGAI** CAPTURED A BRIDE, **OELUN-EKE,** WHO WAS DISLIKED FOR SOME REASON BY YESUGAI'S KINFOLK.

FOUR CHILDREN LATER (TWO BY OELUN-EKE AND TWO BY AN-OTHER), YESUGAI WAS MURDERED.

HIS KINSWOMEN THEN DROVE THE WIDOW AND CHILDREN OUT OF CAMP.

FOR SEVERAL YEARS, THIS LITTLE FAMILY LIVED OFF RODENTS IN THE WILDERNESS.

NOT RAT **AGAIN?**

THE STRAIN TOOK ITS TOLL... ONE OF OELUN-EKE'S BOYS, **TEMUJIN,** MURDERED HIS OWN HALF-BROTHER... HOT-TEMPERED BOY...

HE WOULDN'T **SHARE,** MOMMY!

UM... WELL... JUST DON'T DO IT AGAIN...

A BIT LATER, ON HIS MOTHER'S ADVICE, THIS TEMUJIN WENT TO CLAIM A BRIDE, **BORTE,** WHO HAD BEEN PROMISED TO HIM YEARS EARLIER, WHEN HIS FATHER WAS STILL ALIVE.

WITH BORTE CAME A DOWRY: A VALUABLE SABLE-FUR COAT.

NEXT TEMUJIN WENT TO ANOTH-ER OF HIS FATHER'S FRIENDS AND TRADED THE COAT FOR **FIGHT-ING MEN.**

230

HE AND HIS MEN SERVED ONE LORD AFTER ANOTHER, AT LAST JOINING THE **WANG-KHAN**, ("KING-KING"), MONGOLIA'S GREATEST.

HE'S TOO EFFECTIVE FOR COMFORT...

BUT SOON TEMUJIN PICKED A FIGHT WITH THE WANG-KHAN... ATTACKED THE KHAN'S PEOPLE, THE KERIAT... BEAT THEM... ATTACKED THE TATARS... BEAT THEM... THE NAIMAIN... BEAT THEM...

LET'S SEE... ANYONE LEFT?

IN **1206**, TWO YEARS AFTER THE SACK OF CONSTANTINOPLE, ALL THE MONGOL TRIBES GATHERED TO ACCLAIM TEMUJIN AS THEIR LEADER, WITH THE TITLE **JENGHIS KHAN.***
(THE MONGOLS, LIKE THE CRUSADERS, DID NOT BATHE!)

HEAVEN WILLS IT!! (OR WORDS TO THAT EFFECT)

*NOTE: THE FAMILIAR SPELLING "GENGHIS" DISGUISES THE SOFT INITIAL "G." SOME HISTORIANS EVEN WRITE "CHINGIZ" AS THE BEST RENDERING OF THE MONGOLIAN. WE'LL USE THE "J."

NEXT, FOLLOWING MONGOL TRADITION, THE KHAN'S ARMY BEGAN LOOTING **CHINA**, THE CLOSEST, RICHEST PLACE TO LOOT, WITH SILK BEING THE FAVORITE ITEM.

EVEN THESE GRUBBY LITTLE HUTS HAVE IT!

BUT MOST OF THE BEST LOOT LAY BEHIND **CITY WALLS**, LIKE NOTHING SEEN IN MONGOLIA!

THEY MAKE ME FEEL SO SMALL...

JENGHIS GAVE AN ORDER: CAPTURE CHINESE **MILITARY ENGINEERS** TO TEACH THE MONGOLS HOW TO ATTACK WALLS WITH TOWERS, RAMS, ARTILLERY, TUNNELS, EXPLOSIVES.

FWIP

BOOM

CRUNCH

SUDDENLY I FEEL BIGGER!

DONE—AND IN 1215, THE MONGOLS POUNDED INTO **BEIJING**, THE NORTHERN CAPITAL, AND LOOTED IT THOROUGHLY.

THIS IS MORE LIKE IT!

NEXT JENGHIS ADDRESSED A LINGERING PROBLEM: AN OLD ENEMY, **KUCHLUG** THE NAIMAN, HAD FLED WEST WITH HIS PEOPLE AND SET HIMSELF UP AS A KING.

ARAL SEA

KUCHLUG COUNTRY

LAKE BALKHASH

MONGOLS

KHWARISM

UIGHURS

CHINA

TIBET

INDIA

BY THIS TIME, THE MONGOLS WERE A HIGHLY ORGANIZED, SUPERBLY EQUIPPED, PERFECTLY OBEDIENT ARMY AS NUMEROUS AS BLADES OF GRASS. IN 1218, THEY HEADED WEST.

I HATE TO LEAVE AN ENEMY ALIVE!

THEY MADE SHORT WORK OF KUCHLUG THE NAIMAN AND IN THE PROCESS DOUBLED THE MONGOL DOMAIN!

JENGHIS DECIDED TO INTRODUCE HIMSELF TO HIS NEW NEIGHBORS IN KHWARISM,* SENDING TWO AMBASSADORS AND A HUNDRED MERCHANTS.

TELL HIM YOU COME FROM THE SCARIEST PRINCE IN THE WORLD!

*BIRTHPLACE OF AL-KHWARIZMI, 9TH-CENTURY AUTHOR OF "ALGEBRA."

AT THE BORDER, THE KHWARISMIAN IN CHARGE SEIZED THE GOODS AND HAD EVERYONE MURDERED. **WHAT** WAS HE THINKING?

MY PRINCE IS SCARIER THAN **YOUR** PRINCE!

THE MONGOL ARMY CLIMBED THE MOUNTAINS, TOOK THE TOWN, AND KILLED THE OFFICIAL BY POURING **MOLTEN SILVER** IN HIS EARS.

WAIT! I'M STILL WILLING TO DISCUSS THIS!

JENGHIS THEN LED THE MONGOLS FARTHER WEST, TOWARD KHWARISM AND THE MUSLIM WORLD.

TRULY, IN EVERY GREAT HORDE, SOME GUY GOES LAST.

TRULY.

I SAY! MEN! WAIT UP!

233

BUKHARA, SAMARKAND, BALKH... ONE BY ONE, THE FABLED
CITIES FELL... THE MONGOLS CONQUERED AND SACKED WITH
UNPARALLELED FEROCITY—WHAT USE HAD THEY FOR CITIES
OR CITIZENS? BALKH THEY LEVELED TO THE GROUND (I'VE
SEEN IT!)... THEY KILLED WITHOUT MERCY, TAKING CAPTIVES
ONLY TO SERVE AS **HUMAN SHIELDS,** LEADING THE CHARGE
UP THE LADDERS INTO THE NEXT CITY...

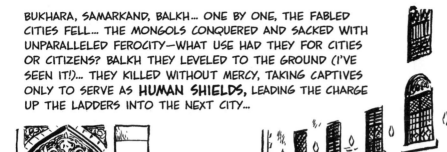

AFTER THE PILLAGE, THE MONGOLS WOULD
ORDER EVERYONE TO GATHER OUTSIDE TOWN,
AND THEN SEPARATE OUT ALL THE **ARTISTS.**

WHAT KIND OF
ART DO YOU DO?

NONE,
YET!

SPARING THE ARTISTS FOR DECORATIVE PUR-
POSES, THEY DIVIDED THE REST INTO GROUPS,
ASSIGNED EACH GROUP TO AN ARMY UNIT, AND
SYSTEMATICALLY BUTCHERED THEM.

BUT I FEEL **EVERYONE**
HAS UNEXPLORED ARTISTIC
POTENTIAL, DON'T YOU?

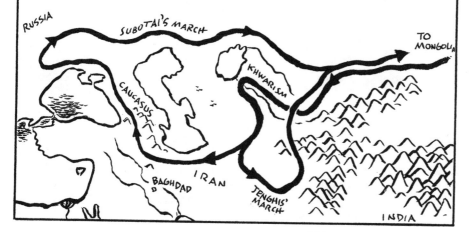

FOR FOUR YEARS, JENGHIS KHAN'S MAIN ARMY GAVE THIS TREATMENT TO THE LAND SOUTH OF KHWARISM, WHILE ANOTHER DIVISION MARCHED ON THROUGH NORTHERN IRAQ, THE CAUCASUS, AND SOUTHERN RUSSIA. IN 1225 THEY REUNITED AND WENT BACK TO MONGOLIA.

AND THIS WAS ONLY THE BEGINNING...

ALMOST AS SOON AS THEY REACHED HOME, JENGHIS SENT HIS WARRIORS AGAINST CHINA AGAIN FOR MORE OF THE SAME. A TOP MONGOL SUGGESTED:

BUT BY NOW THE KHAN HAD SOME MORE SOPHISTICATED AIDES. ONE OF THE UIGHURS POINTED OUT:

THE CHINESE ARE USELESS FOR WAR! WE SHOULD KILL EVERY ONE OF THEM!*

KILL EVERYONE, AND YOU TAKE A MILLION BOLTS OF SILK ALL AT ONCE. LET THE PEOPLE LIVE, AND YOU CAN HAVE **500,000** BOLTS OF SILK **EVERY YEAR.**

JENGHIS KHAN LIKED THE SECOND IDEA AND SHIFTED HIS POLICY FROM SIMPLE WRECKING TO CONQUER-ING AND GOVERNING.

TAXATION... INTERESTING CONCEPT...

THE LESSON OF A LIFETIME!

AND THEN, IN 1227, HE DIED, LEAVING BEHIND AN ARMY, A BODY OF LAW (WRITTEN DOWN BY THE UIGHUR), IMMENSE WRECKAGE, AND AN OPPORTUNITY FOR HIS SONS. THEY THANKED HIM BY "SENDING FORTY MAIDENS TO JENGHIS."

AND ALL I GOT OUT OF THE DEAL WAS THIS FUR COAT...

WHY DID JENGHIS'S MONGOLS WRECK SO THOROUGHLY? SOME HISTORIANS SAY THAT THE NOMADIC MONGOLS HAD NO APPRECIATION OF CIVILIZA-TION AND WANTED **OPEN RANGELAND** EVERYWHERE FOR THEIR PONIES.

"THEY BURN AND SLAY NOT SO MUCH FROM CRUELTY AS FROM PERPLEXITY, AND BECAUSE THEY KNOW OF NOTHING BETTER TO DO."
—GROUSSET

OTHER STRESS THEIR **MILITARY CALCULATION.** THE MONGOLS WERE FAR FROM HOME AND WANTED TO LEAVE NO ENEMIES IN THEIR REAR.

A **PSYCHOLOGICAL** INTERPRE-TATION MIGHT ALSO MAKE SENSE, BASED ON TEMUJIN'S HARSH CHILDHOOD WITH A DISRESPEC-TED MOTHER.

"I ENJOY NOTHING SO MUCH AS HEARING THE GROANS OF THE DYING, THE WEEPING OF WOMEN..."

UM... HOW LONG HAVE YOU FELT THIS WAY?

THE NEW KHAN, JENGHIS'S SON OGODAI, RESUMED THE RAMPAGE, SENDING ONE ARMY WESTWARD TO RUSSIA, POLAND, AND HUNGARY... ANOTHER BACK TO IRAN... AND TWO MORE TO SQUEEZE CHINA AND OCCUPY KOREA.

RELIEF CAME IN 1241, WHEN OGODAI DIED, AND THE COMMANDERS RUSHED BACK TO MONGOLIA TO ELECT HIS HEIR.

FOR ALMOST A DECADE, THE WORLD WAITED FOR THE MONGOLS TO SORT THINGS OUT... AT LAST, IN 1251, A SHREWD WOMAN, JENGHIS'S DAUGHTER-IN-LAW SORGHAQ-TANI, A CHRISTIAN* NIECE OF THE OLD WANG-KHAN, STEERED HER SON **MONGKA** ONTO THE THRONE.

FROM AS FAR AWAY AS PARIS AND ROME, AMBASSADORS CAME TO CONGRATULATE MONGKA, AND TO MAKE A SPECIAL REQUEST.

HELP!

EUROPE, IN ITS DARK-AGE ISO-LATION, HAD A VAGUE IDEA THAT SOMEWHERE A CHRISTIAN WIZARD NAMED **PRESTER JOHN** RULED A RICH AND DISTANT KINGDOM... AND WHEN EUROPEANS REACHED MONGOLIA, THEY SAW THE TRUTH.

IN FACT, CHRISTIANITY HAD SPREAD FAR INTO ASIA. **NESTORIAN** MIS-SIONARIES—FROM A SYRIAN CHURCH CONSIDERED HERETICAL IN THE WEST—MADE MANY CONVERTS IN MONGOLIA, WHERE SEVERAL KHANS HAD NAMES LIKE GEORGE AND MARK (BUT NO JOHN).

AND THE RICHES?

YOU'RE LOOKING AT THEM.

SO—NOT SO ODD THAT THE KHAN'S MOTHER WAS CHRISTIAN. MONGKA'S OWN BELIEF WAS THIS:

THE RELIGIONS ARE LIKE THE FINGERS OF A SINGLE HAND— BUT **BUDDHISM** IS THE PALM!

UM... WHICH FINGER AM I?

HULAGU

BY THIS TIME, REMEMBER, THE CRUSADERS HAD LOST ALL BUT A FEW SYRIAN COASTAL TOWNS. THEY FELT THREATENED, VULNERABLE, NEEDY.

DO THEY NEED AN ARMY OR A THERAPIST?

THE WESTERN AMBASSADORS BEGGED MONGKA KHAN TO HELP... TO SMASH THE STILL-UNCONQUERED MUSLIM POWERS IN **BAGHDAD** AND **CAIRO,** THE ENEMIES OF FRANK AND MONGOL ALIKE.

THESE PEOPLE, YOUR HIGHNESS— THEY BATHE!

AND MONGKA AGREED. IN 1253, HE SENT HIS BROTHER **HULAGU** WITH A HORDE AIMED AT BAGHDAD.

TEACH THESE PEOPLE SOMETHING ABOUT WATER CONSERVATION...

(ALONG THE WAY, THE MONGOLS DID THE IMPOSSIBLE AND STORMED THE **ASSASSINS'** LAIR, PUTTING AN END TO THE SECT.)

OHH, WOWWW...

THEN ON TO BAGHDAD, WHERE THE CALIPH— THE **LAST** CALIPH—RAILED AT THEM UNTIL THE END, WHICH CAME IN 1258 WHEN HULAGU ENTERED BAGHDAD.

TO THE MONGOLS, SHEDDING ROYAL BLOOD WAS A SIGN OF DISRESPECT.

SO YOU WON'T KILL ME?

I DIDN'T SAY THAT...

SO THEY ROLLED UP THE CALIPH IN A RUG AND TRAMPLED HIM TO DEATH... AND SINCE THAT DAY, MAINSTREAM ISLAM HAS HAD NO SINGLE LEADER.

THEN ON TO **SYRIA**, AS THE CRUSADERS CHEERED—RATHER HALFHEARTEDLY, ONCE THEY ACTUALLY MET THEIR RESCUERS!

HIP, HIP—HELLO?

POISED TO ATTACK EGYPT, HULAGU SUDDENLY HAD **BAD NEWS:** HIS BROTHER MONGKA WAS DEAD... HULAGU HAD TO HURRY HOME TO HELP ELECT A NEW GRAND KHAN... SO, LEAVING SOME SOLDIERS BEHIND, HE DEPARTED.

REMEMBER: DEFEAT IS NOT AN OPTION!

THIS LITTLE HORDE FELL TO THE EGYPTIANS, WHO TURNED OUT IN FORCE IN 1260.

HULAGU, WHERE ARE YOOUUU?

AFTER ROUTING THE MONGOLS, THE EGYPTIANS CHASED THE LAST CRUSADERS OUT OF THEIR COASTAL FORTS.

THIS MARKED THE END OF THE CRUSADER STATES AND THE LIMIT OF MONGOL EXPANSION IN THE WEST.

HULAGUUUU...

KUBLAI

MEANWHILE, MONGKA'S OTHER BROTHER **KUBLAI** HAD INVADED SOUTHERN CHINA, BEYOND THE YANGTZE RIVER, A RICH COUNTRY DEFENDED BY THE WORLD'S MOST ADVANCED **MILITARY TECHNOLOGY**, LIKE THESE PADDLE-WHEEL RIVER CRAFT.

BELOWDECKS, ALL WAS LOW-TECH: MANY FEET POWERED THOSE PADDLES!

ABOVE DECKS WAS HIGHER-TECH: THE CHINESE HAD **CANNON**.

IT LOOKED TO BE A LONG WAR...

WE HAVE **GOT** TO GET HOLD OF THOSE THINGS...

WHEN MONGKA DIED IN 1259, KUBLAI ALSO WENT HOME FOR THE ELECTION, AND A GOOD THING FOR HIM: HE **WON** IT—AND SENT HULAGU BACK TO THE WEST.

YOU GO, 'GU!

WHY DID I EVEN BOTHER COMING HOME...? HISTORY MIGHT HAVE TURNED OUT DIFFERENTLY IF I'D STAYED IN SYRIA...

THIS EXPLAINS WHY THE MONGOLS EXPANDED NO FARTHER WEST: AS GRAND KHAN, KUBLAI WANTED TO CONCENTRATE ON THE RICHES CLOSER TO HAND.

AND WHERE IN MONGOLIA WILL YOUR HIGHNESS BE PITCHING YOUR DRAFTY, FLEA-INFESTED TENT?

KUBLAI GAVE UP HIS TENT IN MONGOLIA FOR A PALACE IN BEIJING AND ALL THE TRAPPINGS OF A **CHINESE EMPEROR.** HE RESTARTED THE WAR IN THE SOUTH—THE FIRST IN HISTORY WITH GUNS ON BOTH SIDES. IT LASTED ANOTHER 18 YEARS... MILLIONS DIED... AND IN THE END, KUBLAI RULED ALL CHINA, PLUS THE REST OF THE MONGOLS' VAST DOMAINS: THE BIGGEST EMPIRE IN HISTORY.

GRAMPA JENGHIS ALWAYS SAID WE'D GO SOFT, AND I SAY, IT'S ABOUT TIME!

THE MONGOLS TRIED TWICE TO INVADE **JAPAN,** BUT SEA TRAVEL DISAGREED WITH THESE HORSEMEN.

BJORK BJORK BJORK

THE JAPANESE ORGANIZED THEIR DEFENSES WELL, AND BOTH TIMES DEFEATED THE INVADERS—WITH A LITTLE HELP FROM THE WEATHER.

BUT THE EFFORT BANKRUPTED THE JAPANESE COURT. THE EMPEROR LOST POWER... WAR-LORDS BICKERED... FINALLY THE MOST POWERFUL ONE TOOK CON-TROL... NOW THIS **SHOGUN** AND HIS **SAMURAI,** OR HIRED SWORDS, HELD POWER BY **FORCE,** RATHER THAN THE SMOOTH DIPLOMACY OF EARLIER YEARS.

EXCUSE ME!

HOW DID CHINA FARE UNDER THE MONGOLS? IT DEPENDS ON WHOM YOU ASKED... IT SIMPLY **AMAZED** FOREIGN MERCHANTS LIKE **MARCO POLO,** * A VENETIAN WHO LIVED IN CHINA FOR NEARLY 20 YEARS. POLO SAW HEAVY TRAFFIC, ALL SORTS OF MERCHANDISE, PAPER MONEY, A FAST POSTAL SERVICE... IN SHORT, A MONEYMAKING MACHINE! THE **CHINESE,** ON THE OTHER HAND, SAW BARBARIAN OVERLORDS, RACE DISCRIMINATION, RISING PRICES, FOREIGNERS MAKING OFF WITH THE NATION'S WEALTH... AND THEY REMEMBERED HOW MANY CHINESE HAD DIED IN THE WARS.

THE DUCK NOODLES ARE SUPERB!

MY BACK IS KILLING ME...

MARCO POLO DESCRIBES AN UNUSUALLY FRIENDLY TRADING POST SOMEWHERE IN CENTRAL ASIA, WHERE LOCAL FAMILIES WELCOMED MERCHANTS INTO THEIR HOMES—IN FACT, INTO THEIR BEDS!

THIS **IS** THE GUEST ROOM!

IN EXCHANGE, THE MERCHANT WAS EXPECTED TO GIVE HIS HOSTS A NICE PIECE OF CLOTH OR OTHER TRINKET.

AT VISIT'S END, SAYS POLO, THE FAMILY WOULD HANG THE CLOTH OUT THE WINDOW AND TAUNT THE DEPARTING MERCHANT LIKE SO:

HA! **WE** GOT THIS NICE PIECE OF CLOTH! WHAT DID **YOU** GET THAT YOU CAN TAKE WITH YOU?

MEMORIES AND LICE?

CHINESE SCHOLARS, DENIED POSITIONS AT
COURT, SPENT A LOT OF TIME CONTEMPLATING
NATURE DURING THE MONGOL YEARS.

PAX MONGOLICA (MONGOLIAN PEACE)

AS THE LATE 1200s PASS INTO THE 13s, WE SEE MOST OF EURASIA AT PEACE, MOST OF THE TIME, WITH THE MONGOLS IN CHARGE OF MOST OF THE CONTINENT. HERE ARE SOME MINI-HISTORIES:

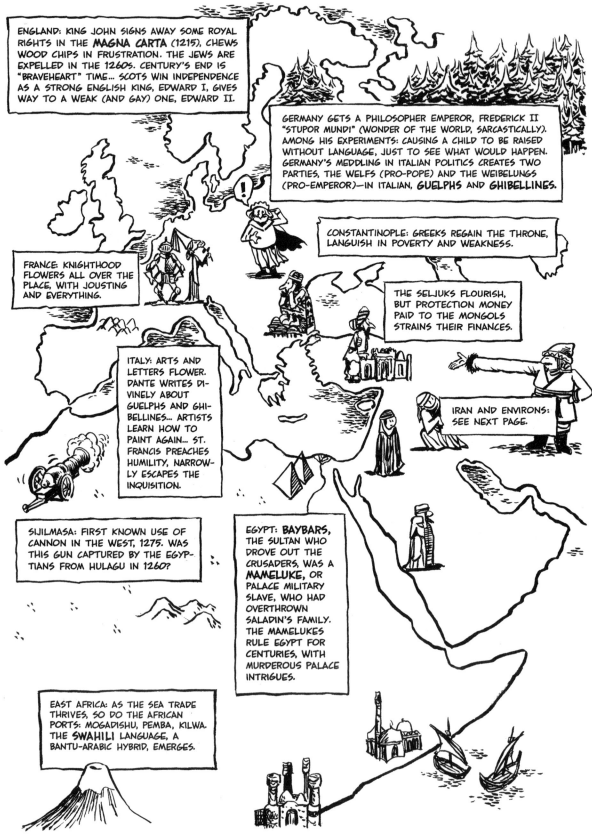

ENGLAND: KING JOHN SIGNS AWAY SOME ROYAL RIGHTS IN THE **MAGNA CARTA** (1215), CHEWS WOOD CHIPS IN FRUSTRATION. THE JEWS ARE EXPELLED IN THE 1260s. CENTURY'S END IS "BRAVEHEART" TIME... SCOTS WIN INDEPENDENCE AS A STRONG ENGLISH KING, EDWARD I, GIVES WAY TO A WEAK (AND GAY) ONE, EDWARD II.

GERMANY GETS A PHILOSOPHER EMPEROR, FREDERICK II "STUPOR MUNDI" (WONDER OF THE WORLD, SARCASTICALLY). AMONG HIS EXPERIMENTS: CAUSING A CHILD TO BE RAISED WITHOUT LANGUAGE, JUST TO SEE WHAT WOULD HAPPEN. GERMANY'S MEDDLING IN ITALIAN POLITICS CREATES TWO PARTIES, THE WELFS (PRO-POPE) AND THE WEIBELUNGS (PRO-EMPEROR)—IN ITALIAN, **GUELPHS** AND **GHIBELLINES**.

CONSTANTINOPLE: GREEKS REGAIN THE THRONE, LANGUISH IN POVERTY AND WEAKNESS.

FRANCE: KNIGHTHOOD FLOWERS ALL OVER THE PLACE, WITH JOUSTING AND EVERYTHING.

THE SELJUKS FLOURISH, BUT PROTECTION MONEY PAID TO THE MONGOLS STRAINS THEIR FINANCES.

ITALY: ARTS AND LETTERS FLOWER. DANTE WRITES DIVINELY ABOUT GUELPHS AND GHIBELLINES... ARTISTS LEARN HOW TO PAINT AGAIN... ST. FRANCIS PREACHES HUMILITY, NARROWLY ESCAPES THE INQUISITION.

IRAN AND ENVIRONS: SEE NEXT PAGE.

SIJILMASA: FIRST KNOWN USE OF CANNON IN THE WEST, 1275. WAS THIS GUN CAPTURED BY THE EGYPTIANS FROM HULAGU IN 1260?

EGYPT: **BAYBARS**, THE SULTAN WHO DROVE OUT THE CRUSADERS, WAS A **MAMELUKE**, OR PALACE MILITARY SLAVE, WHO HAD OVERTHROWN SALADIN'S FAMILY. THE MAMELUKES RULE EGYPT FOR CENTURIES, WITH MURDEROUS PALACE INTRIGUES.

EAST AFRICA: AS THE SEA TRADE THRIVES, SO DO THE AFRICAN PORTS: MOGADISHU, PEMBA, KILWA. THE **SWAHILI** LANGUAGE, A BANTU-ARABIC HYBRID, EMERGES.

BY NOW, THE MONGOLS HAD COME TO APPRECIATE SOME OF CIVILIZATION'S BETTER POINTS, SUCH AS TECHNOLOGY AND VEGETABLES... DURING THESE PEACEFUL YEARS, PLENTY OF BOTH PASSED BETWEEN ASIA AND EUROPE: PAPER, CLOCKS, GUNPOWDER AND CANNON, THE SHIP'S COMPASS AND RUDDER ALL WENT WEST... ALSO: PEACHES, ROSES, ORANGES, NUTMEG, CINNAMON, GINGER, ETC.

A NUMBER OF EUROPEANS WENT TO CHINA, THOUGH ONLY MARCO POLO CAME BACK TO DO A BOOK. ISLAM ALSO HAD ITS GREAT TRAVEL WRITER, THE NORTH AFRICAN **IBN BATTUTA**, WHO VISITED AFRICA (EAST AND WEST), ARABIA, INDIA,* SOUTHEAST ASIA, AND (MAYBE) CHINA. READ HIM!

IN THE NORTHERN STEPPE, THE MONGOLS MERGE WITH MANY OTHER TRIBES AND KEEP UP THE NOMAD TRADITIONS AS THE GOLDEN HORDE.

IRAN & ENVIRONS: WE SAW KUBLAI SEND HULAGU BACK TO THE WEST. AS "IL-KHAN" OF PERSIA, HULAGU FAVORS CHRISTIANS OVER MUSLIMS, BUT NEVER AGAIN ATTACKS EGYPT OR HELPS THE CRUSADERS. HIS OFFSPRING, INTERMARRYING WITH TURKS AND PERSIANS, EVENTUALLY CONVERT TO ISLAM.

CHINA KNOWS THE MONGOLS AS THE **YUAN DYNASTY**, BUT NEVER STOPS THINKING OF THEM AS FOREIGN.

INDIA: AFGHAN ADVENTURERS, FLEEING THE MONGOLS, FORM A SULTANATE IN DELHI.

MALDIVE ISLANDS

THE SULTAN OF DELHI MADE **IBN BATTUTA** A JUDGE IN THE MALDIVE ISLANDS, WHERE, THE TRAVELER COMPLAINED, THE ISLAM WAS DISAPPOINTINGLY LAX. "THE FIRST TIME I SENTENCED A THIEF TO HAVE HIS HAND CUT OFF," WROTE IBN BATTUTA, "PEOPLE FAINTED IN THE COURTROOM."

TSK! SOFT, SOFT, SOFT!

GOLDEN OPPORTUNITY

AT THE SAME TIME, THE HEMISPHERE'S **SECOND**-BIGGEST EMPIRE WAS IN WEST AFRICA. IN THE MID-1200S, A MUSLIM PEOPLE, THE **MALINKE**, HAD CONQUERED A WIDE KINGDOM CENTERED ON THE NIGER RIVER: **MALI**. THIS WAS GOLD COUNTRY, REMEMBER!

YOU HAVE TO BE STRONG JUST TO **WEAR** ALL THIS STUFF!

AT FIRST, MALI'S GREAT FOUNDER **SUNDIATTA** (REIGNED UNTIL 1250) AND HIS SUCCESSORS PILED UP THE GOLD... THEN HIS NEPHEW **MANSA MUSA** (KING MOSES) BEGAN TO SPEND IT...

IN 1324, MANSA MUSA SET OFF ON HIS PILGRIMAGE TO MECCA... THIS INVOLVED A TREK ACROSS THE SAHARA IN ROYAL STYLE, WITH THOUSANDS OF PEOPLE, COUNTLESS CAMELS, ENDLESS BAGGAGE, MANY BAGFULS OF WATER, AND PLENTY OF GOLD... ALMOST INCONCEIVABLE!!

IN EGYPT, MEANWHILE, A FEW PEOPLE SUDDENLY FOUND THEMSELVES VERY RICH.

I DON'T KNOW HOW... IT JUST HAPPENED!!

THEY BID UP THE PRICE OF EVERYTHING...

20,000 DINARS FOR THE HOUSE!

30,000!

40,000!

AT LEAST, THEY DID IF IT WAS ANYTHING LIKE SAN FRANCISCO IN THE LATE 1990s...

POOR, OR EVEN ORDINARY, EGYPTIANS WERE IN SHOCK AND OUT OF A HOME...

WELL, IF YOU CAN'T AFFORD CAIRO, TRY THE SUBURBS.

INFLATION PLAGUED EGYPT FOR A DECADE AFTER THE MALIANS' VISIT.

THOSE ARE THE KIDS. I CAN ONLY AFFORD CLOTHES FOR ONE OF US...

AS WE'VE MENTIONED BEFORE, MANY **ITALIANS** WERE DOING BUSINESS IN EGYPT, WHO WERE ENTIRELY HAPPY TO SELL THEIR WARES AT THE NEW, HIGH EGYPTIAN PRICES!

GLASS

EROTICA (ITALIAN)

EROTICA (FRENCH)

SO LOADS OF MANSA MUSA'S GOLD PASSED INTO ITALIAN HANDS...

JUST THE ONE BAG?

FROM EGYPT, THE GOLD TRAVELED TO PARTNERS AND BANKERS IN ITALY...

WHERE IT WAS ABOUT TO PAY FOR THE ART AND LUXURIES OF THE **ITALIAN RENAISSANCE**— BUT NOT BEFORE A CERTAIN **MAJOR PROBLEM** WAS OVERCOME!

NEXT:

PLAGUE

THE CARTOON HISTORY OF THE UNIVERSE

Volume 19

THE PEST AND THE WEST

BY 1330, LEARNING HAD REVIVED IN WESTERN EUROPE... UNIVERSITIES HAD OPENED... WEALTH AND COMMERCE HAD GROWN... NEW TECHNOLOGY AND IDEAS HAD ARRIVED FROM THE EAST: PRINTED BOOKS, ARABIC NUMERALS, FIREARMS, AND CLOCKS... AND YET, DESPITE THE CLOCKS, EUROPE'S TIME HAD NOT YET COME.

THE REASON WAS A **PLAGUE** THAT RAVAGED THREE CONTINENTS... WE CAN BARELY IMAGINE IT TODAY... WE THINK OF PLAGUE AS MERELY AN ILLNESS, BUT PLAGUES CAN **CHANGE HISTORY...** THIS ONE DID: IT DELAYED EUROPE'S RENAISSANCE FOR A CENTURY... OUSTED THE MONGOLS FROM CHINA... HELPED THE TURKS ENTER EUROPE... AND SO PUSHED EUROPEAN EXPANSION WESTWARD.

AROUND 1300, GLOBAL CLIMATE BEGAN A CENTURY-LONG COOLING TREND, THE "LITTLE ICE AGE." WINTERS GREW HARSHER AND LONGER... ANIMALS MIGRATED, JUST AS THEY'RE DOING TODAY. NOW, AS CLIMATE IS WARMING, THEY MOVE UPHILL AND POLEWARD... THEN, IN THE LITTLE ICE AGE, THEY SCURRIED OUT OF THE NORTH AND DOWN FROM THE HILLS, INTO MORE **CIVILIZED ENVIRONMENTS.**

SOMETIME IN THE 14TH CENTURY, A DANISH BISHOP LOOKED THROUGH HIS FILES, FOUND OLD LETTERS FROM **GREENLAND,** AND WONDERED WHAT HAD HAPPENED TO THE OLD NORSE COLONY.

IN FACT, THE HARD WINTERS OF THE LITTLE ICE AGE DOOMED THE NORSE SETTLEMENT. VIKINGS AND LIVESTOCK GRADUALLY STARVED AND FROZE, UNTIL THE LAST ONES WERE FINISHED OFF IN A FIGHT WITH THEIR INUIT NEIGHBORS.

WHY DID THE NORSE PERISH AND THE INUIT SURVIVE? BECAUSE THE VIKINGS KNEW ONLY **ONE WAY TO LIVE**—CATTLE RAISING—AND WERE TOO BUSY OR TOO RIGID TO TAKE UP THE **KAYAKING** AND **SEAL-HUNTING** THAT SAW THE INUIT THROUGH THE COLD.

LAST WE'LL SEE OF THEM, I RECKON!

THE MONGOLS COUGH IT UP!

SOME OF THESE RODENTS CARRIED CERTAIN **BACTERIA** IN THEIR BLOOD... LICE AND FLEAS BIT RATS AND ATE THE STUFF... WHEN RATS MOVED INTO WARM, SNUG KITCHENS, THE INSECTS JUMPED OFF AND BIT PEOPLE... AND SO BEGAN THE **BLACK DEATH.** TODAY A **COUGH,** TOMORROW A **CORPSE.**

IT STRUCK IN THE 1330S, FIRST IN INDIA, THEN IN CHINA. MILLIONS DIED QUICKLY.*

PLAGUE KILLS **UNEVENLY.** IT MAY SPARE ONE VILLAGE AND WIPE OUT ANOTHER... SPARE ONE FAMILY AND KILL ANOTHER... SPARE THE BAD AND KILL THE GOOD. TO THE SURVIVORS, PLAGUE MAKES **NO SENSE!**

WHEN A FAMILY DIES OUT, IT LEAVES NO ONE TO INHERIT ITS GOODS... SURVIVORS JUST GRAB THE STUFF... SO PLAGUE CAN **ENRICH** PEOPLE TOO!

I'M SO CONFUSED, I THINK THIS STUFF IS MINE!

A GERM NEEDS A **LIVING HOST** IN ORDER TO SURVIVE, SO GERMS DON'T "LIKE" IT WHEN A INFECTED PERSON DIES. IT'S NOT GOOD TO BE TOO DEADLY!

☆@#!

IN A PLAGUE'S EARLY STAGES, THE MOST SUSCEPTIBLE PEOPLE AND THE DEADLIEST BACTERIA DIE OUT TOGETHER, SO SURVIVING PEOPLE ARE **MORE RESISTANT** AND SURVIVING GERMS ARE **LESS DEADLY.** THIS IS WHY LATER STAGES OF PLAGUE ARE LESS HARSH.

BETTER!

DEADLINESS IS ALSO AFFECTED BY HOW EASILY GERMS CAN TRAVEL FROM A DEAD HOST TO A LIVING ONE. IF SANITATION IS GOOD, AND CORPSES ARE DISPOSED OF, THE DEADLIEST GERMS HAVE LESS OPPORTUNITY TO ESCAPE TO A NEW HOST, AND SO DIE OUT. IN OTHER WORDS, **PUBLIC SANITATION BREEDS MILDER DISEASES.**

A SEWER IS AS GOOD AS A DOCTOR!

IN TIME OF PLAGUE, TEMPERS RISE.

HEY! I WAS GONNA TAKE THAT!

ME!

HERE NOW... STOP THAT!

WHILE SOME PEOPLE TREMBLE IN FEAR, OTHERS ARE FEARLESS... THEY LIVE FOR THE MOMENT... SOCIAL ORDER BREAKS DOWN...

WHY FIGHT **EACH OTHER?** LET'S KILL THE **MONGOL!**

AS PLAGUE FLARED IN CHINA, SO DID REVOLT.

EVEN MONGOLS AREN'T AS SCARY AS THE PLAGUE!

FINALLY, AROUND 1360, THE MONGOLS QUIT THE COUNTRY FOR GOOD.

FROM TENT TO PALACE TO TENT IN THREE GENERATIONS!

THE REBEL ARMY WAS LED BY AN ILLITERATE PEASANT BANDIT, **ZHU YUAN-ZHANG**, KNOWN FOR HIS PIGLIKE FACE AND POLITICAL SKILLS. ZHU FOUNDED A DURABLE DYNASTY, THE **MING**—MEANING "BRIGHT"—A WORD CHOSEN TO GLOSS OVER THE FOUNDER'S FAMILY BACKGROUND.

FORWARD, MEN!

RIGHT... JUST GIVE US A LITTLE DISTANCE...

WOULD YOU LIKE A COVERED CARRIAGE?

EVENTUALLY, THE PLAGUE LET UP... BIRTHS AGAIN OUTNUMBERED DEATHS... AND A NEW EMPEROR SAW A UNIQUE **FUND-RAISING** OPPORTUNITY.

THE EMPEROR OWNED A VAST TRACT OF LAND, OVER A THOUSAND SQUARE MILES, WHICH THE MONGOLS HAD "EMPTIED" TO MAKE A **HUNTING PARK** FOR THE KHAN.

THE BRILLIANT IDEA WAS TO SELL IT OFF IN SMALL LOTS TO FARMERS.

UM... ANYTHING WE SHOULD KNOW ABOUT?

ALL SALES "AS IS"!

THIS PLAN PROVIDED LAND FOR CHINA'S GROWING POPULATION AS WELL AS A STEADY STREAM OF CASH FOR THE EMPEROR.

REALLY BRILLIANT!

MONEY FLOWED IN FAST... HE HARDLY KNEW HOW TO SPEND IT... THE PALACE MUST HAVE BUZZED WITH SCHEMES.

IMPERIAL RESTAURANT CHAIN

WORLD LARGEST SCULPTURE OF A BOUND FOOT

FLYING MACHINES

LACQUER EVERY TREE IN THE EMPIRE

A EUNUCH, ZHENG-HE,* SUGGESTED BUILDING **SHIPS**—TO BE PRECISE, A GIANT FLOTILLA OF GIANT SHIPS THAT WOULD SPREAD CHINESE INFLUENCE AROUND THE WORLD.

WAIT! HAVE WE CONSIDERED MAKING ATHLETIC FOOTWEAR?

*ALSO SOMETIMES WRITTEN CHENG-HO.

THE EMPEROR SAID YES—AND IT WAS DONE!! ON A HUGE SCALE, TOO... WHEN THE FLEET FIRST SAILED IN 1405, WITH ZHENG-HE IN COMMAND, IT CARRIED **70,000 MEN.**

WHAT ARE **YOU** DOING **HERE?**

I'M TOO TALL FOR THE OTHER PANEL...

FOR THE NEXT 28 YEARS, THE NEUTERED ADMIRAL LED **SEVEN VOYAGES** TO SOUTHEAST ASIA, THE ISLANDS, INDIA, AND EAST AFRICA, ORDERING EVERYONE TO SUBMIT TO CHINA.

HE'S GOT A LOT OF—

NERVE! A LOT OF NERVE!

AND HE BROUGHT BACK SOME AMAZING STUFF!

A GIFT FROM SOMEPLACE COMPLETELY UNPRONOUNCEABLE!

WHEREVER IT WENT, THE FLEET LEFT A COLONY OF CHINESE TRADERS AND AGENTS.

SOME OF THESE COLONIES DID VERY WELL INDEED!

WAIT! WE'RE GETTING AHEAD OF OURSELVES!

MEANWHILE, BACK IN CHINA, THE LAST OF THE "MONGOL LOTS" WAS SOLD, ENDING THIS SOURCE OF IMPERIAL FUNDS.

SIGH... THERE GOES MY RETURN TICKET...

THE EMPEROR HAD TO FACE IT: THESE NAVAL JAUNTS COST FAR MORE THAN THEY EARNED!

SO WHAT SHOULD WE DO?

ARREST THE ADMIRAL!

SO AT LAST, WHEN THE NAVY CAME HOME AFTER THE 1433 EXPEDITION, TIMES HAD CHANGED IN THE CAPITAL.

WHAT? WHAT?

A NEW EMPEROR QUESTIONED WHY THE BUSINESS HADN'T MADE ENOUGH MONEY BY NOW TO **PAY FOR ITSELF?** WHERE WAS THE **PROFIT?**

WELL?

HASN'T THE SON OF HEAVEN EVER HEARD OF GOVERNMENT SUBSIDIES TO PRIVATE ENTERPRISE?

A CIVIL-SERVANT CHORUS CHIMED IN.

JUST LOOK AT THE INTERNET...

THE GENTLEMAN'S PROGRAM FLIRTS WITH FOREIGNERS AND DEPARTS FROM ANCIENT CUSTOM!

DEPARTING AND FLIRTING HARM THE EMPEROR!

THE ARGUMENT, AS ARGUMENTS WILL, GREW MORE EXTREME THAN NECESSARY.

HARMING THE EMPEROR DESERVES DEATH!

NO FOREIGNERS! NO FOREIGNERS!

OLD WAYS! OLD WAYS!

THE EMPEROR CANCELED THE PROJECT, AND CHINA ENDED ITS EXPERIMENT IN WORLD DOMINATION JUST AS **SPAIN** AND **PORTUGAL** WERE ABOUT TO BEGIN THEIRS.

WHAT GOOD ARE FOREIGNERS, ANYWAY?

THE MING DYNASTY TURNED INWARD AND CONSERVATIVE... AND TODAY SCHOLARS DEBATE WHY CHINA FAILED TO INDUSTRIALIZE AND DOMINATE THE WORLD.

WE LIKE THINGS FINE AS THEY **ARE**, THANK YOU!

THE OVERSEAS CHINESE STILL REVERE ZHENG-HE AS A SORT OF **ANCESTRAL SPIRIT!**

NOT A **REAL** ANCESTOR, MIND YOU!

COULDN'T HAVE BEEN THAT...

An OTTOMAN IS NO FOOTSTOOL!

MEANWHILE, FAR TO THE WEST, THE **GOLDEN HORDE** WAS AT WAR WITH THE **ITALIANS** WHO TRADED AMONG THEM... THE KHAN TOOK HIS HORDE ON THE OFFENSIVE... THE VENETIANS, GENOESE, AND PISANS TOOK REFUGE IN **KAFFA**, GENOA'S PORT ON THE CRIMEAN COAST... THE HORDE BESIEGED THE CITY... AND THEN, IN 1346, **PLAGUE** BROKE OUT IN THE MONGOL CAMP.

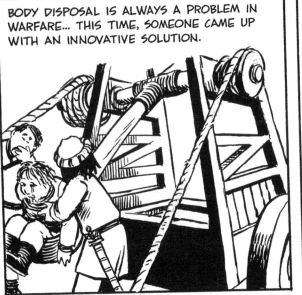

BODY DISPOSAL IS ALWAYS A PROBLEM IN WARFARE... THIS TIME, SOMEONE CAME UP WITH AN INNOVATIVE SOLUTION.

THEY FLUNG THE PLAGUE-RIDDEN CORPSES INTO THE CITY WITH CATAPULTS.

SPROING

THE ITALIANS ARRIVED TOWARD THE END OF A BYZANTINE **CIVIL WAR,** AS A REBELLIOUS GENERAL FOUGHT AN EMPRESS OVER THE EMPIRE'S PATHETIC REMNANTS.

WITH A LITTLE HELP FROM **US,** THANK YOU!

IN THE COURSE OF THIS WAR, ARMED GROUPS OF **TURKS** HAD CROSSED OVER FROM ASIA TO EUROPE—INVITED BY THE GREEK GENERAL, WHO WAS RELATED TO THEIR EMIR BY MARRIAGE.

THE EMPRESS SURRENDERED... THE GENERAL BECAME EMPEROR... THE VENETIANS BROUGHT IN THE PLAGUE... AND BY LATE 1347 MORE THAN HALF OF CONSTANTINOPLE DIED.*

KAFFA KAFFA

THE TURKS DECIDED TO STAY ON THE EUROPEAN SHORE, AND THE BYZANTINES WERE NOW POWERLESS TO SEND THEM BACK!

WHAT A BLESSING!

TO SEE HOW PLAGUE CAN AFFECT THE SURVIVORS, CONSIDER THE "BATTLE" WAGED BY THE BYZANTINES AGAINST **GENOA** TWO YEARS LATER, IN 1349.

THE GREEK NAVY ROWED OUT INTO ITS OWN, FAMILIAR HOME WATERS... ARMED MEN LINED THE DECKS IN THE USUAL WAY...

AND THEN **SOMETHING** HAPPENED—A SUDDEN ROLLING WAVE OR A LOUD NOISE—AND THE GREEK SOLDIERS **JUMPED OVERBOARD** WITH A BAD CASE OF THE POST-PLAGUE JITTERS!

THE TURKS SAW THE PLAGUE AS A **GODSEND**: IT WIPED OUT WHOLE CITIES FULL OF GREEKS, WHILE MOSTLY SPARING THE COUNTRYSIDE, WHERE THE TURKS MADE THEIR CAMPS.

EUROPE

CONSTANTINOPLE

ASIA

IN 1354 CAME GODSEND #2: AN IMMENSE **EARTHQUAKE** TUMBLED THOSE CITY WALLS.

CRASH

NOW TURKISH FAMILIES MOVED ACROSS AND JOINED THE FIGHTING MEN IN EUROPE.

AH! A FIXER-UPPER!

THE EMPEROR BEGGED THEM TO GO HOME... THEY REPLIED THAT WHEN GOD SENDS, YOU DON'T SEND BACK! TO DO SO, THEY SAID, WOULD BE AN **INSULT TO GOD**.

CAN'T DO THAT!

THE EMPEROR (HIS NAME WAS JOHN CANTACUZENUS, BY THE WAY) RETIRED TO A MONASTERY TO WRITE HIS MEMOIRS, WHICH WERE ALMOST AS LONG AS HIS BEARD AND HIS LIST OF EXCUSES...

AND SO, AIDED BY PLAGUE, THE TURKISH CONQUESTS IN EUROPE BEGAN!

DURING THE 1300s, THESE TURKS—ALSO CALLED OSMANLI OR **OTTOMAN** BECAUSE THEIR SULTANS WERE DESCENDED FROM OSMAN, EMIR OF BURSA—SLOWLY EXPANDED THEIR RULE THROUGH THE POST-PLAGUE BALKANS, WHERE SERBS, ALBANIANS, MACEDONIANS, GREEKS, BULGARS, ITALIANS, AND FRANKS WERE OFTEN TOO BUSY FIGHTING EACH OTHER TO UNITE AGAINST ANYONE.

THIS IS **YOUR** FAULT, YOU KNOW!

NO, **YOURS!**

IN SERBIA, FOR EXAMPLE, ARGUMENTS AMONG THE BARONS SEALED THE SERBIAN DEFEAT AT THE BATTLE OF **KOSSOVO** IN 1389,* AND BY 1390, THE OTTOMANS RULED MOST OF THE OLD BYZANTINE EMPIRE—MINUS ONLY CONSTANTINOPLE ITSELF.

THE OTTOMAN SULTAN MURAD WAS KILLED AT KOSSOVO... HIS SON **BAYAZIT** BECAME SULTAN... THE FIRST ITEM ON BAYAZIT'S AGENDA WAS: WHAT TO DO WITH HIS OWN **BROTHERS?**

SHOULD I GIVE 'EM HIGH OFFICE AND HAVE THEM LOOKING OVER MY SHOULDER, SECOND-GUESSING ME ALL THE TIME?

BAYAZIT KNEW THAT SIBLING RIVALRY IN ROYAL FAMILIES CAN RUIN COUNTRIES, LEAD TO CIVIL WAR, SPLIT KINGDOMS, ETC., AND BAYAZIT WANTED NONE OF IT!

SHOULD I BANISH THEM TO REMOTE OUTPOSTS, WHERE THEY CAN PLOT AGAINST ME WITHOUT MY KNOWLEDGE?

SO HE ORDERED HIS BROTHERS **STRANGLED**... AND THEREBY SET A PRECEDENT... LATER SULTANS DID THE SAME TO THEIR BROTHERS... AND EVENTUALLY THIS CUSTOM WAS LEGALIZED IN WRITING—FOR SULTANS ONLY, OF COURSE!

WHAT'S THE BIG DEAL? THERE ARE ONLY 19 OF THEM!

ONCE IN POWER, THE OTTO-MANS RAN A MULTICULTURAL EMPIRE, WHERE EACH COM-MUNITY WAS ALLOWED TO KEEP ITS OWN IDENTITY.

ISN'T THAT WONDERFUL?

UM...

TOLERANT? NOT ENTIRELY... FOR INSTANCE, THE SULTAN'S **ELITE MILITARY GUARD** WAS RECRUITED STRICTLY FROM THE RANKS OF **CHRISTIAN BOYS.**

THAT ONE.

EVERY COUPLE OF YEARS, THE SULTAN'S DRAFT BOARD WOULD TOUR THE COUNTRY AND TAKE A LEVY OF BOYS AWAY FROM THEIR HOMES.

THE BOYS BECAME THE SUL-TAN'S **PERSONAL SLAVES...** THEY WERE RAISED AS MUSLIMS AND TRAINED IN STRICT MILITARY SCHOOLS.

IT'S FUNNY... THO WE HAVE NO SAY IN OUR OWN FATE, WE DO GET TO PLAY WITH BOWS AND ARROWS, SWAGGER AROUND, AND LORD IT OVER THE CIVILIANS...

THIS SLAVE UNIT, THE **JANIS-SARIES,** WAS A POWERFUL FIGHTING FORCE LOYAL TO NO ONE BUT THE SULTAN.

BUT I MISS MY MOMMY!

(BESIDES THE JANISSARIES AND REGULARS, THE SULTAN ALSO HAD **SHOCK TROOPS** WHOSE JOB WAS TO PILLAGE AND TER-RORIZE CIVILIANS. ALL EUROPE FEARED THEM, AND COMICS FANS STILL TREMBLE AT THE NAME OF THE **BASHI-BAZOUKS!**)

BILLIONS OF BLUE, BLISTERING BARNACLES!

SO... MULTICULTURAL OR NO, OTTOMAN RULE IRRITATED THE BALKANS, WHICH REMAIN IRRITATED TO THIS DAY, OVER SIX HUNDRED YEARS LATER.

&£#!!

★@!!

##!!

€@#

AFTER THE SERBS FELL AT KOSSOVO IN 1389, THE HUNGARIANS APPEARED TO BE NEXT IN LINE... THE KING OF HUNGARY, A CATHOLIC, BEGGED THE POPE FOR A NEW CRUSADE... AND SO WE RETURN TO THE WEST...

COELOCANTHS!

SEA-GHERKINS!

CATAPHRACTS!

KNIGHTHOOD'S FLOWER FADES

WESTERN CHRISTENDOM, MEANWHILE, HAD MOVED ALONG NICELY IN THE EARLY 1300s. THANKS TO THE HORSE-DRAWN PLOW, FARMERS REAPED BOUNTIFUL HARVESTS, WHICH ENCOURAGED THEM TO MAKE **MANY BABIES**... EVERYWHERE PEOPLE **DRAINED SWAMPS** AND **FELLED FORESTS** FOR LAND AND FUEL... MONEY FLOWED... TOWNS GREW... PEOPLE GRIPED ABOUT CROWDING...

DESPITE ALL THESE CHANGES, THE **ARISTOCRACY** STILL CLUNG TO ITS **FEUDAL PERKS.** ESPECIALLY IN FRANCE, WHERE THE KING WAS WEAK, THE DUKES AND COUNTS AND SEIGNEURS WERE PROUDER THAN EVER. THEIR ARMOR GREW **HEAVIER**... THEIR ATTITUDES **HIGHER**... IN THEIR OWN OPINION, THEY WERE THE **WORLD'S GREATEST FIGHTERS,** EVEN AFTER LOSING ALL THOSE CRUSADES.

HRRRAF!

BUT EVEN A KNIGHT HAD TO FACE REALITY NOW AND THEN...

IN 1340, ENGLAND'S KING **EDWARD III**, CLAIMING THE FRENCH THRONE ON HIS MOTHER'S SIDE,* INVADED FRANCE AND STARTED SOMETHING WE CALL THE **HUNDRED YEARS' WAR,** THOUGH WHAT THEY CALLED IT AT THE TIME DOES RATHER PUZZLE ONE.

MEN! TODAY WE BEGIN A SIX MONTHS' WAR!

EDWARD, A DRILL SERGEANT OF A KING, RELIED ON **STRATEGY, TACTICS,** AND **DISCIPLINE...** ON THE OTHER SIDE, THE PROUD FRENCH DISDAINED ALL THAT STUFF—EVERY KNIGHT WANTED TO GO FIRST!

ARCHERS, STAND YOUR GROUND!

CAVALRY, OUTFLANK THEIR LEFT!

WHEN THEY FALL BACK, WE PURSUE! ETC. ETC. ETC.

RESULT: A MAJOR DEFEAT FOR THE FRENCH AT THE BATTLE OF **CRECY** IN 1346.

THIS IS **SO** NOT FAIR!

THE MOVIE **BRAVEHEART** (WHICH I LIKED!) TELLS THE STORY OF **ED 3'S** PARENTS. IN THE FILM, ED 2, A HOMOSEXUAL, HAS NO INTEREST IN HIS WIFE THE FRENCH PRINCESS, WHO TRAVELS TO SCOTLAND AND CONCEIVES **MEL GIBSON'S** BABY.

AH, M'SIEUR LE SCOT, LET US NEGOTIATE...

IN FACT, MEL GIBSON WASN'T BORN YET, AND **WILLIAM WALLACE,** HIS CHARACTER, WAS ALREADY **DEAD** BY THE TIME THE PRINCESS FIRST CAME TO ENGLAND... SO ED 3 MAY WELL HAVE BEEN THE SON OF ED 2 AFTER ALL.

I'M AFRAID SO...

ED 2 REALLY WAS GAY, AND HIS LOVER REALLY WAS KILLED, THOUGH NOT BY BEING PITCHED OUT THE WINDOW, AS IN THE FILM. YOU CAN READ THE HIDEOUS DETAILS IN MARLOWE'S PLAY **EDWARD II.**

WHAT'S MY MOTIVATION?

GOOD VISUALS!

WHILE THE FLAGELLANTS FLAGELLATED, OTHERS RESPONDED TO THE BLACK DEATH WITH COMPLETE **RATIONALITY.** CONSIDER...

WHAT'S SO IRRATIONAL ABOUT A LITTLE FLAGELLATION?

A PLAGUE LEAVES THE WORLD WITH A LOT OF WORK TO BE DONE AND NOT ENOUGH WORKERS TO DO IT.

WHERE DO YOU GET BREAD WHEN THE MILLER'S DEAD?

THE SURVIVING BREWERS AND MILLERS AND MASONS AND SMITHS DID THE **REASONABLE** THING: ASKED FOR **HIGHER WAGES.**

HIGHER WAGES? ARE YOU OUT OF YOUR **MIND?**

WE'VE NEVER BEEN CLEARER.

THE UPPER CLASSES AGREED: **BAD IDEA!** EVERYWHERE, KINGS DECREED THAT WAGES MUST STAY AT **PRE-PLAGUE LEVELS.**

REASON IS THE DEVIL'S ARSE-TRUMPET!

THESE LAWS, OF COURSE, IGNORED THE BASIC PROBLEM: EMPLOYERS HAD TO BID AGAINST EACH OTHER FOR SCARCE WORKERS.

CART & CARTER FOR HIRE—

THIS COMBINATION OF WAGE CONTROLS AND LABOR SHORTAGE MAY HAVE BEEN THE PARENT OF THE "STRUCTURED DEAL."

O.K.... WAGES MAY BE FIXED... BUT I CAN GIVE YOU A **SIGNING BONUS** AND **DEFERRED COMPENSATION** OF A **PREGNANT SOW!** WHAT DO YOU SAY?

CALL MY AGENT!

AFTER A PLAGUE, THE SAME NUMBER OF COINS PILE UP IN FEWER HANDS... IN OTHER WORDS, SOME PEOPLE GET RICH!

NOT NECESSARILY TRUE IN A MODERN ECONOMY, WHERE MONEY IS BASED ON CREDIT, NOT COINS!

AND SO THE FEUDAL LORDS BEGAN "FREEING"—I.E., EVICTING—THEIR SERFS. THEY KICKED THEM OFF THE LAND AND REPLACED THEM WITH SOMETHING MORE PROFITABLE, LIKE SHEEP.

GOOD NEWS! YOU'RE **FREE!** FREE TO DO ANYTHING BUT STAY...

FEUDAL LORDS, COMPETING WITH BUSINESSMEN, LOOKED FOR WAYS TO "RATIONALIZE" THEIR OWN OPERATIONS.

AS LONG AS EVERYONE'S BEING SO DAMN RATIONAL!

A FEW WORKERS MIGHT STAY ON, LABOR FOR WAGES, AND PAY RENT.

AND IF I CAN'T MAKE RENT?

AS I SAID, YOU'RE **FREE!**

WHAT THEY SAW WAS THAT **SERFS** WERE **COSTLY.** DOWNTRODDEN THEY MAY HAVE BEEN, BUT THESE **SEMI-FREE WORKERS** HAD A CLAIM ON THE LAND, AND THE LORD OWED THEM VARIOUS ANNOYING FEUDAL OBLIGATIONS.

FOR SOME PEOPLE, FREEDOM WAS A GRAND OPPORTUNITY TO HIT THE ROAD—THE VAGRANT **DICK WHITTINGTON** BECAME MAYOR OF LONDON—BUT MANY, MANY OTHERS JUST HIT THE STREET.

WHEN THEY'RE NOT SLAVING AWAY FOR ME, THEY DRINK ALL MY BEER!

WE DO APPRECIATE YOUR HELP IN BUILDING A RATIONAL ECONOMY!

SO THE RICH GOT RICHER AND THE POOR GOT POORER... A CLICHE BUT TRUE... AND IN EUROPE'S PLAGUE YEARS, AS IN CHINA'S, THE POOR LOST THEIR FEAR.

LET'S TEACH THESE VARLETS A LESSON!

"THE SEIGNEURS WITH THEIR ENDLESS GREED WOULD TAKE FROM YOU, IF THEY COULD, EVEN YOUR SHARE OF DAYLIGHT... THESE MEN WHO FEED ON OUR SUBSTANCE HAVE NO OTHER THOUGHT THAN TO GLITTER WITH GOLD AND JEWELS... AND TO RAISE NEW TAXES TO OPPRESS US."

—UNNAMED PARISIAN COBBLER

ALL ACROSS EUROPE, THE COMMONERS ROSE IN REVOLT IN THE 1370s AND '80s. THEY FOUGHT AGAINST WAGE CONTROLS... ATTACKED FEUDAL BONDAGE (AND THE JUDGES AND LAWYERS WHO ENFORCED IT)... RESISTED THE ENDLESS WAR TAXES... AND DEMANDED A VOICE IN GOVERNMENT.

WUP! AND THE LESSON IS—?

"MATTERS CANNOT GO WELL IN ENGLAND UNTIL ALL THINGS ARE HELD IN COMMON, WHEN THERE SHALL BE NEITHER VASSALS NOR LORDS, WHEN THE LORDS SHALL BE NO MORE MASTERS THAN OURSELVES..."

—JOHN BALL

VIVA LA POPOLO!

—ITALIAN WORKERS' CRY

AFTER SOME SUCCESS, THE REBELLIOUS WORKERS AND PEASANTS WERE PUT DOWN WITH UNSPARING FEROCITY... LANDLORDS TOOK BACK THEIR PLACE AT THE TOP... BUT KNIGHTHOOD HAD BEEN BADLY SHAKEN, EVEN THOUGH THE KNIGHTS THEMSELVES WOULD NEVER ADMIT IT!

BY GOD, THE NATURAL ORDER IS BACK FOREVER!

ALL THIS TIME, THE ENGLISH AND FRENCH FOUGHT EACH OTHER WHEN THEY COULD... BUT DURING THE POPULAR UPRISING, BOTH SIDES CALLED "TIME OUT."

SHALL WE MAKE IT THE FORTY-FIVE YEARS' WAR, THEN?

BIEN SUR...

THEN, IN 1389, CAME KOS-SOVO... AND AS THE TURKS ADVANCED, THE POPE—BOTH POPES, ACTUALLY*—CALLED FOR A NEW CRUSADE.

BON IDEE!

IN 1396, A THOUSAND FRENCH KNIGHTS (A MERE 10% AS MANY AS IN THE FIRST CRU-SADE) HEADED FOR HUNGARY, WHERE THE KING HAD 60,000 MEN UNDER ARMS.

THOSE HUNGARIANS WILL BE SO GLAD TO HAVE US...

IF THEY CAN CONTAIN THEIR ENVY...

THE HUNGARIANS ADVISED CAUTION... THE FRENCH SNEERED... AND WHEN THEY FOUND THE TURKS NEAR NICOPOLIS, BULGARIA, OUR PROUD GALLIC KNIGHTS WENT RIGHT AT THEM!

ME FIRST!

ME!

ME!

BUT—!

AFTER CHOPPING DOWN ENEMIES FOR HOURS, THE FRENCH FELT VERY PROUD OF THEM-SELVES INDEED!

ZUT!

OUR SELF-ESTEEM IS COM-PLETELY VINDICATED!

IN 1309, A PRO-FRENCH POPE, CLEMENT V, FEARING THE ROMAN MOB, MOVED HIS COURT TO FRANCE... IN 1377, POPE GRE-GORY XI MOVED BACK TO ROME, BUT THE FRENCH DEFIANTLY ELECTED THEIR OWN POPE, SO NOW THERE WERE TWO.

NO, THERE'S ONLY ONE, AND YOU'RE NOT IT!

IN 1414, A COUNCIL OF BISHOPS MET TO MEND THE SPLIT. THEY DECLARED THAT THE CHURCH CAME BEFORE THE POPE, THE CHURCH COULD "DESELECT" POPES, AND THAT POPES WERE NOT PERFECT, BUT SOMETIMES MADE MISTAKES.

THEY CAN'T BOTH BE RIGHT!

WHEN THE COUNCIL CHOSE A NEW POPE IN 1418, THE 2-POPE ERA ENDED... BUT THE POPE'S PRESTIGE HAD SUFFERED... HE COULD NOW OFFICIALLY ERR... UNTIL 1870, THAT IS, WHEN A CHURCH COUNCIL DECLARED HIM COMPLETELY INFALLIBLE!

EVERYTHING I SAY IS TRUE, INCLUDING THIS!

THEN BAYAZIT'S MAIN ARMY CAME INTO VIEW. THE MORNING'S WORKOUT, IT SEEMED, HAD BEEN JUST A WARM-UP...

NICOPOLIS: ANOTHER TOTAL VICTORY FOR THE TURKS, ANOTHER TOTAL LOSS FOR FRENCH KNIGHTHOOD.

WE'LL GET IT RIGHT ONE OF THESE YEARS...

HOW COULD EUROPE SAVE IT-SELF NOW? NO WAY, MAYBE... SOMEONE ELSE HAD TO DO IT: **TAMERLANE**, A CHESS-PLAYING WARLORD FAR TO THE EAST.

SAMARKAND, TAMERLANE'S CAPITAL

IN THE LATE 1300s, THIS **TIMUR** THE **LAME** HAD CON-QUERED AN EMPIRE IN THE JENGHIS KHAN MODE: PYRAMIDS OF SKULLS, ARTISTS SPARED.

WHOA! MUCH SCARIER THAN A FEW STUPID FRENCH!

IN 1402, TIMUR TURNED AGAINST THE OTTOMAN TURKS, SO BAYAZIT HAD TO BID EUR-OPE GOOD-BYE.

BAYAZIT

TIMUR

TAMERLANE DEFEATED BAYAZIT, LOCKED HIM IN AN IRON CAGE, AND TOOK OVER HIS EASTERN TERRITORY.

IS THIS A PLACE FOR MIGHTY BAJAZETH? CONFUSION LIGHT ON HIM THAT HELPS THEE THUS!

THERE WHILES HE LIVES, SHAL BAJAZETH BE KEPT, AND WHERE I GOE BE THUS IN TRIUMPH DRAWN: AND THOU HIS WIFE SHALT FEED HIM WITH THE SCRAPS MY SERVITURES SHALL BRING THEE FROM MY BOARD. FOR HE THAT GIVES HIM OTHER FOOD THAN THIS SHALL SIT BY HIM AND STARVE TO DEATH HIMSELFE. THIS IS MY MINDE, AND I SHALL HAVE IT SO.

—MARLOWE, TAMBURLAINE, PART I, ACT 4, SCENE 2

THE OTTOMANS WERE FORCED TO MAKE PEACE WITH THE WEST, SAVING EUROPE FROM FURTHER TURKISH INVASIONS—TEMPORARILY.

THANK YOU, TAMERLANE, YOU VICIOUS, TRYANNICAL MAN, YOU!

TIMUR'S TOMB, SAMARKAND

NOW, OF COURSE, **ENGLAND** AND **FRANCE** COULD GO AT IT AGAIN—JUST AS SOON AS A NEW GENERATION OF KNIGHTS CAME OF AGE!

SO CUTE!

BY NOW, THESE KNIGHTS HAD LEARNED SOMETHING: **MISTAKES** HAD BEEN MADE... CHANGES WERE NEEDED...

WE NEED EVEN HEAVIER ARMOR.

RESULT: THE FAMOUS BATTLE OF **AGINCOURT** (1415): RAIN POURED THE NIGHT BEFORE... IN THEIR WET ARMOR, THE FRENCH WERE HOISTED ONTO THEIR MOUNTS... THEY ADVANCED, OR TRIED TO... MUD SUCKED DOWN EVERYTHING... THE "WAR-SUVS" COULD BARELY MOVE... AND ENGLAND'S YEOMAN BOWMEN MOWED THEM DOWN.

LET'S MAKE IT THE **75 YEARS'** WAR, SHALL WE?

ENGLAND'S KING **HENRY V** TRIED TO END THE WAR WITH THIS ONE—HE KILLED ALL HIS PRISONERS—BUT THE FRENCH REFUSED TO GIVE UP, AS LEADERS AROSE FROM AMONG THE COMMON PEOPLE.

TO KNIGHTHOOD'S CHAGRIN, FRANCE'S NEW HEROINE WAS A 19-YEAR-OLD GIRL: **JOAN OF ARC**, WHO HEARD VOICES TELLING HER TO TAKE ON THE ENGLISH.

WELL, OBVIOUSLY, HEAVIER ARMOR ISN'T QUITE ENOUGH.

JOAN LED THE FRENCH TO SEVERAL VICTORIES...

BUT ALSO TO SEVERAL DEFEATS... AND AT LAST SHE FELL INTO ENEMY HANDS.

TO DISCREDIT HER, THE ENGLISH HAD HER TRIED BY PRIESTS, ON THE GROUNDS THAT HER VOICES MADE HER A **WITCH**.

FOUND GUILTY, SHE WAS BURNED AT THE STAKE... BUT THE FRENCH STILL ADORED HER, AND TODAY SHE'S A SAINT.

THE WAR DRAGGED ON FOR ANOTHER QUARTER CENTURY... UNTIL AT LAST ENGLAND NOTICED THAT IT COST MORE THAN IT WAS WORTH. IN 1453, ENGLAND PULLED OUT OF FRANCE ALMOST COMPLETELY, LEAVING THINGS JUST AS THEY HAD STOOD IN 1340 WHEN THE WAR BEGAN—EXCEPT THAT EUROPE WAS NOW A DIFFERENT PLACE...

WE FOLLOW THE FATES OF GREAT, STABLE NATIONS BECAUSE WE KNOW WHAT THEIR POWER CAN DO... JUST LOOK AROUND! TODAY THE **WHOLE WORLD** IS TOUCHED BY THE CULTURE OF **ONE LARGE COUNTRY.**

BUT THINK OF ALL THE **LIT-TLE, TURBULENT** STATES THAT HAVE DONE **BIG THINGS:** CHINA'S WARRING KINGDOMS, EMBATTLED ISRAEL, THE GREEK CITIES, MECCA...

IN THE 1300s AND 1400s, A SMALL ITALIAN CITY DID MORE THAN ITS SHARE FOR THE WORLD OF ART AND IDEAS.

FLORENCE, LIKE MANY ITALIAN CITIES, GOVERNED ITSELF. IN 1290, THE FLORENTINES VOTED TO END FEUDALISM, AND THEN THEY TORE DOWN THE ARISTOCRATS' CASTLES.

THE TOWN BECAME A SORT OF REPUBLIC, WITH ASSEMBLIES, COUNCILS, JUDGES, ELECTIONS, ARGUMENTS, RIOTS, AND POLITICAL PARTIES.* THE DETAILS ARE UNIMPORTANT BECAUSE THEY CHANGED ALMOST EVERY YEAR.

TSK! THOSE FLORENTINES—ALWAYS SEEKING PERFECTION!

AT FIRST THE TWO PARTIES WERE THE **GUELPHS,** WHO FOLLOWED THE POPE, AND THE **GHIBELLINES,** WHO FAVORED THE GERMAN EMPEROR. THE GUELPHS LATER SPLIT INTO ARIS-TOCRATIC **BLACKS** AND MORE MIDDLE-CLASS **WHITES.**

NO PLACE FOR GRAY IN THIS TOWN!

AFTER A VIOLENT ARGUMENT IN 1302, THE BLACKS BANISHED THE WHITES FROM FLORENCE. ONE OF THE EXILES, **DANTE ALIGHIERI,** WAS ITALY'S GREATEST POET.

I'LL MAKE YOU RUE THE DAY, YOU'LL PAY AND PAY AND PAY!

DANTE, WHO NEVER RETURNED TO FLORENCE, GOT HIS REVENGE BY WRITING THE **INFERNO** (HELL), IN WHICH HE PUTS HIS ENEMIES TO ETERNAL, POETIC TORTURE.

WHA'D I DO?

REFUSED TO LET ME MARRY YOUR DAUGHTER!

IN ALL THIS TURMOIL, FLORENCE SOMEHOW NURTURED AN ARTISTIC AND LITERARY TRADITION.

TURMOIL MAKES GOOD MATERIAL!

DANTE

THE MIDDLE AGES' GREAT ITALIAN WRITERS—**DANTE, PETRARCH, BOCCACCIO**—ALL HAD A FLORENCE CONNECTION... AND MODERN EUROPEAN PAINTING BEGAN WITH A FLORENTINE NATIVE, **CIMABUE** (1240-1302), WHO TAUGHT HIS POLISHED, VIGOROUS CHOPS TO **GIOTTO** (1276-1337).

YOU'RE A SQUAT, UGLY LITTLE MUG, JO, BUT YOU HAVE A BEAUTIFUL BRUSH!

IN 1348, THE PLAGUE CAME TO FLORENCE, AND ART CLASSES SUFFERED.

AHEM **AHEM!!** PEOPLE AREN'T PICKING UP THEIR CRAYONS HERE!!

FLORENCE'S POST-PLAGUE POLITICS WERE AS EXTREME AS ANYONE'S... THE WORKERS' REVOLT OF THE '70s BURNED DOWN EVERY CHURCH IN THE CITY.

THE WORK OF A FEW FANATICS!

THE BURNING, OR THE CHURCH?

BY THAT TIME, SAYS A WITNESS, FLORENCE HAD 100,000 PEOPLE AND 17,000 BEGGARS... BUT FINALLY, TOWARD CENTURY'S END, THE PLAGUE ABATED... THE CITY REVIVED... MONEY BEGAN TO FLOW... AND (THIS BEING FLORENCE) SOME OF IT FLOWED INTO **ARTISTS' POCKETS.**

I HEAR **JENGHIS KHAN** LIKED ARTISTS TOO!

AND THEN, AROUND 1400, A FLORENTINE MADE A STARTLING DISCOVERY...

277

TO ITALIANS, THE FINEST ART WAS **ANCIENT ROMAN** ART... EVERYTHING SINCE THEN WAS JUST JUNK... AND NOW, SUDDENLY, THE FLORENTINES COULD DREAM OF BEING JUST AS GOOD AS THE ANCIENT ROMANS!

WE ARE SO COOL!

BRUNELLESCHI AND HIS YOUNG FRIEND, THE SCULPTOR **DONATELLO** (BORN 1386), WENT TO ROME TOGETHER AND SPENT YEARS MEASURING AND SKETCHING THE RUINS.

MUST BE A COUPLE OF ANTIQUE FORGERS!

NOT SO FAR-FETCHED! MICHELANGELO HIMSELF WAS KNOWN TO "ANTIQUE" A DRAWING TO BRING UP THE PRICE.

BRUNELLESCHI SOON LEARNED ENOUGH ABOUT ANCIENT ARCHITECTURE TO DO NEW BUILDINGS IN PERFECT, CLASSICAL STYLE* (DRAWN PERFECTLY, TOO!).

BEAUTIFUL BUILDING, FIL!

AND THAT'S ONLY THE DRAWING!

BUT CLASSICAL SCULPTORS HAD WORKED IN **BRONZE**... AND LUCKILY FOR DONATELLO, THE FOUNDRIES HAD JUST LATELY GOTTEN THE HANG OF CASTING **LARGE BRONZE OBJECTS.**

WHAT OBJECTS?

SORRY. STATE SECRET.

MANY OF BRUNELLESCHI'S BUILDINGS STILL ADORN FLORENCE, INCLUDING ITS LANDMARK: THE CATHEDRAL'S GREAT DOME, WHICH THE ARCHITECT BUILT ON POINTED ARCHES FOR EXTRA STRENGTH— NOT ROUND AND CLASSICAL AT ALL.

THE PROJECT WAS ALMOST NEVER BEGUN. THE COMMITTEE IN CHARGE, DAUNTED BY THE SIZE OF THE THING, HAD TROUBLE DECIDING AMONG TWENTY DIFFERENT DESIGN PROPOSALS.

WHAT IF IT FAILS?

WHAT IF IT FAILS?

A FRENCH ARCHITECT SUGGESTED SUPPORTING THE CONSTRUCTION ON A HUGE MOUND OF EARTH WITH **COINS** SPRINKLED THROUGHOUT. WHEN THE DOME WAS DONE, HE SAID, PEOPLE WOULD DIG OUT THE DIRT IN NO TIME!

GET BRUNELLESCHI!

WHAT'S WRONG WITH THIS?

WE DON'T GIVE AWAY COINS HERE.

ONE LITTLE PROBLEM WITH USING ANCIENT ROMANS AS ROLE MODELS, AND NO GETTING AROUND IT: THEY WERE **PAGANS,** DEVOTED TO THE PALPABLE PLEASURES OF **THIS** WORLD, NOT THE DUBIOUS JOYS OF THE NEXT.

HM!

HOW COULD ONE EMULATE PAGANS, AND STILL AVOID THE INQUISITION?

HMM!

NO... PAGAN WAS **OUT**... OUR FORWARD-BACKWARD-LOOKING ITALIANS NEEDED A **BETTER LABEL** FOR THEMSELVES...

HMMMMM...

THEY SETTLED ON "HUMANISTS."

SOUNDS HARMLESS ENOUGH...

WHAT WAS HUMANISM? THEY MADE IT UP AS THEY WENT ALONG, TALKING LONG AND LATE AT DINNER PARTIES THROWN BY **COSIMO DE' MEDICI,** THE RICHEST BANKER IN FLORENCE.

TO ME, HUMANISM IS ABOUT... IS ABOUT......

HUMANS?

YES! YES! YES!

COSIMO, THREE YEARS YOUNGER THAN DONATELLO, ADDED STUDIO SPACE TO THE FAMILY MANSION FOR FAVORITE ARTISTS. DONATELLO MOVED IN AND NEVER MOVED OUT!

LATER, WE'LL BURY YOU IN THE FAMILY CRYPT!

THERE, IN 1436, HE CREATED HIS BRONZE **DAVID:** BIBLICAL SUBJECT, CLASSICAL STYLE!

AND IT'S NAKED!!!

COSIMO LIKED THE STATUE—IT WAS **HUMANISTIC**—SO THE CITY ACCEPTED IT... BECAUSE BY NOW COSIMO WAS **BOSS OF FLORENCE**... EVERYONE OWED HIM MONEY... HIS WORD WAS LAW, MORE OR LESS...

WHAT'S THAT IN HIS POCKET?

THE CITY COUNCIL!

IN 1439, HE SPONSORED A CONFERENCE ON THE ANCIENT GREEKS. (THE HUMANISTS, STRONG ON LATIN, WERE WEAK ON GREEK.)

LET'S DO "GREEK WEEK"!

SCHISM ANATHEMA DAMNATION

A CONCLAVE OF CLASSICS PROFESSORS FROM CONSTAN-TINOPLE FLOCKED TO FLOR-ENCE FOR THE MEETING.

PHI BETA KAPPA

SIGMA CHI

MANY OF THEM DECIDED TO STAY. FLORENCE SEEMED SO HOPEFUL AND GAY—VERY GAY, ACTUALLY.

WHAT A STATUE!

WOULD YOU LIKE TO MEET THE MODEL?

LORD KNEW, CONSTANTINOPLE HAD FALLEN TO RUIN... THE RESIDENTS OF THE ONE-CITY EM-PIRE WERE REDUCED TO GROWING THEIR OWN FOOD ON VACANT LOTS... BUT AT LEAST THE WALLS STILL STOOD...

NOT FOR LONG... IN 1453, THE TURKS POINTED THIS THING AT CONSTANTINOPLE: 27 FEET LONG, ALMOST 3 FEET IN DIAMETER WITH WALLS 8 INCHES THICK, AND ABLE TO THROW A 1,300-POUND BALL OVER A MILE.

THE FALL

THE GUN'S MAKER, A GERMAN ENGINEER, HAD OFFERED HIS SERVICES TO THE HIGHEST BIDDER, AND THE TURKS WON THE AUCTION...

WE'LL GIVE YOU OUR BLESSING AND A NAME AMONG THE SAINTS...

WE'LL GIVE YOU WHATEVER YOU ASK, PLUS A LITTLE...

A NEW SULTAN, **MEHMET II,** JUST 19 YEARS OLD, HAD DECIDED IT WAS FINALLY TIME FOR AN **ALL-OUT ASSAULT** ON CONSTANTINOPLE.

HAVE YOU NO LOYALTY?

I'M A TECHNICIAN WHO LIKES TO EAT.

IN SPRING 1453, THE MONSTER GUN BEGAN BLASTING CHUNKS OUT OF THE FABLED LAND WALLS...

BOOM

THE DEFENDERS WORKED LIKE MAD ALL NIGHT LONG...

TO PATCH UP THE HOLES GOOD AS NEW, ALMOST!

MEHMET WANTED TO ATTACK BY **SEA** AS WELL, BUT HIS NAVY BASHED HELPLESSLY AGAINST A THICK **IRON CHAIN** STRETCHED ACROSS THE WATERWAY CALLED THE **GOLDEN HORN.**

GOLDEN HORN

CHAIN

SEA WALLS

LAND WALLS

SO HE ORDERED HIS SHIPS HAULED **OVERLAND,** AROUND THE CITY, AND BACK INTO THE WATER.

THE GREEKS COULD BARELY BELIEVE THEIR EYES...

POUNDED FROM TWO SIDES, THEY FALTERED AND FINALLY FELL... THE TURKS DID WHAT WAS CUSTOMARY TO A RESISTING CITY: THREE DAYS OF NONSTOP RAPE, MURDER, AND PILLAGE.

BUT NO WRECKING! I WANT TO **LIVE** HERE, YOU KNOW!

AFTERWARD, MEHMET CONVERTED THE ST. SOPHIA CATHEDRAL TO A MOSQUE, SLATHERED ITS MOSAICS WITH WHITEWASH (WHICH PRESERVED THEM!), AND PRAYED. THE LAST REMNANT OF THE "ROME" WAS GONE, AND CONSTANTINOPLE BECAME **ISTANBUL.**

EUROPE WAS SHOCKED.

YEAH, YEAH... EVERYTHING'S **DIFFERENT** NOW... WELL... **SOMETHING** IS DIFFERENT... A LITTLE BIT, ANYWAY...

AFTER TAKING CONSTANTINOPLE, THE TURKS WENT ON THE OFFENSIVE IN EASTERN EUROPE, BUT CAME UP AGAINST AN ENEMY SO **SADISTIC** HE BROUGHT THEM UP SHORT: COUNT **VLAD** OF WALLACHIA.

VLAD LIKED TO HAVE PEOPLE **SKEWERED** ON STAKES... AND AS THE TURKS APPROACHED, THEY SAW A FOREST OF IMPALED VICTIMS. THE TROOPS QUAILED, AND VLAD PREVAILED.

THEY CALLED HIM **VLAD THE IMPALER,** BUT HIS OWN PEOPLE CALLED HIM **DRAKUL,** MEANING DRAGON OR DEVIL—THE ORIGINAL **COUNT DRACULA.**

THE GUY'S BATS!

HOW DOES HE LOOK AT HIMSELF IN THE MIRROR?

RENAISSANCE MARZIPAN

IN 1452,* ONE YEAR BEFORE CONSTANTINOPLE FELL, **LEONARDO DA VINCI** WAS BORN TO AN UNWED MOTHER ON A FARM NEAR FLORENCE.

THE RENAISSANCE MUST HAVE ARRIVED, BECAUSE HERE WAS THE **RENAISSANCE MAN:** MUSICIAN, PAINTER, SCULPTOR, DRAFTSMAN, ENGINEER, ARCHITECT, SCIENTIST, RACONTEUR, POET... AND HOMOSEXUAL!

"THE THINGS THAT MAKE BABIES ARE SO UGLY, THAT IF IT WEREN'T FOR PRETTY FACES, THE HUMAN RACE WOULD PERISH."

HE CAME OF AGE IN FLORENCE'S GLORY YEARS, UNDER THE MOST FREE-SPENDING MEDICI OF ALL, **LORENZO THE MAGNIFICENT**—JUST THREE YEARS OLDER THAN LEONARDO.

LEONARDO, IN FACT, WITNESSED FLORENCE'S BIGGEST NEWS STORY: AN **ASSASSINATION ATTEMPT** ON LORENZO AND HIS BROTHER GIULIANO IN CHURCH ON EASTER SUNDAY, 1478.

AT THE SAME TIME, A GERMAN NAMED GUTENBERG WAS BUILDING A PRINTING PRESS... MORE ON THIS LATER... BUT EUROPE ALREADY HAD **PRINTED BOOKS**, IN WHICH MANY COPIES OF EACH PAGE WERE PRESSED FROM A SINGLE CARVED WOODEN BLOCK.

CARVING A MESS OF TYPE INTO WOOD SEEMED LIKE A BOTHER (THOUGH THE CHINESE DID IT)... SO THESE WERE **PICTURE BOOKS** EXPLAINING THE BIBLE WITH ILLUSTRATIONS AND A FEW WELL-CHOSEN WORDS.

YES, EUROPE'S FIRST PRINTED BOOKS, THE **"PAUPER'S BIBLES,"** WERE **COMIC BOOKS!** LIKE MOST COMICS, THEY WERE PRODUCED CHEAPLY AND FELL TO BITS OVER THE YEARS, MAKING THEM EXTREMELY RARE TODAY.

COMICON

OH, MANNN! WHY DIDN'T THEY BAG THEM IN PLASTIC?

THE COUP, HATCHED* BY FAILED LITIGANTS IN A CASE WHERE LORENZO HAD BRIBED THE JUDGE, PARTLY SUCCEEDED... GIULIANO DIED, BUT LORENZO ESCAPED WITH A WOUNDED ARM.

*WITH THE POPE'S KNOWLEDGE AND TACIT CONSENT

A MEDICI-FRIENDLY MOB CHASED DOWN THE ASSASSINS AND HANGED THEM FROM A BALCONY, AS LEONARDO FURIOUSLY SKETCHED BELOW!

THE APPRECIATIVE MEDICI COMMISSIONED HIM TO MAKE A PAINTING OF THE EVENT... BUT HE NEVER QUITE FINISHED IT.

I'M A **VERY** GREAT ARTIST—HAVEN'T I TOLD YOU?—AND WHO KNOWS WHEN INSPIRATION MAY STRIKE?

IN FACT, LEONARDO HAD A HARD TIME FINISHING ANYTHING, AND LORENZO TOOK A DISLIKE TO THE MAN!

NOW **THERE'S** A NICE LINE!

THIS GUY IS ALL TALK!!

SO DA VINCI DECIDED TO GO. IN 1482, HE SENT A FAMOUS **SELF-PROMOTIONAL PIECE** TO THE RULER OF MILAN.

I CAN BUILD BRIDGES, SIEGE EQUIPMENT, CANNON THAT SPRAY SMALL SHOT, CANNON THAT SHOOT BIG BALLS, MORTARS, LIGHT ORDINANCE, NAVAL WEAPONS, CATAPULTS, BUILDINGS, WATERWORKS... OH, YES, AND PAINTING AND SCULPTURE.

MILAN WAS INTERESTED, AND AWAY HE WENT.

IN MILAN, LEONARDO MADE MILITARY MACHINES, COSTUMES FOR MASKED BALLS, A FEW MASTERPIECES OF ART, AND SOME **MARZIPAN SCULPTURES** FOR DESSERT.

BE JUST A MINUTE!

LEONARDO GONE? NO PROBLEM! LORENZO AND THE OTHER ART BUYERS STILL HAD **VERROCCHIO**, **GHIRLANDAIO**, **LIPPI**, AND **BOTTICELLI**, THAT LAST ONE A WILD MAN WHO DID A LOT OF NUDE FEMALES—PAINTED THEM, THAT IS (BUT MAYBE NOT ONLY)—AND MADE **PAGAN PICTURES** LIKE THE **BIRTH OF VENUS**, GODDESS OF LOVE...

OH, YEAH, BABY!

THEN, IN 1492, NOT LONG AFTER BRINGING A TEENAGER NAMED **MICHELANGELO** INTO THE FAMILY STUDIOS, LORENZO DIED AT AGE 43.

TAKE A LAST LOOK, MIKE... FLORENCE WILL NEVER BE THE SAME!

WHEN THE LAWYERS TRIED TO SORT OUT HIS ESTATE, THEY FOUND THAT LORENZO HAD PAID PERSONAL DEBTS WITH PUBLIC MONEY, LEAVING THE CITY'S FINANCES IN SHAMBLES.

IPSE &%$# DIXIT!

A PURITANICAL PRIEST, FATHER **SAVANAROLA**, CALLED FOR AN END TO THIS LUXURY, WASTE, AND PAGANISM—AN END, IN FACT, TO **MEDICI RULE!** HUGE CROWDS GATHERED TO LISTEN...

I ALWAYS ENJOY HEARING WELL-PHRASED INSULTS.

HEARING THESE SERMONS, BOTTICELLI HAD A CHANGE OF HEART AND SWORE OFF PAGAN THEMES... BUT MICHELANGELO AND OTHER MEDICI "PETS" SMELLED **REVOLUTION** AND **LEFT TOWN**—AND SO, RE-GRETFULLY, MUST WE...

'BYE, GUYS! I'LL PRAY FOR YOUR ETERNAL SOULS!

YEAH, YEAH...

FISH STORY

IN THE EARLY 1400s, WHILE FLORENCE DREAMED OF REVIVING ANCIENT GLORIES, ANOTHER SMALL COUNTRY, **PORTUGAL**, DREAMED OF FISH.

AND NO WONDER... WITH AN ALL-ATLANTIC COAST, THE PORTUGUESE CAUGHT FISH, ATE FISH, SOLD FISH, DRIED FISH, SALTED FISH—WHAT ELSE WAS THERE TO DREAM ABOUT?

NOT SURPRISINGLY, ONE OF PORTUGAL'S ROYAL PRINCES, **ENRIQUE**, OWNED A TOTAL MONOPOLY ON TUNA.

THIS ENRIQUE—OR **HENRY**, AS HIS ENGLISH GRANDFATHER CALLED HIM—NATURALLY TOOK AN INTEREST WHEN PORTUGAL IN 1418 SENT SETTLERS TO THE UNINHABITED, FORESTED ISLAND OF **MADEIRA** (="WOOD").

WHEN MADEIRA'S TREES TURNED INTO **SPARS, MASTS,** AND **PLANKS,** PRINCE HENRY'S TUNA FLEET PROSPERED!

NOW THE FISH-PRINCE DROVE HIS SHIPWRIGHTS TO BUILD THE MOST OCEAN-WORTHY CRAFT ON THE PLANET.*

HE'S OBSESSED!

*EXCEPT FOR POLYNESIA, WHICH THEY KNEW NOTHING ABOUT.

IN 1427, PORTUGAL COLONIZED MORE DESERT ISLANDS, THE **AZORES**, AND FROM THESE BASES, HENRY'S SHIPS BEGAN EXPLORING THE AFRICAN COAST...

AZORES

MADERA

ALGUIN

SENEGAL R.

CAPE VERDE

AT FIRST, ALL WAS SAND AND WATER...

IT'S A BIRD!

IT'S A FISH!

IN 1441, AT A SAND-BLOWN TRADING POST, ALGUIN, THE PORTUGUESE KIDNAPPED THEIR FIRST AFRICANS.

(NOT COUNTING NORTH AFRICANS TAKEN IN WARS WITH MOROCCO)

IN 1444, THEY FIRST SAW GREEN AT THE SENEGAL RIVER (KIDNAPPING MORE AFRICANS) AND THEN PASSED **CAPE VERDE**, WHERE THE TROPICS BEGIN (KIDNAPPING MORE AFRICANS).

WHEN HE HEARD THE REPORTS AND SAW THE HAUL, HENRY BEGAN TO DREAM OF BIGGER FISH THAN TUNA...

SH! YOU'RE DISTURBING THE ENTRE-PRENEURIAL MIND!

ON FIRST MEET-ING WEST AFRI-CANS, THE EURO-PEANS **LAUGHED** AT SOME OF THEIR HABITS, SUCH AS JUMPING AWAY FROM PUDDLES IN TERROR WHENEVER IT RAINED.

HA HA HA HA HA

THE EUROPEANS DECIDED TO GIVE THEM A LESSON IN OVERCOMING **SILLY SUPERSTITIONS.**

A FEW MONTHS LATER, THEY DIS-COVERED THAT THE PUDDLES HAR-BORED TINY **WORMS**, WHICH BURROWED INTO FEET, GREW IN THE BLOODSTREAM, AND SOME-TIMES **POPPED THEIR HEADS OUT** THROUGH THE SKIN!!

HELLO!

HA HA HA

THE PORTUGUESE, WHO KNEW ALL ABOUT THE TRANS-SAHARAN TRAFFIC IN GOLD AND SLAVES, DECIDED TO BYPASS THE ARAB WORLD AND SAIL DIRECTLY TO THE SOURCE. SOON, AS MANY AS 25 SHIPS A YEAR WERE GOING OUT...

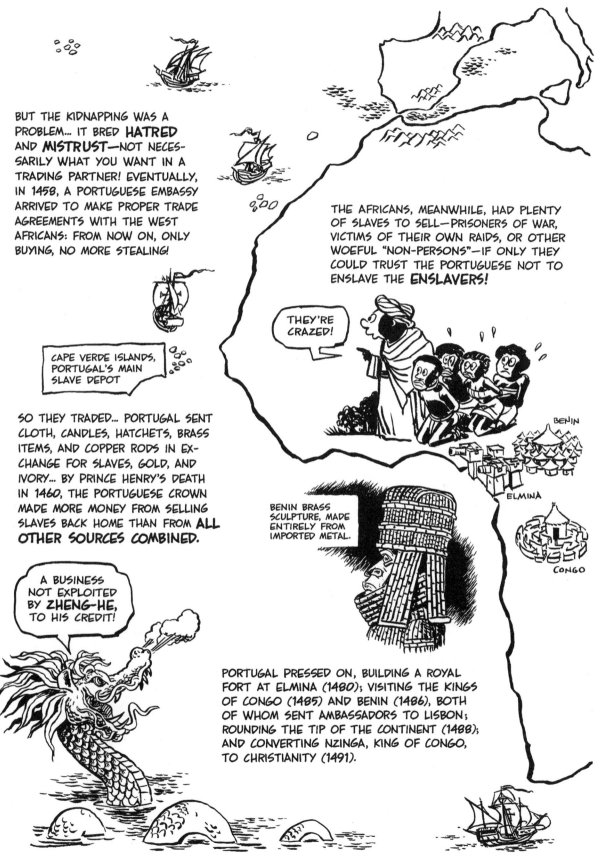

BUT THE KIDNAPPING WAS A PROBLEM... IT BRED **HATRED** AND **MISTRUST**—NOT NECESSARILY WHAT YOU WANT IN A TRADING PARTNER! EVENTUALLY, IN 1458, A PORTUGUESE EMBASSY ARRIVED TO MAKE PROPER TRADE AGREEMENTS WITH THE WEST AFRICANS: FROM NOW ON, ONLY BUYING, NO MORE STEALING!

CAPE VERDE ISLANDS, PORTUGAL'S MAIN SLAVE DEPOT

SO THEY TRADED... PORTUGAL SENT CLOTH, CANDLES, HATCHETS, BRASS ITEMS, AND COPPER RODS IN EXCHANGE FOR SLAVES, GOLD, AND IVORY... BY PRINCE HENRY'S DEATH IN 1460, THE PORTUGUESE CROWN MADE MORE MONEY FROM SELLING SLAVES BACK HOME THAN FROM **ALL OTHER SOURCES COMBINED.**

A BUSINESS NOT EXPLOITED BY **ZHENG-HE**, TO HIS CREDIT!

THE AFRICANS, MEANWHILE, HAD PLENTY OF SLAVES TO SELL—PRISONERS OF WAR, VICTIMS OF THEIR OWN RAIDS, OR OTHER WOEFUL "NON-PERSONS"—IF ONLY THEY COULD TRUST THE PORTUGUESE NOT TO ENSLAVE THE **ENSLAVERS!**

THEY'RE CRAZED!

BENIN

ELMINA

CONGO

BENIN BRASS SCULPTURE, MADE ENTIRELY FROM IMPORTED METAL.

PORTUGAL PRESSED ON, BUILDING A ROYAL FORT AT ELMINA (1480); VISITING THE KINGS OF CONGO (1485) AND BENIN (1486), BOTH OF WHOM SENT AMBASSADORS TO LISBON; ROUNDING THE TIP OF THE CONTINENT (1488); AND CONVERTING NZINGA, KING OF CONGO, TO CHRISTIANITY (1491).

IN THE MIDST OF ALL THIS, THE **ITALIANS** BEGAN TO ARRIVE... BEFORE 1453, ITALIAN FORTUNES HAD DEPENDED ON CLEAR SAILING IN THE BLACK SEA... BUT WHEN THE TURKS TOOK CONSTANTINOPLE—AND KAFFA TOO—ALL THE PROFIT WENT OUT OF THE BLACK SEA TRADE...

SO ITALIAN SAILORS—AND INVESTORS—WENT WEST, LOOKING FOR ACTION IN SPAIN, PORTUGAL, AND ENGLAND...

LORENZO DE MEDICI HAD AN AGENT IN LISBON (HE LOST MONEY)... SPAIN'S BIGGEST SLAVE DEALER, BARTOLOMMEO MARCHIONNI, WAS ITALIAN... AND GENOESE SAILORS LIKE **CHRISTOPHER COLUMBUS** FOUND THEMSELVES SAILING THE **ATLANTIC** IN THE 1470s, INSTEAD OF THE BLACK SEA!

☆✱@!!

COLUMBUS WAS THERE WHEN THE BUZZ BEGAN... WHEN PEOPLE STARTED SAYING THEY COULD SAIL ALL THE WAY AROUND AFRICA TO THE INDIES... COULD BYPASS THE TURKS, THE PERSIANS, THE SYRIANS, AND ALL THE MIDDLEMEN... COULD PICK UP **SPICES** AT THE SOURCE—SPICES, EVEN MORE PROFITABLE THAN SLAVES!

PLUS SPICES DON'T EAT, REBEL, FOUL THE SHIP, OR MAKE YOU FEEL GUILTY...

SO NOW, TO THE SAILORS AND BUSINESSMEN, ADD ONE MORE TYPE: THE VISIONARY **CAPTAIN-SALESMAN**, EAGER TO LAY HIS SCHEME OF WORLD DOMINATION BEFORE A FRIENDLY MONARCH. COLUMBUS JOINED THIS CROWD.

WE ALL KNOW WHAT HIS IDEA WAS: TO REACH THE INDIES BY SAILING **WEST**. HOW WACKY WAS THAT? IT'S HARD TO SAY... EVERYONE KNEW THE WORLD WAS ROUND (YES, THEY DID!)... ICELANDERS KNEW THE ATLANTIC HAD BEEN CROSSED... COLUMBUS HAD A PRETTY FAIR IDEA HOW WIDE IT WAS... HE HAD HIS SOURCES.

HE TOOK HIS IDEA TO SPAIN... NO LUCK... HE WENT TO PORTUGAL... BAD LUCK: WHILE HE WAS THERE, IN 1488, **BARTOLOMEU DIAS** SAILED IN, JUST BACK FROM ROUNDING THE SOUTHERN TIP OF AFRICA... PORTUGAL WAS GOING **EAST!**

COLUMBUS WENT BACK TO SPAIN.

WHY, YOU MIGHT ASK, HAD GREAT, BIG SPAIN LAGGED SO FAR BEHIND LITTLE, BITTY PORTUGAL?

FOR ONE THING, SPAIN HAD NO BUSINESSMAN-PRINCE LIKE PORTUGAL'S HENRY... IN FACT, THE SPANISH ROYAL FAMILY WAS DISTURBINGLY INBRED, WEIRD, AND DEGENERATE.

HOLA! I'M PEDRO EL CRUEL! WHAT CAN I DO TO YOU?

FOR ANOTHER, THERE WAS NO "SPAIN" IN THE EARLY 1400s, ONLY THE TWO KINGDOMS OF **ARAGON** AND **CASTILE**, FOREVER AT WAR WITH SEVERAL SMALL MOORISH EMIRATES.*

CASTILE, WHICH HAD ATLANTIC PORTS, DID SEND SHIPS TO AFRICA, BUT PORTUGAL ATTACKED THEM... WAR BEGAN... AND THE POPE SIDED WITH PORTUGAL.

BOOM

IN 1479, THE QUEEN OF CASTILE MARRIED THE KING OF ARAGON: **ISABELLA** AND **FERDINAND**, "LOS REYES CATOLICOS," THE CATHOLIC RULERS. THEY DEVOUTLY OBEYED THE POPE AND GAVE IN TO PORTUGAL, THE BETTER TO CONCENTRATE ON A RELIGIOUS DUTY...

NAMELY, "RECONQUERING" THE LAST OF MUSLIM SPAIN... AND THAT IS EXACTLY WHAT THEY WERE DOING WHEN COLUMBUS ARRIVED...

IN THE 1300s, THE DYING WISH OF SCOTLAND'S KING ROBERT "THE BRUCE" WAS FOR HIS HEART TO BE BURIED IN THE HOLY LAND. THE SURGERY WAS DONE, THE HEART SEALED IN A LEADEN CASKET, AND OFF IT WENT.

BWEE BWEE

A TROOP OF SCOTS CARRIED THE HEART ACROSS SPAIN... THEY HAPPENED ON A BATTLE... THE MOORS WERE WINNING... SO THE SCOTTISH LEADER FLUNG THE BRUCE'S HEART AT THE ENEMY!

THE SCOTS CHARGED AFTER IT, WON THE BATTLE, AND RECOVERED THE RELIC. (FOR SOME REASON, THE HEART RETURNED TO SCOTLAND, WHERE IT RESURFACED IN THE 1990s.)

ALL RIGHT, MEN! LET'S HAVE ANOTHER ROUND OF "MY HEART'S IN THE HIGHLANDS"!

NO! NO!

ONE BY ONE, ALL THE ISLAMIC STRONGHOLDS FELL... IN 1491, COLUMBUS FOLLOWED THE COURT TO THE LAST OF THEM, **GRANADA.** FERDINAND HAD JUST DOUBLE-CROSSED ITS EMIR, **ABU ABDULLAH,** WHO SIX MONTHS EARLIER HAD BEEN HIS ALLY... TOGETHER THEY HAD STORMED MUSLIM MALAGA... BUT NOW THE CATHOLICS TURNED AGAINST HIM, BESIEGED GRANADA, AND WASTED THE COUNTRYSIDE. IN THE ROYAL CAMP, COLUMBUS MADE HIS CASE.

WEST? TELL ME THIS FISH STORY AGAIN!

BY GOING WEST, YOUR MAJESTIES, WE CAN AVOID THE PORTUGUESE COMPLETELY... REACH THE INDIES AHEAD OF THEM... GET AN EXCLUSIVE FROM THE POPE... AND HAVE ALL THE **WEALTH OF ASIA!** BUT WE MUST ACT FAST! PORTUGAL IS ON THE MOVE...

YES, YES... IT'S JUST WE'RE RATHER **BUSY,** YOU SEE...

AMAZING PLACE, GRANADA! AN ELEGANT MOORISH PALACE, THE ALHAMBRA, CROWNS A COOL, FORESTED HILL WATERED BY MELTING SNOW FROM MOUNTAINS 20 MILES TO THE SOUTH. TODAY YOU CAN DRIVE FROM GRANADA TO A SKI LODGE IN THE MORNING AND THE BEACH IN THE AFTERNOON.

MEANWHILE, INSIDE GRANADA, THE SIEGE THREATENED EMIR ABU ABDULLAH PERSONALLY... EVERYONE BLAMED HIM FOR THIS FIASCO... HE EXPECTED A DAGGER IN THE RIBS ANYTIME...

MUTTER MUTTER MUTTER

TO SAVE HIMSELF—AND AS MUCH OF GRANADA AS POSSIBLE—HE BEGAN A SECRET EXCHANGE OF NOTES WITH THE CATHOLIC CAMP.

IN DECEMBER, THEY CAME TO TERMS: THE CITY WOULD SURRENDER... FERDINAND WOULD ALLOW THE EMIR TO SLIP SAFELY AWAY... THE CHRISTIANS WOULD COMMIT NO PILLAGE, ENSLAVEMENT, OR DESPOLIATION IN GRANADA—AS THEY HAD IN MALAGA—AND FERDINAND PUT ALL THESE PROMISES IN WRITING.

IN THE EARLY MORNING OF JANUARY 1, 1492, ABU ABDULLAH AND ABOUT 50 OTHERS SLIPPED OUT OF TOWN IN THE DARK.

AT DAWN, THEY REACHED A MOUNTAIN PASS TO THE SOUTH AND LOOKED BACK AT GRANADA FOR THE LAST TIME. ABU ABDULLAH LET OUT A SOB OR A SIGH, WHICH HAS GIVEN THE PASS ITS NAME (EL SOSPIRO DEL MORO, THE SIGH OF THE MOOR), AND WHICH CAUSED HIS MOTHER TO BERATE HIM FOR BEHAVING LIKE A WOMAN, EVEN THOUGH SHE WAS ONE HERSELF.

THE ROYAL ARMY TRAMPED INTO GRANADA AND BROKE ALL THE PROMISES. THEY PILLAGED, THEY ENSLAVED THOUSANDS, AND THEY EMPTIED LIBRARIES FULL OF "INFIDEL BOOKS" INTO A GREAT HEAP, WHICH THEY TORCHED.

THE BEST THING ABOUT BOOKS IS THEY'RE SELF-KINDLING!

COLUMBUS, WHO HAD BEEN ON THE VERGE OF DESPAIR AND DEPARTURE, NOW FOUND NEW HOPE... MAYBE THE CATHOLIC SOVEREIGNS WOULD HAVE TIME FOR HIM AFTER ALL!

TELL MISTER COLUMBUS WE HAVE **ONE MORE THING** TO DO FIRST...

NOW WHAT?

FRESH FROM TROUNCING THE MUSLIMS, THE ROYALS CONTINUED THEIR PURIFICATION DRIVE. IN MARCH, THEY DECREED THAT EVERY JEW IN SPAIN MUST BECOME CATHOLIC OR LEAVE THE COUNTRY BY AUGUST 31.

NO MORE WEIRD MIDDLE-EASTERN RELIGIONS HERE—ONLY CHRISTIANITY!

YES, THE KING AND QUEEN WERE PIOUS, SINCERE, EVEN (LET'S FACE IT) FANATICAL... ALSO THEY NEEDED **CASH**—DID I MENTION THAT DEPARTING JEWS WERE REQUIRED TO LEAVE ALL THEIR MONEY BEHIND?

SINCE WHEN HAS RELIGION DECLARED WAR ON SELF-INTEREST?

SO—GO OR CONVERT? THOSE WHO LEFT WOULD FACE POVERTY... THOSE WHO STAYED FACED THE **INQUISITION**—TO PROVE THEY WERE NOW "REAL" CHRISTIANS!

LIFE... LAW... LIVELIHOOD... YOU'VE GOT TO **PRIORITIZE**, MAN!

A FUNNY THING ABOUT THE INQUISITION: IT SEIZED THE ASSETS OF THE GUILTY... MADE MONEY BY CONVICTING... HAD A "PERVERSE INCENTIVE" TO SEND RICH CONVERTS TO THE FLAMES.

MY ROBE NEEDS MENDING, YOU MUST BE GUILTY!

IN THE END, ABOUT 100,000 SPANISH JEWS CONVERTED AND STAYED... ABOUT DOUBLE THAT NUMBER PACKED AND WENT.

WE HAD TO CONVERT—WE COULDN'T AFFORD A TICKET!

AMONG THOSE PLANNING TO LEAVE WERE THE "COURT JEWS" ISAAC ABRABANEL, JUAN CABRERO, AND ABRAHAM SENIOR, BANKERS WHO HELPED FINANCE THE GOVERNMENT.

WITH OUR MONEY, STAYING WOULD MEAN THE STAKE!

THEY COULDN'T TAKE IT WITH THEM, SO THEY HANDED A FORTUNE TO THE CHANCELLOR OF THE EXCHEQUER (HIMSELF A CONVERT) AS A "LOAN."

GOD WILLING, WE'LL INVEST IT IN SOMETHING PROFITABLE, AND YOU'LL SEE A RETURN ON CAPITAL SOMEDAY...

YOU HEAR? THE JEWS HAVE A SECRET LANGUAGE!

SEVERAL DAYS LATER, ON APRIL 17, QUEEN ISABELLA GAVE COLUMBUS THE GOOD NEWS.

YOU'VE GOT FUNDING!

COLUMBUS STILL FACED ONE LAST PROBLEM: SPAIN'S MAJOR PORTS WERE ALL CLOGGED WITH **JEWISH REFUGEES** TRYING TO GET OUT BY THE AUGUST 31 DEADLINE. FINDING A SHIP FROM CADIZ, SEVILLA, MALAGA, BILBAO, OR BARCELONA SEEMED IMPOSSIBLE.

THIS HAS BEEN SUCH A TRIAL FOR ME!

SO COLUMBUS AND HIS CREW OF 88 HAD TO SAIL THEIR THREE VESSELS FROM A VILLAGE CALLED **PALOS** ON A SWAMPY, MOSQUITO-INFESTED STRETCH OF SPAIN'S ATLANTIC COAST. IT WAS AUGUST 12, 1492.

NEXT: QUETZALCOATL!

BIBLIOGRAPHY

ASHTOR, ELIYAHU, *THE JEWS OF MUSLIM SPAIN, VOLUMES I AND II*, PHILADELPHIA: THE JEWISH PUBLICATION SOCIETY, 1992. OVERWROUGHT AT TIMES, BUT AN IMMENSE SCHOLARLY ACHIEVEMENT AND FULL OF JUICY STUFF!

ASTON, W. G., TR., *NIHONGI*, RUTLAND, VERMONT: CHARLES TUTTLE CO., INC., 1972. THE CHRONICLES OF EARLY JAPAN.

ATTAR, FARID UD-DIN, *THE CONFERENCE OF THE BIRDS*, TR. BY A. DARBANDI AND D. DAVIS, LONDON: PENGUIN BOOKS, 1984.

BOAHEN, CLARK, ET. AL., *THE HORIZON HISTORY OF AFRICA*, NEW YORK: AMERICAN HERITAGE, 1971. AS MEDIOCRE AS THE HORIZON CHINA IS EXCELLENT. GOOD PIX, BUT SKETCHY HISTORY. THE TIME-LIFE AFRICA IS BETTER.

BOULTING, WILLIAM, *FOUR PILGRIMS*, LONDON, KEGAN PAUL, YEAR NOT GIVEN. PILGRIMS ARE HSIUEN-TSIANG, SAEWULF OF BRITAIN, IBN BATUTTA, AND LUDOVICO VARTHEMA OF BOLOGNA.

BROOKS, LESTER, *GREAT CIVILIZATIONS OF ANCIENT AFRICA*, NEW YORK: FOUR WINDS PRESS, 1971. NO FRILLS, BUT GOOD AND ACCURATE.

BURROUGHS, BETTY, ED., *VASARI'S LIVES OF THE ARTISTS* (ABRIDGED), NEW YORK: SIMON AND SCHUSTER, 1946. NOT 100% RELIABLE, BUT WHAT DO YOU WANT FROM AN ARTIST?

CAHEN, CLAUDE, *PRE-OTTOMAN TURKEY*, NEW YORK: TAPLINGER, 1968. WAY MORE DETAILS THAN YOU CAN FOLLOW, OR MAY WANT TO KNOW!

CLEAVES, F. W., TR., *THE SECRET HISTORY OF THE MONGOLS*, CAMBRIDGE, MASS.: HARVARD UNIVERSITY PRESS, 1982. THE MONGOLS' OWN VERSION OF JENGHIS KHAN. THE VERY LITERAL TRANSLATION IS OFTEN HARD TO FOLLOW, BUT WELL WORTH THE EFFORT!

COEDES, G., *THE INDIANIZED STATES OF SOUTHEAST ASIA*, TR. BY W. VELLA, HONOLULU: EAST-WEST PRESS, 1968. GREAT FIRST CHAPTER.

COMNENA, ANNA, *THE ALEXIAD*, NEW YORK: PENGUIN, 1969. "PROFESSIONAL" HISTORIANS LOVE TO DUMP ON THIS DAUGHTER OF EMPEROR ALEXIUS, BUT HER BOOK IS STILL A MUST-READ ON THE FIRST CRUSADE. SHE WAS THERE!

COOK, HARRY, *SAMURAI, THE STORY OF A WARRIOR TRADITION*, NEW YORK: STERLING, 1993. GOOD PIX.

DAVIDSON, BASIL, *AFRICAN KINGDOMS*, NEW YORK: TIME-LIFE BOOKS, 1966. GOOD PICTURE BOOK.

DAVIDSON, BASIL, *THE AFRICAN GENIUS*, BOSTON: LITTLE, BROWN, 1969. CULTURAL HISTORY BY AN EXPERT.

DE MAREES, PIETER, *DESCRIPTION AND HISTORICAL ACCOUNT OF THE GOLD KINGDOM OF GUINEA* (1602), TR. BY A. VAN DANTZIG AND A. JONES, OXFORD: OXFORD UNIVERSITY PRESS, 1987.

DUNBABIN, JEAN, *FRANCE IN THE MAKING, 830-1130*, NEW YORK: OXFORD UNIVERSITY PRESS, 1985. ON THE CHANGES WROUGHT BY THE VIKING RAIDS.

DURANT, WILL AND ARIEL, *THE AGE OF FAITH*, NEW YORK: SIMON AND SCHUSTER, 1950. MUCH BETTER THAN I EXPECTED. VERY DETAILED, GOOD ON ISLAM, FAIRLY BALANCED, THOUGH WITH LITTLE AFRICAN HISTORY, AND THEIR ECONOMIC HISTORY IS SOMETIMES LESS THAN CLEAR.

DURANT, WILL AND ARIEL, *THE REFORMATION*, NEW YORK: SIMON AND SCHUSTER, 1957. MOSTLY COVERS MATERIAL LATER THAN WHAT'S IN THIS BOOK, BUT DOES DO COLUMBUS.

DURANT, WILL AND ARIEL, *THE RENAISSANCE*, NEW YORK: SIMON AND SCHUSTER, 1953. MUCH ADO ABOUT ITALY.

EBERHARD, WOLFRAM, *A HISTORY OF CHINA*, BERKELEY: U. OF CALIFORNIA PRESS, 1966.

EINHARD, *THE LIFE OF CHARLEMAGNE*, ANN ARBOR: UNIVERSITY OF MICHIGAN PRESS, 1979. THE GREAT ONE'S SECRETARY SPEAKS!

FAGE, J. D. AND ROLAND OLIVER, *THE CAMBRIDGE HISTORY OF AFRICA, VOL. 2, FROM C. 500 BC TO AD 1050*, AND *VOLUME 3, FROM 1050 TO 1600*, CAMBRIDGE: CAMBRIDGE UNIVERSITY PRESS 1978, 1977 RESPECTIVELY (YES, VOL. 3 CAME OUT FIRST).

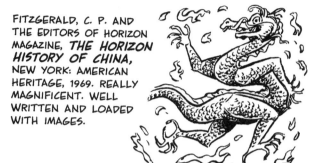

FITZGERALD, C. P. AND THE EDITORS OF HORIZON MAGAZINE, *THE HORIZON HISTORY OF CHINA*, NEW YORK: AMERICAN HERITAGE, 1969. REALLY MAGNIFICENT. WELL WRITTEN AND LOADED WITH IMAGES.

FOX-DAVIES, A. C., *A COMPLETE GUIDE TO HERALDRY*, LONDON: BRACKEN BOOKS, 1993.

GABRIELI, F., TR., *ARAB HISTORIANS OF THE CRUSADES*, BERKELEY: UNIVERSITY OF CALIFORNIA PRESS, 1984. THE VIEW FROM THE DEFENSE.

GAILEY, HARRY A., *HISTORY OF AFRICA FROM EARLIEST TIMES TO 1800*, NEW YORK: HOLT, RINEHART AND WINSTON, 1970.

GENDEL, MILTON, ED., *AN ILLUSTRATED HISTORY OF ITALY*, NEW YORK: McGRAW-HILL, 1966. THE MEDIEVAL SECTION IS BY MY MAN NORWICH.

GLUBB, SIR JOHN, *THE LIFE AND TIMES OF MUHAMMAD*, CHELSEA, MICHIGAN: SCARBOROUGH HOUSE, 1991. A VERY GOOD, SYMPATHETIC, POPULAR ACCOUNT.

GROUSSET, R., *THE EMPIRE OF THE STEPPES*, NEW BRUNSWICK, N.J.: RUTGERS UNIVERSITY PRESS, 1970. ALL ABOUT CENTRAL ASIA. INVALUABLE!

GUICCIARDINI, *HISTORY OF ITALY* AND *HISTORY OF FLORENCE* (ABRIDGED), NEW YORK: WASHINGTON SQ. PRESS, 1964. CLOSE-UP OF ITALY, YEAR BY YEAR, BY A MAN ON THE SCENE. THE EDITORS NEVER MENTION GUICCIARDINI'S FIRST NAME!

GUILLAUME, A., TR., *THE LIFE OF MUHAMMAD*, KARACHI, PAKISTAN: OXFORD UNIVERSITY PRESS, 1996. *THIS IS THE BOOK!!* A TRANSLATION OF IBN ISHAQ'S 8TH-CENTURY MASTERPIECE, THE SOURCE OF ALL OTHERS. DETAILED, FRANK, AND JUDICIOUS. FAIRLY HARD TO FIND.

HALLAM, ELIZABETH, GEN. ED., *CHRONICLES OF THE AGE OF CHIVALRY*, NEW YORK: CRESCENT BOOKS, 1995. FLAVORFUL.

HALLETT, ROBIN, *AFRICA TO 1875*, ANN ARBOR: THE UNIVERSITY OF MICHIGAN PRESS, 1970.

HITTI, PHILIP K., *HISTORY OF THE ARABS*, 9TH EDITION, NEW YORK: ST. MARTIN'S PRESS, 1967. ESSENTIAL, MAGISTERIAL, DETAILED, OUT OF PRINT, MAYBE OUT OF FASHION TOO.

HODGKIN, THOMAS, *NIGERIAN PERSPECTIVES, AN HISTORICAL ANTHOLOGY*, LONDON: OXFORD UNIVERSITY PRESS, 1960. EXCERPTS FROM ORIGINAL TEXTS.

HOOKHAM, HILDA, *TAMBURLAINE THE CONQUEROR*, LONDON: HODDER AND STOUGHTON, 1962. MUCH TOO WORSHIPFUL. (EUROPE HAS TENDED TO ADMIRE THIS CITY-LEVELER FOR DISTRACTING THE TURKS IN 1402.)

HOWARTH, DAVID, *1066, THE YEAR OF THE CONQUEST*, NEW YORK: VIKING PRESS, 1978. INCLUDES THE RIPPING YARN OF NORWAY'S HARALD HARDRADA.

HRBEK, I., ED., *AFRICA FROM THE SEVENTH TO THE ELEVENTH CENTURY*, ABRIDGED EDITION, BERKELEY: U. OF CALIFORNIA PRESS, 1992. AUTHORED BY A BEVY OF EXPERTS; EXCELLENT SOURCE ON MANY SUBJECTS.

IBN BATUTTA, *TRAVELS IN ASIA AND AFRICA*, LONDON: GEORGE ROUTLEDGE & SONS, 1929. WHATTA GUY...

IRVING, CLIVE, *CROSSROADS OF CIVILIZATION, 3000 YEARS OF PERSIAN HISTORY,* NEW YORK: BARNES & NOBLE, 1979.

JACOBS, JOSEPH, *THE JEWS OF ANGEVIN ENGLAND,* NEW YORK: G. P. PUTNAM & SONS, 1893.

LABOURET, HENRI, *AFRICA BEFORE THE WHITE MAN,* NEW YORK: WALKER AND COMPANY, 1962. IF THERE EVER WAS SUCH A THING...

LEWIS, BERNARD, ED., *THE WORLD OF ISLAM,* LONDON: THAMES AND HUDSON, 1976. SUMPTUOUS, WITH GREAT PIX AND ESSAYS.

MAGOCSI, PAUL, *A HISTORY OF THE UKRAINE,* SEATTLE: U. OF WASHINGTON PRESS, 1996. THICK BOOK, WITH A THIN BIT ABOUT THE KHAZARS.

MASON, R. H. P., AND J. G. CAIGER, *A HISTORY OF JAPAN,* NEW YORK: FREE PRESS, 1972.

MICHELL, G., ED., *ARCHITECTURE OF THE ISLAMIC WORLD,* NEW YORK: THAMES AND HUDSON, PAPERBACK EDITION 1995. BEAUTIFUL.

MORRIS, A. E. J., *HISTORY OF URBAN FORM,* 3RD EDITION, NEW YORK: JOHN WILEY & SONS, 1994.

MURASAKI SHIBUKU, *THE TALE OF GENJI,* TR. BY E. SEIDENSTICKER, NEW YORK: KNOPF, 1978. WAR AND PEACE WITHOUT THE WAR.

NAHN, ANDREW C., *KOREA, TRADITION AND TRANSFORMATION,* ELIZABETH, N.J.: HOLLYM INTERNATIONAL, 1988.

NEWBY, GORDON D., *A HISTORY OF THE JEWS OF ARABIA,* COLUMBIA, S.C.: U. OF SOUTH CAROLINA PRESS, 1988. CAUTIOUS BUT INFORMATIVE.

NEWMAN, J. L., *THE PEOPLING OF AFRICA,* NEW HAVEN: YALE U. PRESS, 1995. MIGRATIONS.

NIANE, D. T., ED., *GENERAL HISTORY OF AFRICA IV, FROM THE TWELFTH TO THE SIXTEENTH CENTURY,* BERKELEY: U. OF CALIFORNIA PRESS, 1984.

NORWICH, JOHN J., *BYZANTIUM, THE EARLY CENTURIES,* NEW YORK: KNOPF, 1996. GREAT GOSSIP, TERRIFIC STYLE, AND AN EYE FOR THE GROTESQUE.

NORWICH, JOHN J., *BYZANTIUM, THE APOGEE,* NEW YORK: KNOPF, 1996. AS GOOD AS THE FIRST ONE.

NORWICH, JOHN J., *BYZANTIUM, DECLINE AND FALL,* NEW YORK: KNOPF, 1996. EXCELLENT ACCOUNT OF THE FALL OF CONSTANTINOPLE.

NORWICH, JOHN J., *A HISTORY OF VENICE,* NEW YORK: KNOPF, 1982. ANOTHER RIP-SNORTER BY THE MAN.

OLDENBOURG, ZOE, *THE CRUSADES,* TRANSLATED BY A. CARTER, NEW YORK: PANTHEON BOOKS, 1966. VIVID, WELL ARGUED, CONVINCING.

PACHOCINSKI, RYSZARD, *PROVERBS OF AFRICA,* ST. PAUL: PROFESSORS WORLD PEACE ACADEMY, 1996. "ONE WHO IS FRIENDLY WITH THUNDER NEED NOT FEAR RAIN."

PANKHURST, RICHARD, *A SOCIAL HISTORY OF ETHIOPIA,* TRENTON, N.J.: THE RED SEA PRESS, 1992. HARD TO FOLLOW WITHOUT A BASIC HISTORY.

PARKES, JAMES, *THE JEW IN THE MEDIEVAL COMMUNITY,* EXCELLENT ANALYSIS OF THE JEWS' ROYAL CHARTERS, BY AN ANGLICAN PRIEST ON HITLER'S (S)HIT LIST FOR HELPING JEWS. I CAN'T FIND THE PUBLISHING REFERENCES!!!

POLO, MARCO, *THE TRAVELS OF MARCO POLO;* MANY EDITIONS EXIST. THE ONE I USED WAS TRANSLATED BY R. LATHAM, NEW YORK: ABARIS BOOKS, 1982.

PRUSSIN, LABELLE, *AFRICAN NOMADIC ARCHITECTURE, SPACE, PLACE, AND GENDER,* WASHINGTON, D.C.: SMITHSONIAN INSTITUTION PRESS, 1995. FANTASTIC PIX, AND YOU'VE GOTTA LOVE THAT SUBTITLE!

RICE, TAMARA TALBOT, *THE SELJUKS IN ASIA MINOR,* NEW YORK: FREDERICK A. PRAEGER, 1961.

RIDDLE, JOHN, *EVE'S HERBS,* CAMBRIDGE MASS.: HARVARD, 1997. CONTRACEPTION AND ABORTION IN EUROPE, GOING WAY BACK.

RILEY-SMITH, JONATHAN, *THE OXFORD ILLUSTRATED HISTORY OF THE CRUSADES,* OXFORD: OXFORD U. PRESS, 1997. GREAT PIX. TYPIFIES AN UNFORTUNATE KIND OF NEW HISTORY, FULL OF "WHY" BUT SHORT ON WHO, WHAT, WHERE, AND WHEN. AN ILLUSTRATED SCHOLARLY TOME MASQUERADING AS A POPULAR BOOK.

RUNCIMAN, STEVEN, *THE MEDIEVAL MANICHEE; A STUDY OF THE CHRISTIAN DUALIST HERESY,* NEW YORK: VIKING PRESS, 1961. ASTONISHING! FULLY DETAILED, JUDICIOUSLY ARGUED ACCOUNT OF THE "BOUGRES."

SANSOM, GEORGE, *A HISTORY OF JAPAN TO 1334,* STANFORD, CALIFORNIA: STANFORD UNIVERSITY PRESS, 1958.

SAWYER, PETER, *FROM ROMAN BRITAIN TO NORMAN ENGLAND,* NEW YORK: ST. MARTIN'S PRESS, 1978. DENSE, BUT INCLUDES PRECIOUS NUGGETS OF INFO.

SAWYER, PETER, ED., *THE OXFORD ILLUSTRATED HISTORY OF THE VIKINGS,* OXFORD: OXFORD U PRESS, 1997. GREAT PIX.

SCHAFER, EDWARD, *THE GOLDEN PEACHES OF SAMARKAND,* BERKELEY: U. OF CALIFORNIA PRESS, 1985. A LEARNED ACCOUNT OF FOREIGN IMPORTS TO CHINA UNDER THE TANG.

SCHEVILL, FERDINAND, *HISTORY OF THE BALKAN PENINSULA,* NEW YORK: FREDERICK UNGAR, 1966 (ORIGINALLY PUBLISHED IN 1922). WRITTEN JUST AFTER WWI, WHICH STARTED IN THE BALKANS. DEPRESSING.

SHERRARD, PHILIP AND EDITORS OF TIME-LIFE BOOKS, *BYZANTIUM,* NEW YORK: TIME, INC., 1966.

SWIFT, JEREMY, AND THE EDITORS OF TIME-LIFE BOOKS, *THE SAHARA,* AMSTERDAM, TIME-LIFE INTERNATIONAL (NEDERLAND) B.V. 1975. SOME CUTE LI'L ANIMALS WITH BIG EARS.

SYKES, PERCY, *A HISTORY OF PERSIA, VOLUME II,* NEW YORK: BARNES & NOBLE, INC., 1969.

THOMAS, HUGH, *THE SLAVE TRADE,* NEW YORK: SIMON & SCHUSTER, 1997. INDISPENSABLE, BUT SMALL ERRORS MAKE YOU DOUBT THE BIG STUFF.

TREECE, HENRY, *THE CRUSADES,* NEW YORK: RANDOM HOUSE, 1963. ERRATIC AND ODDLY ORGANIZED, BUT TELLS THE TALE WELL.

TSUNODA, R., DE BARY, W. T., AND D. KEENE, *SOURCES OF JAPANESE TRADITION,* NEW YORK: COLUMBIA UNIVERSITY PRESS, 1958. EXCERPTS FROM ORIGINAL TEXTS.

TUCHMAN, BARBARA, *A DISTANT MIRROR,* NEW YORK: BALLANTINE, 1978. WOW. THE BLACK DEATH, IN ALL ITS GORY GLORY. AN EXCEPTIONAL BOOK.

VLEKKE, BERNARD H. M., *NUSANTARA, A HISTORY OF INDONESIA,* CHICAGO: QUADRANGLE BOOKS, 1960.

WATT, W. MONTGOMERY, *MUHAMMAD AT MEDINA,* LONDON: OXFORD UNIVERSITY PRESS, 1962. EXACTLY HOW MANY CAMELS DID HE GIVE TO ABU SUFYAN, ANYWAY?

ZINSSER, HANS, *RATS, LICE, AND HISTORY,* NEW YORK: BLUE RIBBON BOOKS, 1935. WONDERFULLY ECCENTRIC CLASSIC ABOUT PLAGUE.

NAMES

IF YOU'RE INTERESTED IN READING FURTHER ABOUT ANY OF THE PEOPLE OR PLACES IN THIS BOOK, PLEASE REMEMBER THAT NON-LATIN NAMES HAVE BEEN TRANSLITERATED MANY WAYS. HERE ARE SOME ALTERNATIVE SPELLINGS THAT YOU MAY FIND USED ELSEWHERE.

ABDAR RAHMAN, ABDAL RAHMAN, ABD AR-RAHMAN, ABD AL-RAHMAN

ABRAHAM (THE SPLIT-FACED OF ETHIOPIA), ABRAHA

ABU ABDULLAH (EMIR OF GRANADA), BOABDIL

ABU AL-ABBAS (FOUNDER OF ABASSID DYNASTY), ABUL ABBAS

ABU BAKR, ABU-BAKR, ABU BEKR

ABU SUFYAN, ABU SOFYAN, ABU SOFIAN

ALMORAVID, AL-MURABIT

AN LU-SHAN, RUKHSHAN

ANDALUCIA, ANDALUSIA, AL-ANDALUS

BAYBARS, BAIBARS

BOHEMOND, BOHEMUND

BUKHARA, BOKHARA

CAIRO, AL-KAHIRA

CALIPH, KHALIF, KHALIFA

CATHARS, CATHARI

CONRAD, KONRAD

CORDOBA, CORDOVA

ETHIOPIA, ABYSSINIA

FERDINAND, FERNANDO

FIRDAUSI, FIRDAWSI

GHAZNI, GHAZNA, GHAZNAH

HARUN, HAROUN

IBN SENA, IBN SINA, AVICENNA

JENGHIS, GENGHIS (COMMON, BUT NOT TO BE PREFERRED!), JINGHIS, CHINGHIZ, CHINGGHIS

JIDDA, JIDDAH

KABA, KA'ABA

KAIBAR, KHAYBAR, KHAIBAR

KHITAI, KHITAN

KHWARISM, KHWARIZM, KHIVA

AL-KHWARISMI, AL-KHWARIZMI

KILIJ ARSLAN, QILIJ ARSLAN

KORAN, QURAN

KUBLAI, KUBILAI, QUBILAI

KURAISH, QURAISH, QURAYSH, KOREISH

KUSAILA, KUSAYLA, KOSAILA, ETC.

LOTHAR, LOTHAIR, CHLOTHAIR

MAHMOUD, MAHMUD

MAMELUKE, MAMLUK

MANZIKERT, MALAZGIRT

MECCA, MAKKAH

MEDINA, MADINAH, AL-MADINAH

MUHAMMAD, MOHAMMED, MAHOMET

NUR AD-DIN, NUR AL-DIN

PIPPIN, PEPIN

QURAIZA, QURAYZAH

ROMANOS, ROMANUS

SALADIN, SALAH AD-DIN, SALAH AL-DIN

SELJUK, SALJUK, SALJUQ

SEVILLA, SEVILLE

SHEBA, SABA

SUNG (DYNASTY), SONG

TANG, T'ANG

TAI-TSUNG, T'AI-T'SUNG

TIMBUKTU, TIMBUCTOO, ETC.

TOBA, TO-PA

TOKHARIAN, TOCHARIAN

TUGHRIL BEY, TUGHRIL BEG

TURKISTAN, TURKESTAN

UMAR, OMAR

UMAYYAD, OMAYYAD

UTHMAN, OTHMAN

YANG GUEI-FEI, YANG KWEI-FEI

ZENGI, ZANGI

ZHU YUAN-ZHANG, CHU YUAN-CHANG

Index

305

INDEX

About the Author

LARRY GONICK, WINNER OF THE 1999 INKPOT AWARD FOR EXCELLENCE IN CARTOON-ING, IS A PROFESSIONAL CARTOONIST AND AUTHOR OF *THE CARTOON HISTORY OF THE UNIVERSE* SERIES, AMONG OTHER ILLUSTRATED BOOKS. HE GRADUATED FROM HARVARD COLLEGE WITH A SUMMA CUM LAUDE DEGREE IN MATHEMATICS AND PHI BETA KAPPA HONORS. AFTER EARNING A MASTER'S DEGREE IN MATHEMATICS FROM HARVARD UNIVERSITY, HE LEFT ACADEMIA TO PURSUE NONFICTION CARTOONING FULL TIME.

GONICK RECEIVED KNIGHT SCIENCE JOURNALISM FELLOWSHIPS AT THE MASSACHUSETTS INSTITUTE OF TECHNOLOGY IN 1994 AND 1995. HE WAS ALSO A 2000 JOURNALISM FELLOW AT THE MATHEMATICAL SCIENCES RESEARCH INSTITUTE IN BERKELEY.

THE CARTOON HISTORY OF THE UNIVERSE SERIES WAS NAMED AMONG THE TOP 100 COMIC BOOKS OF THE TWENTIETH CENTURY BY THE AUTHORITATIVE FAN MAGA-ZINE *THE COMICS JOURNAL*, PUBLISHED BY FANTAGRAPHICS BOOKS OF SEATTLE. THE SERIES'S CD-ROM RECEIVED THE EDDIE (*MACUSER* EDITOR'S CHOICE) AWARD AS BEST "EDUTAINMENT" PRODUCT OF 1994.